Teaching Legal Education in the Digital Age

Teaching Legal Education in the Digital Age explores how legal pedagogy and curriculum design should be modernised to ensure that law students have a realistic view of the future of the legal profession.

Using future readiness and digital empowerment as central themes, chapters discuss the use of technology to enhance the design and delivery of the curriculum and argue the need for the curriculum to be developed to prepare students for the use of technology in the workplace. The volume draws together a range of contributions to consider the impact of digital pedagogies in legal education and propose how technology can be used in the law curriculum to enhance student learning in law schools and lead excellence in teaching. Throughout, the authors consider what it means to be future-ready and what law academics can do to facilitate the knowledge, skills, and dispositions needed by future-ready graduates.

Part of Routledge's series on Legal Pedagogy, this book will be of great interest to academics, post-graduate students, teachers and researchers of law, as well as those with a wider interest in legal pedagogy or legal practice. It is dedicated to the memory of Helen Edwards, 1969-2022.

Ann Thanaraj is Founder and Host of Digital Lawyering, an international initiative which brings together a global interdisciplinary audience to shape the direction of legal education fit for a digital age. Ann is Assistant Academic Registrar at Teesside University where she leads the digital transformation of learning and teaching institutionally. Ann is a Principal Fellow and National Teaching Fellow (AdvanceHE).

Kris Gledhill is based at AUT Law School, Auckland, New Zealand and is the Series Editor of the Legal Pedagogy Series.

Legal Pedagogy

Series Editor: Kris Gledhill

Auckland University of Technology, New Zealand

This series consists of high-quality monographs, each of which explores best practices in an aspect of the law school curriculum. Books cover teaching methods and curriculum design in the main areas of law, how to integrate themes and areas of jurisprudential thought, and wider questions about legal education more generally. With contributions from around the world, this series explores innovative thinking and practice within the context of a generally conservative branch of academia, with the aim of promoting discussion as to how best to teach the various aspects of the law degree and ensure the ongoing validity of the law degree as a whole. Typical topics addressed include the value of variety in teaching methods and curriculum design, how best to incorporate educational research, the role for more practical courses, and the need to ensure that law schools provide degrees of relevance to the needs of students and of society.
The books in this series will be of great interest to academics, researchers, and postgraduates in the fields of law and education, as well as teachers of the law who may be interested in revising curricula and need guidance in doing so. In addition, the legal profession, and in particular those who regulate entry into the profession, will find much to interest them within the series.

Recent books in this series:

Key Directions in Legal Education
National and International Perspectives
Edited by Emma Jones and Fiona Cownie

Teaching Migration and Asylum Law
Theory and Practice
Edited by Richard Grimes, Věra Honuskova and Ulrich Stege

Teaching Evidence Law
Contemporary Trends and Innovations
Edited by Yvonne Daly, Jeremy Gans and PJ Schwikkard

For more information about books in this series, please visit https://www.routledge.com/Legal-Pedagogy/book-series/LEGPED

Teaching Legal Education in the Digital Age

Pedagogical Practices to Digitally Empower Law Graduates

Edited by Ann Thanaraj and Kris Gledhill

Routledge
Taylor & Francis Group
LONDON AND NEW YORK

First published 2023
by Routledge
4 Park Square, Milton Park, Abingdon, Oxon OX14 4RN

and by Routledge
605 Third Avenue, New York, NY 10158

Routledge is an imprint of the Taylor & Francis Group, an informa business

British Library Cataloguing-in-Publication Data
A catalogue record for this book is available from the British Library

Library of Congress Cataloging-in-Publication Data
Names: Thanaraj, Ann, editor. | Gledhill, Kris, editor.
Title: Teaching legal education in the digital age : pedagogical practices to digitally empower law graduates / edited by Ann Thanaraj and Kris Gledhill.
Description: Abingdon, Oxon ; New York, NY : Routledge, 2023. | Series: Legal pedagogy | Includes bibliographical references and index. |
Identifiers: LCCN 2022020133 (print) | LCCN 2022020134 (ebook) | ISBN 9780367367404 (hardback) | ISBN 9781032362267 (paperback) | ISBN 9780429351082 (ebook)
Subjects: LCSH: Law--Study and teaching. | Education, Higher--Effect of technological innovations on.
Classification: LCC K100 .T43 2023 (print) | LCC K100 (ebook) | DDC 340.071/1--dc23/eng/20220630
LC record available at https://lccn.loc.gov/2022020133
LC ebook record available at https://lccn.loc.gov/2022020134

ISBN: 978-0-367-36740-4 (hbk)
ISBN: 978-1-032-36226-7 (pbk)
ISBN: 978-0-429-35108-2 (ebk)

DOI: 10.4324/9780429351082

Typeset in Bembo
by MPS Limited, Dehradun

Contents

Contributors

Cemile Cakir is the Head of Online Post Graduate Academic studies at the Online Campus at the University of Law. She qualified as a solicitor with a Law Degree from the London School of Economics, has an MA(Dist) in Education Technology from the University College London, Institute of Education and is a Teaching Fellow. She has taught and designed many programmes including the Masters in Law, Legal Practice Course, and Law Conversion Programmes. She is a founding member of the ULaw Tech Research Academy (ULTRA), led the project implementing the introduction of legal tech education and developed the Technoethics in Law module for the MSC Legal Technology. She has published her work on legal technology and education technology in law which she has also presented at conferences. She has a keen interest in human rights, ethics and equality, particularly in the context of technology and innovation.

David Chaplin is a legal publisher and writer with his own company – Bath Publishing. He is also Editor of Computers & Law – the magazine and website of the Society for Computers and Law – for whom he writes a weekly newsletter on topical techlaw issues and hosts regular webinars and podcasts. He was in at the start of the digital revolution, and over the years he has been involved in setting up several innovative legal information websites and helped design practice management software.

Alex Cook is an Adjunct Lecturer at the University of Western Australia. He holds a Masters in Law and Finance from the University of Oxford, and a Juris Doctor from the University of Western Australia. Alex has taught postgraduate law students for more than six years and designed Legal APPtitude together with Kate Offer. Outside of teaching, Alex helped design smart legal contract infrastructure for Australia and has founded technology companies in both Europe and Australia.

Jamie Daniels is an experienced educational software developer working in The Open University's Learning Innovation team. He has a passion for exploring the boundaries of new technologies to deliver and underpin impactful learning. He has been at the forefront of many landmark educational technologies, including e-learning websites, mobile apps and most recently Virtual Reality.

Sara de Freitas is an educator, author, researcher, and public speaker with 25 years in education. She has worked in six universities in Australia and the United Kingdom in various roles from Research Fellow to Deputy Vice-Chancellor, with experience in education and research portfolios. Moving into the industry as a Director of Education for a PLC company and a School Leader for InterHigh and Academy21, Sara is now Executive Director at StudyGroup focusing on international and transnational education. She is a passionate advocate for high-quality learning and teaching and applied, translational and discovery research that creates social and economic benefits for local, regional and international growth and renewal. She has published seven books and 100 peer-reviewed journal articles and conference papers, as well as over 20 book chapters and 100 technical reports and strategies. Her cross-disciplinary and cross-sectoral influence on the academic domains of educational technology and higher education policy and leadership development has been fostered by sitting on over 80 programme committees and advisory groups and undertaking over 160 international keynotes, presentations and public lectures in four continents. Sara is currently working as a University Governor and holds a Visiting Professorship and Fellowships.

Thomas Dunk joined the University of Hertfordshire in August 2015 and is currently a Principal Lecturer and LLB Programme leader. Thomas's research interests include Public International law, Land Law, and British Politics.

Paul Durston is Digital Learning Manager at Teesside University, working with the Digital Transformation Management Team to lead digital excellence through digital learning, managing, and delivering key strategic digital projects relating to the digital transformation of learning and teaching, in alignment with the University's Education 4.0 ambitions. A Senior Fellow of AdvanceHE, Paul is co-author of the Digital Learning Design Framework & Toolkit (developed with support from Jisc and currently used by 80+ learning organisations globally) which provides a mechanism through which course teams can pursue a reflective and collaborative approach to course design. Paul leads a team of digital learning specialists and has contributed to Teesside gaining recognition as a sector leader in Digital Learning across the UK. Between 2018–2020, Paul led a mandatory Digital Development Programme for all teaching staff which reported a 96% satisfaction rating from participants, enabling the University to accrue the largest concentration of Microsoft Innovative Educator Experts (MIEEs) in the UK.

Helen Edwards was called to the Bar in 1994 and practised in criminal and family law on the Welsh circuit. She specialised in teaching professional skills and preparing students for professional practice. As a former course leader and head of the professional programmes at Nottingham Trent University, she delivered many advocacy training courses including advocacy training for the judicial institute of Malaysia. In 2017 she joined De Montfort University, Leicester. Her teaching and research interests were criminal law and evidence and language in court. Her experience and understanding of the requirements of professional practice informed her teaching and research and she was an advocate for innovative forms of teaching practice.

Sam Elkington is Principal Lecturer in Learning and Teaching Excellence at Teesside University. He is an experienced education practitioner, researcher, and leader with a track record of innovation at a senior, strategic level in the higher education sector. Sam has significant expertise in change leadership and management in higher education and learning and development settings, with wider expertise in areas such as curricula and academic development, educational technology, instructional design for learning, student engagement, and creativity. Sam has developed a reputation for delivering high-impact practice-based and industry-applied research leadership through knowledge transfer partnerships and externally funded research projects. Sam has been awarded National Teaching Fellow and Principal Fellowship of the Higher Education Academy in recognition of his excellence in shaping assessments across the sector.

Jeff Giddings is Associate Dean (Experiential Education) and Professor of Law at Monash University. He joined the Monash Law Faculty in 2017 after 22 years at Griffith University in Brisbane, Queensland. Jeff remains an Adjunct Professor at the Griffith Law School. He received an Australia National Teaching Fellowship in 2013 for the Effective Law Student Supervision Project. Jeff also received the Australian Award for University Teaching in Law and Legal Studies in 1999 along with multiple Griffith University teaching awards, including the inaugural Griffith Award for Excellence in Teaching. From 2013 to 2015, Jeff served as an International Scholar for the Academic Fellows Program of the Open Society Foundation, working extensively with the American University of Central Asia, Bishkek, Kyrgyzstan.

Kris Gledhill is a professor of law at AUT Law School in Auckland, New Zealand; he was a London-based barrister before moving into academia. His many roles include being the Series Editor of the Legal Pedagogy Series.

Matthew J Homewood is the Deputy Dean at Nottingham Law School where he has taught numerous law modules with a particular specialism in European Union Law and aspects of free movement – an area within which he has authored a number of best-selling academic texts. In 2016 in recognition of his contribution to legal education, he was awarded a Higher

Education Academy National Teaching Fellowship, the most prestigious individual award for excellence in teaching in higher education. Matthew has an international reputation in both legal education and education generally as an expert in the use of technology-enhanced learning and the impact that educational technologies can have on student engagement and outcomes. Matthew's expertise has been recognised by the higher education sector through a number of high-profile awards, including a Highly Commended ALT Learning Technologist of the Year Award, Association of Law Teachers Teaching Law with Technology Prize, Guardian University Awards, Law Teacher of the Year Finalist, and recipient of the Global Legal Skills Award.

Václav Janeček is a Lecturer in Law at the University of Bristol. Previously, he was a Visiting Research Fellow in Law and Technology at Masaryk University in Brno and a Research and Course Development Fellow in Law and Technology at the University of Oxford. He currently explores judicial remedies for illegal online tracking and the role of public interest in the law of damages. His work also seeks to understand how lawyers and computer scientists can learn to work together more efficiently.

Emma Jones is a Senior Lecturer in Law and Director of Student Wellbeing at the University of Sheffield's Law School. Her research interests include digital lawyering and the role of emotions and wellbeing in legal education and the legal profession. She is the lead on the Fit for Law project (www.fitforlaw.org.uk) working with the charity LawCare. Prior to entering academia, Emma was a solicitor in private practice.

Rónán Kennedy researches and teaches environmental law, information technology law, and the intersections between these in the School of Law at the National University of Ireland Galway. In addition to many journal articles on these and other topics, he is co-author of "How to Think, Write and Cite: Key Skills for Irish Law Students" (Round Hall, 2016) and "Information and Communications Technology Law in Ireland" (Clarus Press, 2017). He has a background in information technology and information systems.

Lawrence Kizilkaya is a Product Development Manager for the Learning Innovation team at The Open University. He is responsible for the design and management of many new and innovative approaches to teaching students across all disciplines. His primary focus is on ensuring the robust application of relevant pedagogies and balancing the complexities of function, form and usability.

Yulia Marunchak is a Senior eLearning Technology Developer based in the Learning and Teaching Innovation Centre and a member of the Computer Science Adaptive Systems Research Group at the University of Hertfordshire.

As an educator and 3D artist, she spends much of her time exploring emerging technologies and creative trends in the digital medium.

Hugh McFaul is a Senior Lecturer in Law and was formerly a co-Director of the Open Justice Centre, which focuses on research, teaching and public engagement to deliver legal education for the public good. It has won several awards for its use of technology to widen access to legal education, advice and guidance and has pioneered a series of online and face to face community engagement projects in schools, prisons and community organisations. Hugh has consulted for NGOs and governmental organisations including the UN Office on Drugs and Crime to design and develop open-access education tools to support the rule of law. Hugh was the academic advisor for the critically acclaimed four-part BBC2/Open University television documentary series The Detectives and is currently working on another series.

Ryan Murray is a Principal Lecturer at Nottingham Law School, Nottingham Trent University. He is the School's Learning and Teaching Manager. Ryan leads on projects to enhance teaching practice across the undergraduate and postgraduate portfolio of courses. He is currently involved in a project to develop students' employability via the use of digital skills.

Kate Offer is a Senior Lecturer & the Director of Applied Innovation at UWA's Law School as well as Deputy Head of School (Teaching & Learning). She is the recipient of multiple teaching awards at the university, national, and international levels. She teaches Torts and Evidence in the Juris Doctor degree at UWA as well as the elective unit, Legal APPtitude, which gives students the opportunity to work with not-for-profit organisations to build an app that solves a legal issue. Kate's research interests focus primarily on legal education.

Lucia Otoyo is a Senior Lecturer and Deputy Head of the Computer Science and Informatics Division at London South Bank University. She is interested in developing students' cross-disciplinary team working and project management skills.

Olga M Piaskowska is an Advocate and an Assistant Professor and Researcher at the Institute of Law of the SWPS University of Social Sciences and Humanities. She is also involved in research on new methods of law teaching at the SWPS University and is a co-author of a new curriculum for a law school. For more than 10 years she was a senior judicial law clerk at the Civil Chamber of the Supreme Court of the Republic of Poland. Mrs Piaskowska has written and lectured on legal topics relating primarily to Polish and European regulations governing civil law and human rights, as well as lawyering skills. In 2014 she received the honour in the "Golden Wings 2014" by Dziennik Gazeta Prawna for her

PhD dissertation. She is a laureate of the 4th edition of "The Rising Stars Lawyers – Leaders of Tomorrow 2015". She earned her master's degree (master of law) in 2006 from Silesian University and her PhD in 2013 from Warsaw University. She is a member of the Polish Association of European law. She is also a member of the Warsaw Bar Association.

Piotr F Piesiewicz is an Assistant Professor at the Faculty of Law of the SWPS University of Social Sciences and Humanities and advocate. He practices civil, criminal and intellectual property law. He has worked extensively in matters involving film production, advertising, and media law. He is also involved in research on new methods of law teaching at the SWPS University. He is also a co-author of a new curriculum for a law school and head of the didactic centre for teaching law. Mr Piesiewicz has written and lectured on legal topics relating primarily to Polish and European regulations governing copyright law, criminal law and media law. As an advocate, he is a member of the Warsaw Bar Association. He is also a member of the Press Law Association and the Association of Law Teachers. He earned his masters degree in 2000 from Warsaw University and his PhD in 2007 from Lazarski University in Warsaw. Between 2000 and 2003 he was a judge trainee, and in 2003 he passed the judge examination. In 2007, he was admitted to the Warsaw Bar Association and since 2010 he has his own attorney's practice.

Vernon Rive is an Associate Professor at the School of Law, Auckland University of Technology, where he teaches and researches judicial review, constitutional law, international environmental law, resource management law, and climate change law. He has published widely in the areas of environmental and international environmental law. Vernon is a co-convenor of the New Zealand Resource Management Law Association Academic Advisory Group, member of the managing committee of the New Zealand Centre for Environmental Law, Consultant Editor of the LexisNexis Resource Management Bulletin, and Associated Graduate Scholar with the Peter McMullin Centre on Statelessness at the Melbourne Law School. He has a particular interest in the use of digital and mobile technology in the teaching, learning, and research of public and environmental law and has presented on and contributed to publications on this topic. He is a member of the steering group for the Technology in Legal Education for New Zealand (TeLENZ) project, a New Zealand Law Foundation-funded initiative to assist academics to create papers and develop teaching resources related to technology, cyber security, and AI in various fields of law taught at the New Zealand universities.

Alan Russell is a Senior Lecturer in Law and Deputy Director of the London South Bank University Legal Advice Clinic. He is interested in applying LawTech to support access to justice for the Clinic's clients.

Francine Ryan is a qualified solicitor, Senior Lecturer in Law and Director of the Open Justice Centre at The Open University. Francine has worked to develop a range of innovative and technology-enhanced opportunities for OU law students. She is responsible for creating and managing the Open Justice Online Law Clinic and leads on the digital justice project. Francine's research areas are in technology and the law, focusing on access to justice in clinical legal education.

Kim Silver has recently retired as a Senior Lecturer in Law at London South Bank University, who has also taught with The Open University. She is interested in the impact of LawTech on legal education.

Ann Thanaraj is Assistant Academic Registrar leading the digital transformation of learning and teaching at Teesside University, having successfully led a university-wide strategic and change transformation project in Online Learning. Ann is also the founder and host of Lawyering in a Digital Age, an international initiative which brings together a global interdisciplinary audience to shape the direction of legal education fit for a digital age. In a quest to digitally transform legal education, particularly in today's rapidly changing legal landscape, Ann and her co-authors have developed the first in the world textbook for law students on "Digital Lawyering" as a guide for law schools to reimagine the legal education curriculum. Cited by the House of Lords, and in recognition of her strategic leadership in online learning with impact across the sector, Ann has been awarded National Teaching Fellow and Principal Fellowship of the Higher Education Academy in recognition for her excellence in teaching and strategic leadership in the fields of legal and online education.

Andy Unger is an Associate Professor and Head of the Law Division at London South Bank University. He is interested in the potential of LawTech to increase access to justice and its likely impact on careers for Law students.

David Vince is a Senior Product Development Manager at The Open University focused on developing post-secondary educational technology practice. He is also a Senior Fellow of the Higher Education Academy.

Jacqueline Weinberg is the Academic Director of Springvale Monash Legal Service, Lecturer in Law and Clinical Practice Supervisor in Monash Legal Practice Programs, Monash University. Jacqueline has been committed to education and academic pursuits for over 30 years and has attained graduate and post-graduate qualifications in the areas of legal education and clinical legal education. Her PhD explored the teaching alternative dispute resolution in Australian clinical legal education. Her areas of research include dispute resolution, student wellbeing, and the links between technology and the law in enhancing access to justice. Jacqueline has presented at numerous conferences both internationally and within Australia, including the International Journal of Clinical Legal Education Conferences, The National Wellness for Law Forums, and the ADR Research Network Roundtables.

Rebecca Williams is a Professor of Public Law and Criminal Law at the University of Oxford, in association with Pembroke College. Rebecca's principal teaching interests are criminal law and public law. Her work includes examining optimum methods of decision-making and the use of criminal law as a form of regulation. Increasingly her work also focuses on the relationship between law and technology and the ways in which the law will need to develop in order to keep pace with technological developments.

Foreword

Contrary to perceptions of the remote and isolated 'ivory tower', modern universities in general, and legal educators in particular, are required to prepare their students to deal with unprecedented challenges throughout their adult lives with greater urgency than ever before.

These challenges warrant enumeration. On a global scale, climate change and threats to food security pose grave economic risks and ever widening inequality. The rise of populism, nationalism, and the resurrection of old enmities, underpinned by the proliferation of 'fake news', pose a threat to the nature of liberal democracy itself. Public health challenges around mental health, wellbeing, and the evolution of future pandemics prompt further concern.

Educators have a critical role to play in our global response to these challenges, as demonstrated by the chapters in this collection, through developing those who will address them. In particular, two themes resonate in situating the role of current legal education within this dynamic socioeconomic and political context, namely future readiness and digital empowerment.

Future readiness can be defined as providing students with the skills, knowledge, and expertise to thrive in complex and uncertain futures. It is important to recognise the role of higher education in supporting students to achieve success not just as narrowly defined through concepts of employability and progression in the professional workplace, but more importantly in the contributions that they will make to the communities that they will serve and society more broadly.

The concept of digital empowerment is framed by the potential that tools, networks and platforms hold, when designed and used appropriately, to accelerate and amplify actions and impact beyond physical and geographical limitations. Yet the unique dangers of operating in a digitally connected world must also be recognised, with an imperative to ensure that graduates are prepared to operate safely and critically online. Ultimately, digital must enable and energise innovative pedagogy, rather than warp or replace it.

The chapters in this collection address a broad range of urgent themes relating to legal pedagogy as defined within a digital context, including the impact of artificial intelligence, virtual reality, immersive environments and social media. Providing a global perspective on the modernisation of curriculum design and delivery, this collection makes a unique contribution to the evolution of legal education to meet the challenges of the future.

Jonathan Eaton
Director of Student Learning & Academic Registrar
Teesside University

Chapter 1

Introduction: Exploring Becoming Future Ready

Ann Thanaraj, Sara De Freitas, David Chaplin, and Kris Gledhill

with thanks to Andy Unger and Rónán Kennedy

Introduction

It is, of course, true that law is an academic discipline in its own right: but as with other professional degrees – medicine, engineering, architecture, or a whole host of others – it is also true that the number of students who enrol to study law is conditioned in large part by the desire of many and perhaps most of them to enter the legal profession or other professions for which legal skills are significant. The viability of a law school offering a programme of study that was academically credible but did not prepare students to join the legal profession would be questionable. The practical outcome of this is that law schools have to treat the legal profession as significant stakeholders and have in mind the knowledge and skills that students need to become members of the profession. Naturally, this can be – and invariably is – supplemented by steps that are required between graduation and entry into the profession.

Accordingly, law schools and legal academics have to prepare our students for the future. But the obvious question arises: what does the future hold? The Covid-19 pandemic that occurred as chapters in this book were being written provides the reminder that what is entirely predictable (in the sense that pandemics are a regular feature of human history) is also seemingly unpredictable in terms of when it occurred and the responses to it.

Many developments are predictably going to have an impact on the legal world, and technology is one of them: quite what that impact will be and when it will occur is difficult to say. There will be changes both to the process of law and to the subject matter that law regulates. But will it be evolutionary or revolutionary, building on existing paradigms or requiring new ones?

Similarly, legal research has changed. Readers who went to university in the pre-personal computer and internet age will recall that legal research was different in the days of card indexes and bound volumes. As material moved to discs and then to internet databases, the process has changed, but in an evolutionary fashion: a keyword search in a database rather than looking in a paper index involves the same core skill. Will technology, most obviously, artificial intelligence (AI), change this in a more radical fashion?

DOI: 10.4324/9780429351082-1

There is a range of views as to how different the future will be. Some of the chapters in this book rest on technology opening up a range of new avenues that can build incrementally on what is familiar in the Law School world; but others have more of a focus on the prospect (or risk, perhaps?) that there will be significant changes, amounting to the Fourth Industrial Revolution (4IR) and that we should be preparing students for this future. Higher Education generally is searching for a vision of learning, teaching, assessments and student experience during the 4IR (Schwab, 2016). Some see a time of unprecedented change, opportunities, and challenges through the use of technologies to deliver educational experiences, and encourage institutions to explore how the sector might respond to the future needs of industry and jobs; this has been captioned Education 4.0 (Feldman, 2018).

Similarly, the legal industry seems to be subject to disruption that might bring significant changes to the profession and the services offered. The affordances of digital transformation, particularly through the developments across AI, automation, big data, and analytics, and the use of Internet of Things (IoT), are changing the roles within the legal profession. The way in which legal services are being delivered is changing through tools that are capable of (i) retrieving legal knowledge, reducing the need for lawyers to control the delivery of legal service; (ii) automating lawyering, creating more affordable and standardised services and products, whilst streamlining work requiring fewer lawyers and (iii) augmenting and extending our capabilities (Surden, 2014, McGinnis & Pearce, 2014). Whilst technologies are not as yet capable of replacing our human and intellectual faculties, such as legal reasoning, the art of persuasion and interpreting information in the context of the realities of our world today, they still impact how students prepare for the changing profession.

Digital transformation is also seen in the cutting-edge of reforms of our court system through the emerging use of online courts and online dispute resolution (Canadian Bar Association, 2014, Vos 2018, Susskind, 2015, 2017, Katsh and Rule, 2016). Further, with the emergence of new hybrid roles within the legal profession – such as legal knowledge engineer, legal technologist, legal process analyst, legal project manager, legal management consultant, and legal risk manager (Susskind, 2010) – there is a need for legal expertise in the form of judgement, interpretation, contextualisation, and reasoning that refutes attempts at automation. These skills may become more valuable, and will remain so whilst it is impossible to frame rules to anticipate and provide for every possible combination of circumstances which the future may bring, and whilst datasets have to evolve with interpretations and social norms (Velsberg, 2019).

If there are all-encompassing developments that will reshape the legal systems of the future, a curriculum that is rooted in the Third Industrial Revolution will not suffice. While the day-to-day use of technology is now routinely taught, this is generally with the prosaic aim of ensuring that a new entrant to the profession can query research databases, complete an online form or draft a contract. The profound challenges ahead of us, such as the use of AI in decision making or the ethical dilemmas of using neural interfaces, may require a more fundamental reworking of not just what tomorrow's lawyers are expected to know but what they can expect to do with that training and what responsibilities they will have to bear in their professional lives. Students may need tools, knowledge, and skills for change that will constantly evolve.

These are some of the questions this book addresses through examples of innovative curriculum design and student learning experiences. As a whole, this collection portrays elements of a model for legal education fit for a digital age, identifying the sorts of research, knowledge, skills, competencies, and experiences that should future-proof law graduates so that they can respond to and thrive in a changing world of work and knowledge. However, we do not claim that these are the only approaches. As technologies evolve and as new approaches to learning and working are discovered, the examples presented here are a starting point for a conversation around technology and the future of learning and the preparation of learners for the future.

We take a multidimensional approach to think about learning design that encompasses technology and its influence and impact on the curriculum, alongside leveraging the digital capabilities of academics and the affordances of technologies, to reimagine the learning experiences within the law degree. We also showcase how technology enables innovation, allowing those who are interested in innovating to do so within their own academic practices.

Digital transformation offers law schools an opportunity to re-evaluate how they should be preparing students for their future and reimagine legal education, particularly around how a law degree can provide stewardship to the challenges we face in the evolving environments in the digital age. Identifying the purpose of a law degree is a common quest. In the context of digital transformation and the exponential growth and impact of technologies across professions, industries, and sectors, the relationship of the law degree to the profession, industry, regulators, and market forces should cause legal academia to question the role law plays during this transformation in the legal profession and beyond. Whilst a law degree is a versatile academic course affording a variety of career opportunities, including a solid academic preparation for the vocational stage of studying towards the legal profession, a question remains as to what sorts of knowledge and intellectual pursuits are now necessary and relevant for a changing world. Similarly, the value of a law degree and its use in other professions is also a worthy exploration, since change across every sector, profession and industry is disrupting the future of education, and blurring and re-forming disciplines, identities, professional skills, knowledge.

Authors in this collection share their successful practices and reflections around preparing law students for this changing world of work. Perhaps it is also overdue for policy regulators and professional bodies to reconsider the core subjects taught in law degrees. It begs the question of how our education and training can be reimagined, redesigned, and recreated to become fit for purpose, leading to renewed debate around its telos and axiology once again.

The Collection

This collection is grounded in unpacking the diverse insights into future readiness and digital empowerment as a means to contribute towards the challenges society, the sector, and graduates face. The concept of "future", "readiness", "empowerment", and "digital" are contested (Danvers, 2016, Dunne, 2015).

Many chapters delve into the pedagogic and philosophical approaches to future readiness and digital empowerment, and how approaches in learning and teaching and curriculum development can be reimagined to equip law students for the changing landscape of work – the technologically augmented and mediated legal practice and delivery of legal services. Authors reflect on how their initiatives empower learners to thrive in a complex and uncertain future, drawing on their own perspectives on what future readiness means in the context of legal education and their own academic practice. This covers graduate attributes, skills, knowledge, and experiences inculcated throughout the learning experience and beyond; it may also cover aptitude and a mindset which may be able to contribute towards humans and automation working together. We invite the reader to reflect on the roles and expectations of ourselves as academics using digital technology in legal education to shape the curriculum and the preparation of learners for the future to live and work in a digitally mediated society.

Several chapters focus on examples of excellent strides in harnessing new technologies and new ways of experiencing a module, utilising digital methods to create high impact, interactive, and transformational learning experience. Yulia and Thomas from the University of Hertfordshire bring land law to life in chapter 2. They share their reflections on creating an immersive "Virtual Town", at the University of Hertfordshire, an innovative initiative in the teaching of land law which also became the winner of the Routledge/Association of Law Teachers Teaching Law with Technology Prize 2016. A desire to bring the subject alive in a way that students could relate to, and attempt to make exciting and relevant some convoluted terminologies and principles in a subject that others in academia typically look upon with pity and fear, led to the design of a digital 3D model representing a small, urbanised, area. From this, land law concepts could be demonstrated to students. It was incorporated into lectures, tutorials, and workshops, and then into assessments. With an increasing quantity of third-year dissertations wishing to explore the subject, having studied land law through the backdrop of the virtual town, students were introduced to visual literacies. The effectiveness of digital and visual communication of information may make legal concepts more accessible and user-friendly to clients and organisations. It helps students to visualise arguments, allowing for relationships between numerous elements of facts, propositions, and challenges to surface more readily.

Gamification and Virtual Reality have barely been used in law school curricula. Making the shift towards connecting academic knowledge with real-world applications, and developing students' soft skills, such as interpersonal skills and working as a team, fosters the development of in-depth technical knowledge, industry readiness, and transferable skills in its graduates who "know that" and also "know how". In chapter 3, colleagues at The Open University UK, Emma, Francine, Hugh, David, Lawrence, and Jamie describe the development of virtual reality (VR) app as part of the module on presentation skills. It mimics a prison, school, or community environment through an immersive simulation using a VR headset. The VR app provides an opportunity for students to work with real people and real situations, developing their social awareness, affording opportunities to immerse students in other unfamiliar settings to enhance learning and confidently build on their practical skills in an authentic learning environment. Additionally, students are equipped with future-ready thinking to identify legal and ethical challenges that arise from technological innovations and critically examine how developments in technology may protect or undermine the rule of law. The chapter provides recommendations on how VR can be used to digitally empower students.

Similarly, Matthew analyses an action research project on the use of Twitter as a feedback tool to build Communities of Practice as part of learning at the University of Nottingham Trent. Chapter 4 seeks to add to the body of knowledge concerning social theories of learning with specific reference to the use of and particular characteristics of Twitter. As does the VR App chapter, this shows the multi-dimensional nature of the future readiness and digital empowerment of law students, by using technology to challenge students to use their academic knowledge to solve problems around them. The chapters raise questions around whether we always teach to fit what's required now rather than thinking of ways to change the system to fit the new realities? What are the affordances and challenges of designing a curriculum for law students using technological solutions? And, to what extent can new technologies and approaches be utilised to support learner-interactivity, collaboration, communication, reflection, and skills, and thus provide pedagogically rich learning environments that are authentic, meaningful, and reflective of the goals of preparing students to be future reading and digitally empowered? Many of these questions are addressed in the chapters that follow.

Creating learning opportunities where students can bridge the gap between theoretical research and industrial applications in the form of solving an industry problem equips students with real skills needed to solve in-demand industry and societal problems. Students are often confronted with unique and unstructured problems, forcing them to think outside the box and look for answers beyond their textbooks. Jacqueline and Jeff at Monash University share their design and use of a Virtual Law Clinic and reflect on the innovation and the opportunities it has provided their students in chapter 5. They address the distinctive opportunity a VLC offers to address access to justice as well as preparing students with knowledge, skills, and attributes related to technological proficiency for current and future legal practice. The chapter addresses the key considerations that need to be addressed to prepare students to use technology effectively in assisting and building trust with clients, including developing communication skills for interacting with clients via technology.

Similarly, in chapter 6, Kate and Alex share the development of an innovation at the University of Western Australia where students created apps for community organisations. The apps aided decision-making processes through a series of questions, accompanied by associated documents and advice. The module was supplemented with guest talks and access to external computer science and legal technology experts. Legal design is prevalent and ubiquitous throughout each chapter. The authors have shown how they have used design thinking in their approaches to help students craft accessible and useable outputs for real-world purposes.

The Covid-19 pandemic that is ongoing at the time of writing has impacted the free movement of people all over the world, making clear that digital education is not just a supplement for education but may be "the new normal" in education. The research evidence supports this shift, which some think may be more transformational for education than in other areas of human activity due to the flexibility and adaptability that it allows learners. The evidence is clear in the work by Altbach and colleagues at UNESCO (Altbach et al, 2009) and Means and colleagues at the US Department of education, which found blended learning to provide improvements and a significant difference to either face-to-face or online education when used alone (Means et al, 2009). Vernon from the Auckland University of Technology takes an auto-ethnographic approach to reflecting on the use of online platforms to teach public law and international environmental law in chapter 7. He advocates creating learning opportunities with the right balance between online delivery and the need for non-digital, in-person law teaching, which requires thoughtful and reflective engagement with learning designs. He charts the use of digital tools and solutions most effectively within curriculum design such as audio recordings, video talking heads, online discussion boards, and online workshops. His reflections offer insights into the effective use of online platforms as part of preparing students for the technologically advancing world of work, whilst acknowledging key global issues around digital poverty and social inclusion, digital confidence and reduced opportunities for student engagement and equipping students with the ability to wade through large volumes of documentation and words to distil and analyse the key elements and propositions.

While the Covid-19 pandemic has shown that many universities have the infrastructure for delivering high quality education through physical and virtual spaces, the fragility of the system and the lack of uniform capacity and the digital divide amongst students has exposed the limitations of fully harnessing the adoption of technologies. The nature and scale of the digital learning that is used to support the educational experience for higher education students has been a matter for individual organisations to determine. As a result, terminology such as "digital learning", "online learning", "remote learning", and "blended learning" are used interchangeably to describe quite different educational experiences, resulting also in a wide variation in the quality of digital learning experiences within the sector. It is also difficult to identify when digital delivery may fall short of reasonable standards in the absence of any shared criteria for measuring the impact of digital learning on the achievement of student success. Framed around designing creativity into digital learning in legal education, Ann, Sam, and Paul from Teesside University have developed a blueprint for planning a built-for-digital academic learner journey, underpinned by three principles to aid our role as educators. Chapter 8 defines these principles as: (i) Creating authentic and creative learning experiences and assessments, (ii) Inculcating future readiness and digital empowerment in learners, and (iii) Embedding digital literacies contextualised to the needs of the discipline and profession within the curriculum and learning design.

Creativity and resilience are arguably core to authentic future-facing learning: students need to be able to take ownership of knowledge and be empowered to use their creativity, skills, and knowledge confidently in familiar and unfamiliar circumstances, contextualising and adapting knowledge and skills based on ongoing experience and learning. The three principles outlined in chapter 8 provide pillars that equip graduates with the self-awareness and wide-ranging qualities, abilities, and behaviours to prepare for the future, particularly where there are significant changes in the process of qualifying for the vast array of established and new roles in the legal profession. Both chapters 7 and 8 raise questions around how new digital experiences and pedagogy deliver learning and teaching in legal education that meets the changing needs of the profession and society and the sorts of challenges/advantages to established pedagogies and course design these potentially disruptive technologies present.

Graduates need to be resilient in order to survive and thrive in the future workplace. In determining some of the core curriculum components to build resilience, three pillars of future readiness in law students are emphasised in various parts of the book: sustainability, creativity, and using law for the greater good. Is it worth teaching technology where that tech might be obsolescent by the time the student has graduated? And if so how should it be integrated? In chapter 9, Ryan and Helen draw on their joint perspectives from two institutions, Nottingham Trent and De Montford University, to address the need to incorporate the lens of sustainable teaching and learning practices so as to develop graduates with the skills to adapt to an ever-changing professional environment. The authors develop three pillars of sustainability and apply these to the broader perspective of learning and teaching in legal education, supporting students to develop an understanding of "why" legal tech is used by lawyers and what skills need to be developed. They pose whether a newly qualified lawyer conversant with legal principles and procedures needs any technical skills in order to successfully practice with legal tech? By inviting students to reflect on the pillars of sustainability, using technology as their lens, students will be able to develop skills of adaptability, critical thinking and the ability to navigate change in a digitally advancing practice. The pillars of sustainability also afford an understanding of the commercial realities of legal tech and consequently build an additional dimension of their digital lawyering skills.

In Chapter 10, Olga and Piotr share their interventions to ensure that students and clients have access to legal information in the digital age through the administration of legal clinics at SWPS University of Social Sciences and Humanities in Warsaw (Poland). Framed around the significance of preparing students with an Access to Justice mindset as a foundation for developing future-ready law graduates, their study addressed the extent to which lawyers and law students use digital tools in the form of Internet search engines as a source of legal knowledge and whether they had the skills and tools to verify the usefulness and credibility of the information found on the Internet: otherwise this is a risk and barrier to Access to Justice initiatives. The chapter tackles digital literacies in students by advocating that a law curriculum goes beyond teaching how to use the digital tools due to the exponential changes in the use of technology. Instead, they argue that with the internet being a source of information and misinformation, the ability to recognise the truthfulness of news, and, in particular, legal information, will allow students to be well prepared to exercise their profession in the future. This will help the implementation of the guarantee of Access to Justice and better prepare the students to be future-ready. The authors argue that further research on reliability and trustworthiness of information is important not only to determine the impact on the access to justice itself but also on the legal education. This chapter is a testament to supporting students to go beyond securing a job, and engage with communities and potentially make improvements that impact the social, economic or environmental aspects of the community they live and work within through the experiences and learning they have gained from their legal education. Naturally, its access to justice and clinical legal education foci also link it to chapter 5.

Several authors offer their take on reimagining the law degree and teaching law-tech as a discipline. The restructuring is based on the need for curricula to equip graduates to tackle the world's biggest challenges, which will require interdisciplinary knowledge, flexible and innovative thinking, design thinking to assimilate and work with change, and problem solving. Innovation can be difficult when there are core subjects to teach and these chapters explore a variety of questions – how to work within the prescribed frameworks (namely, where the law degree is regulated by its professional bodies), how to modernise traditional subjects in law, how to teach digital literacies and digital confidence to law students (and what does that mean in the context of legal education, there being several phrases in play, such as digital literacies, digital competencies, digital proficiencies, and more, often used interchangeably and with varying meanings).

Several authors in this book take the position that technology has the potential to go beyond being a tool for innovation and become a subject of teaching and research within the episteme of law and the law degree. The recently coined term "Digital Lawyering" (Thanaraj, 2017, 2018) offers an insight into the theory behind the sorts of learning required for law students and future professionals to thrive in a digital age. Linked to this, Lucia, Alan, Kim, and Andy from London South Bank University discuss their interdisciplinary and collaborative approach, involving law lecturers, computer scientists, and local lawyers to introducing students to lawtech in chapter 11. This innovative module is an example where legal education meets computer science to aid students' development of new literacies in data, technology and humanities, communication, and design. Whilst the authors suggest that law students do not necessarily need to code, skills in project management, teamworking, and legal design are vital. As was the case with other chapters, their module was created with an emphasis on access to justice and legal design, a key future-ready skill for law students to address diverse client needs by breaking down legal solutions into a set of simple rules brought to life by technological solutions. The module develops new ways of thinking in both law students and computer science students, particularly around the impact of technology on legal services and careers in law and computing.

In chapter 12, Rónán shares a real-world experiential initiative called Law and Innovation at the National University of Ireland, Galway, in which students worked on real-world app projects, developing their ability to critically assess the suitability of digital solutions to address practical legal and social issues and to work across disciplines to develop and design a systems solution through design-thinking approaches and assessing its legal implications. He discusses the drivers for this innovation, including inculcating basic skills needed to operate in an increasingly technologically-enabled workplace, equipping students with the knowledge and perspectives required to engage critically with technology and creating opportunities to develop understanding of the role of innovation in modern society, in legal practice, and in their careers. His work has led to developing a partial but influential perspective on the purpose of legal education, one he advocates as focusing more on high-level skills and understanding, and training towards the profession focusing more on efficiently and effectively engaging in repeated behaviours or actions. This project was part-funded by the National Forum for the Enhancement of Teaching and Learning in Higher Education and the Higher Education Authority of Ireland, through the Learning Enhancement Projects scheme.

In both chapters 11 and 12, the authors develop the literature on digital lawyering containing theoretical frameworks created through one's own professional and personal development and reflection, and practical activities such as design thinking, communicating in creative ways through the use of digital solutions. A key factor in the success of being a digital professional is the need to continually learn and evolve our mindset, skills, and knowledge as digital solutions develop in fast-paced environments. Chapters 5, 6, 10, and 11 are linked by their consideration of the affordance between innovation and access to justice initiatives to more effectively communicate rights to vulnerable and disadvantaged groups, and to help unrepresented litigants navigate legal procedures. Embedding design thinking in legal education will become increasingly important for students to be aware of the potential of design thinking to make accessible legal services for everyone.

In setting the direction of change towards future-ready disciplines and curricula, authors have considered the exponential growth of knowledge and the rapid and radical development of technology. Chapters 13 to 15 consider how we ensure that curricula remain relevant and responsive to contextual challenges and to student needs, the competencies future graduates need and how we anticipate them, and how we prepare graduates to be future-ready in a digital world that is constantly changing and inhabited by artificial intelligence. As part of their responsibility to understand and assist this digital transformation, Law Schools should prepare students and can do so through interdisciplinary knowledge, working across a variety of disciplines so that students can exercise leadership on critically important debates at the intersection of law and digital technology through fluency in the key legal frameworks, together with an understanding of the technical, philosophical, ethical, and humanities aspects of technologies and the ways society can work to ensure those technologies serve the public good (Williams, 2020).

In chapter 13, colleagues from Oxford University, Rebecca and Václav, describe and reflect on their practice-oriented Oxford LawTech Education Programme and the academically-oriented Law and Computer Science programme, demonstrating that through collaborative interdisciplinary approaches to learning, learners are being prepared to become future-ready. Their reflections and findings identify gaps within legal education and they advocate for a curriculum that lends itself to developing an interdisciplinary mindset, one that is focused on the use of data and design thinking with robust ethical grounding in the use of technology for lawyering.

In chapter 14, Cemile shares her experience of designing and teaching a Masters in Legal Technology at the University of Law UK, to empower lawyers for the digital age through an in-depth study of how technologies are changing the legal sector, incorporating STEM subjects into the study of law and developing design thinking in lawyers and law graduates. The chapters make a case towards the value of interdisciplinary knowledge to shape law degrees as stewards as the world navigates through the Fourth Industrial Revolution and to train and prepare students for the digital transformation of society by giving them the means to understand and face the challenges that the digital world presents, using law as a lens to identify challenges and develop potential interdisciplinary solutions.

In chapter 15, Ann makes a case for positioning legal education, supported by interdisciplinarity, as an anchor degree, given the need for the law to have a pivotal role in regulating the digital transformation and the 4IR. Two models for a law-tech curriculum are proposed, which will allow a reimagined law degree to contribute to the response to the challenges that are coming, and prepare students for the digital transformation of society by giving them the means to understand and face the challenges that the digital world presents, by drawing on the law's interpretive flexibility and the epistemically constructive nature of law. As an anchor discipline in Higher Education, a law degree can provide stewardship in dealing with the challenges of the 4IR, which are both greater and unknown as digital age environments evolve. The models proposed allow law academics to consider the need for different knowledge and skills from those currently being developed through the academic and vocational stages of legal study.

To teach effectively with technology and to design teaching and learning academic experiences with technology, a programme of development across the law school is needed. It should be aimed to equip staff with the knowledge and skills to enhance their pedagogical practice through the use of various digital tools, by giving them the confidence to embrace new technologies in the delivery of their lessons, including the efficient deployment and management of the right technology; it will require bespoke training and coaching for students and staff and on-going support. The right technology can completely change the way that students learn across the whole academic portfolio. In chapter 16, the first of two concluding chapters, Kim from London South Bank University explores, in this context, the identity of the "legal academic", the roles of faculty and students in modern university teaching, and the pedagogical skills and leadership attitudes needed to foster student-oriented teaching. She draws on the lessons provided from chapters in this book and from another commentary.

In the second part of the conclusion, in chapter 17, Ann from Teesside University explores what it means to be a law school in the fourth industrial revolution. This chapter is grounded in the construct that lawyers should not lose focus on the core competencies the profession has always been known for and should see technology as a way to further expand their skill set. Within the realm of law and technology, the ability to use technology is only one component of a multidimensional approach to formulating what a law-tech degree would look like. An appreciation and understanding of interdisciplinary concepts to collaborate and find solutions that are broader than just the law itself is the crux of the value of a law degree in addressing some of the grand challenges around technology and innovation at this time.

By foregrounding thinking about studying law within the space of nurturing creativity in learners, a student's developing of a "sense of being" is the cornerstone of creativity, as it mediates their emerging personal and professional identities (Solomonides et al, 2012). This chapter aims to address questions such as how do we reconstruct our legal education systems so that they are relevant in the digital age? And what are the key challenges facing the adaptability of law schools and the culture change that is necessary (EDUCAUSE 2016–2020, Clark, 2018). Ann shares a roadmap for law schools to enable them to develop the student's capacity and disposition and strategies to deal with the unknown and the ambiguous–and in doing so, learn how to persevere and navigate their way through it in a way that will make a difference.

Beginning your Journey with us

As you reflect on your own professional digital transformation journey or that of your team, law school or university, and formulate a strategy, the examples in chapters in this book should assist. However, this transformation journey will need to go through several iterations to be able to respond to the changing needs of learners, the evolving purpose of legal education and its role as an anchor for stewardship of the 4IR. As such, as you read the chapters, you may wish to consider how a change of direction in legal education and the approaches we take in learning, teaching, and assessments can prepare our students for the future. This could be captured in the following ways. In other words, here are some questions to consider as you navigate the book:

- Are we teaching to fit what's required now rather than thinking of ways to change the system to fit the new realities?
- What skills and knowledge will these new realities require of lawyers? Will there be more need for interdisciplinary knowledge and skills that support flexibility and innovation?
- As innovation can be difficult when there are core subjects to teach, how can we work within the prescribed frameworks (if the law degree is regulated by its professional bodies in your jurisdiction) and how can traditional subjects in law become modernised?
- What challenges and advantages to established pedagogies and course design do these potentially disruptive technologies present?
- Can new technologies and approaches support learner interactivity, collaboration, communication, reflection, and skills, and so assist to prepare students for the future?
- Should we be teaching law students about technology or digital literacy and confidence, and if so what does that mean in the context of legal education and how should we go about it?

The journey towards reimagining legal education requires consideration of the future role of lawyers. These are some suggested questions to reflect on in this context:

- What will be the role of lawyers in a future where many tasks currently carried out by lawyers might be automated?
- What roles cannot be automated, such that lawyers will always be needed?
- What are the problems and regulatory requirements that the next generation of lawyers will need to solve?

- Will lawyers enjoy being lawyers in this new environment?
- Will there be new roles for lawyers arising from the coming technological and societal changes, and what skills will lawyers need for those?
- What roles outside being a member of the legal profession will be assisted by having a law degree?
- What should be the balance between academia, the legal profession and other stakeholders in deciding what the curriculum should contain?

This collection is an opportunity to draw on various pedagogic narratives on designing law degrees that push the boundaries in knowledge, experience, and learning; one that is not simply focused on preparing for the changing legal profession but also explores what it means to become future-ready and digitally empowered, and socially and ethically engaged, so as to meaningfully address the challenges of regulating the digital world. We hope this work contributes towards reimagining legal education to play a role as legal and regulatory frameworks evolve to address developments in technology. The future of legal education is a complex, contested, rapidly changing, and disruptive space (Christensen et al, 2015, Flood, 2015). The regulatory challenges and the digital transformation brought about by the 4IR allow law schools to question how legal education can become an anchor discipline within Higher Education, providing academic leadership at a time of exponential change. Alongside this, a wider question needs to be addressed around what it means to have a legal education in the changing landscape of the legal profession and also in the changing world of work.

The chapters can be read in a number of ways. Ann and Kris have laid out the book as a collection in which early chapters give accounts of creative and innovative approaches to learning and teaching in legal education, in which authors who have embraced change share best practices around teaching existing topics with technology and developing technology-enhanced approaches to teaching and reflect on where to take their course designs next. Further chapters look ahead at the direction of change required for legal education, and concluding chapters look to the ongoing research agenda. Naturally, there are other ways in which chapters could have been collated, and we trust that readers will be able to discern other themes and links between chapters. The collection is framed around what it means to be future-ready today and what we can do as law academics to facilitate the knowledge, skills, and dispositions needed by future-ready graduates: we trust that debate around securing that is an important one to facilitate.

Bibliography

Altbach, PG, Reisberg, L., & Rumbley, LE (2009). Trends in global higher education: Tracking an academic revolution trends in global higher education. *Higher Education*. Retrieved from http://unesdoc.unesco.org/images/0018/001832/183219e.pdf

Barnett, R (1997). *Higher education: A critical business*. Buckingham: The Society for Research into Higher Education and Open University.

Barnett, R (2000b). University knowledge in an age of supercomplexity, *Higher Education, 40*, 409–422, available at doi:10.1023/A:1004159513741

Barnett, R (August 2014). *The University in an age of supercomplexity: Challenges and possibilities*. Guest lecture, UNESP, Sao Paulo State University, available at: https://www.ronaldbarnett.co.uk/assets/docs/The%20University%20in%20an%20Age%20of%20Supercomplexity%20-%20Sao%20Paulo.pdf

Bradney, A (2003). *Conversations, choices and chances: The liberal law school in the twenty-first century* (Hart Publication).

Canadian Bar Association (August 2014). Futures: Transforming the delivery of legal services in Canada, http://www.cba.org/CBAMediaLibrary/cba_na/PDFs/CBA%20Legal%20Futures%20PDFS/Futures-Final-eng.pdf

Christensen, CM, Raynor, M, & McDonald, R (2015). What is disruptive innovation. *Harvard Business Review, 93*(12), 1–11.

Clark, E (May 2018). Digital transformation: What is it? EDUCAUSE, available at: https://er.educause.edu/articles/2018/5/digital-transformation-what-is-it

Danvers, E (2016). Re-thinking criticality: Undergraduate students, critical thinking and higher education. Doctoral thesis (PhD), University of Sussex, available at: http://sro.sussex.ac.uk/id/eprint/61114/

Dunne, G (2015). Beyond critical thinking to critical being: Criticality in higher education and life. *International Journal of Educational Research, 71*, 86–99, available online at 10.1016/j.ijer.2015.03.003

EDUCAUSE, Digital transformation (resources), available at: https://library.educause.edu/topics/information-technology-management-and-leadership/digital-transformation-dx

EDUCAUSE, Dx: Digital transformation of higher education, available at: https://www.educause.edu/focus-areas-and-initiatives/digital-transformation

Ehlers, UD, & Kellermann, SA (2019). Future skills—The future of learning and higher education. *Results of the international future skills delphi survey*. Karlsruhe. https://nextskills.files.wordpress.com/2019/03/2019-02-23-delphi-report-final.pdf

Feldman, P (2018). *The potential of 4.0 is huge—UK must take the lead*. Blog. https://www.jisc.ac.uk/blog/the-potential-of-education-4-is-huge-the-uk-must-take-the-lead-now-12-sep-2018

Flood, J (2015). Global challenges for legal education: Competing for the world's students. *Nottingham Law Journal, 24*, 79 https://papers.ssrn.com/sol3/papers.cfm?abstract_id=2909891

Katsh, E, & Rule, C (2016). "What We Know and Need to Know about Online Dispute Resolution," South Carolina Law Review: Vol. 67: Iss. 2 , Article 10. Available at: https://scholarcommons.sc.edu/sclr/vol67/iss2/10

Lord Neuberger (2012). Judges and professors – ships passing in the night? Speech Max Planck Institute, Hamburg on 9 July 2012, https://www.judiciary.uk/wp-content/uploads/JCO/Documents/Speeches/mr-speech-hamburg-lecture-09072012.pdf

McGinnis, J, & Pearce, R (2014). The great disruption: How machine intelligence will transform the role of lawyers in the delivery of legal services. *Fordham Law Review, 82*, 3041–3066 https://ir.lawnet.fordham.edu/cgi/viewcontent.cgi?article=5007&context=flr

Means, B, Toyama, Y, Murphy, R, Bakia, M, & Jones, K (2009). *Evaluation of evidence-based practices in online learning: a meta-analysis and review of online learning studies*. US Department of Education.

Nedelkoska, L, & Quintini, G (2018). Automation, skills use and training, OECD Social, Employment and Migration Working Papers, No. 202, Paris: OECD Publishing, (https://www.oecd-ilibrary.org/docserver/2e2f4eea-en.pdf?expires=1554040951&id=id&accname=guest&checksum=06BC7F3A1E72160839AC2189A34B9B8F

Orr, S, & Shreeve, A (2018). *Art and design pedagogy in higher education: Knowledge, values and ambiguity in the creative curriculum*. Routledge.

Surden, H (2014). Machine learning and law. *Washington Law Review*, 89–95 https://www.law.uw.edu/wlr/print-edition/print-edition/vol-89/1/machine-learning-and-law

Sir Geoffrey Vos, Chancellor of the High Court: Lawyers and judges will need different training if they are to resolve modern day business disputes through the adoption of new technology can be accelerated to improve the efficiency of the justice system (20th June 2018) https://www.judiciary.uk/wp-content/uploads/2018/06/speech-chc-the-foundation-for-science-and-technology.pdf

Solomonides, I, Reid, A, & Petocz, P (2012). "A Relational model of student engagement" In *Engaging with learning in higher education*, I. Solomonides, A. Reid, & P. Petocz (Eds.). Faringdon, UK: Libri Publishing.

Susskind R (2017). *Tomorrow's Lawyers*. Oxford University Press.

Susskind, R., & Susskind, D. (2015). *The Future of the Professions*. Oxford University Press.

Schwab, K (2016). The fourth industrial revolution: What it means, how to respond. https://www.weforum.org/agenda/2016/01/the-fourth-industrial-revolution-what-it-means-and-how-torespond/

Thanaraj, A (2017). Making the case for a digital lawyering framework in legal education. *International Review of Law, 2017*(3), 17, available at: https://insight.cumbria.ac.uk/id/eprint/3324/1/Thanaraj_MakingTheCase.pdf

Thanaraj, A (2018). Studying law in a digital age: Preparing law students for participation in a technologically-advanced, *Multidisciplinary and Complex Professional Environment*, 27(2) Nott L J. https://www4.ntu.ac.uk/nls/document_uploads/nlj-vol-27-2-2018.pdf

Velsberg, O (18 June 2019). The technolawgist, government chief data officer of Estonia: robot judges, artificial intelligence and the future of digitalisation reporting on Estonia's project to issue rulings through AI judges http://www.thetechnolawgist.com/2019/06/18/ott-velsberg-government-chief-data-officer-of-estonia-robot-judges-artificial-intelligence-and-the-future-of-digitalisation/

Wegner, J (2015). The values of legal education, *24 Nottingham Law Journal.*, 112 https://www4.ntu.ac.uk/nls/document_uploads/nlj_24.pdf

Williams, R (14th May 2020). 21st century legal education: A university perspective, keynote presentation at the Future of Legal Education and Training Conference 2020 (LegalEdCon London, organised by Legal Cheek), available at: https://www.law.ox.ac.uk/news/2020-05-14-rebecca-williams-delivers-future-legal-education-keynote

World Economic Forum (2017). Accelerating workforce reskilling for the Fourth Industrial Revolution, Geneva http://www3.weforum.org/docs/WEF_EGW_White_Paper_Reskilling.pdf

World Economic Forum (2016). The future of jobs: Employment, skills and workforce strategy for the fourth industrial revolution, global challenge insight report, available at: http://www3.weforum.org/docs/WEF_Future_of_Jobs.pdf

Chapter 2

Bringing Land Law to Life: Lessons From the Development and Deployment of an Immersive "Virtual Town" in the Teaching of Land Law

Yulia Marunchak and Thomas Dunk

Introduction

The teaching of Land Law is often stigmatised for its seeming inability to draw on the inherent intellectual fascination of university students. Indeed, a commonly held belief is that teaching Land Law involves drawing the short straw (perhaps only second to Trusts and Equity). Responding to this challenge, we enhanced the learning and teaching experience by utilising 3D graphics technology to integrate a "Virtual Town" into our second-year Land Law module. A digital 3D model representing a small, urbanised, area whereby Land Law concepts can be demonstrated to students was incorporated into lectures, tutorials, and workshops, and then into assessments. An early version of the Town can be viewed at https://youtu.be/oMiufsm58j4.

This chapter sets out the pedagogical advantages of this approach. It describes how the Town was designed, developed, and integrated seamlessly into the module along with how it assists digital readiness. It explores digital empowerment through incorporating new tools into the learning environment. Finally, it considers how the Virtual Town can be taken forward to enhance legal teaching in the future.

By employing 3D visualisation(s), we ensured that the teaching of Land Law remains future-ready, part of a key role in transforming a usually black letter law module to one using a dynamic visual medium to enhance the learning and teaching experiences of students and staff. Digital empowerment and future readiness are not just qualities that law students need to engage with and embrace: legal educators must also adopt modern practices to enhance their own teaching provision. Digital empowerment for teachers involves the effective use of new technologies to enrich the student experience and contribute towards their legal development. This can be in improved grades, but also enhanced legal skills and graduate attributes. Land Law remains a challenging area in which to implement digital empowerment and future readiness given the inability of the profession to embrace e-conveyancing, almost 20 years after the LRA 2002 (Dixon, 2018, p34) but, certainly, the teaching of this area is ripe for new technologies.

DOI: 10.4324/9780429351082-2

Design, Adoption, and Embedding of the Virtual Town into the Land Law Module

We developed the Virtual Town in-house at the University of Hertfordshire, loosely based on the small Hertfordshire market town of Baldock but with significant changes to ensure that almost every conceivable Land Law conundrum could be explored: as one student remarked "one town has never had so many dodgy conveyances and legal problems". We used Google's 3D editing application, "Sketchup", which integrates seamlessly with the satellite data made available via the "Google Earth" platform, allowing the downloading of regions in isolation of their greater geographical area(s). Manual authoring of the model (and the suitable abstraction of a real-world town) was undertaken to ensure our creative agency. The Virtual Town is used in different ways. For example, in the form of short videos accompanied by audio narratives during online lectures, ad-hoc explanations within skills-based sessions, and question setting and answering for workshops. Using off-the-shelf technology, sometimes in innovative ways, keeps to a minimum the overall cost, ensuring the viability of such projects.

Several variables should be borne in mind when addressing how to convey meaning in a 3D virtual space. Indexicality – best understood as a modality of signage – is a primary factor often overlooked by those seeking to communicate information (as opposed to raw data) visually. This concept draws from a rich field of research on semiotics (Komedchikov, 2005) and is best understood by examining cartography and its multitude of recognisable symbols. Modern-day map making, often referred to as a form of "neo cartography", is largely computer-driven and procedural in nature. It is driven by algorithms designed to work at scales beyond the ability of humans to envisage. Its implementation deviates from traditional cartography which, in addition to conveying spaces visually, also serves as a vehicle for narrative. This ancient art form has found new appreciation in the entertainment industry inside video games, whose designers strive to depict fictional areas whilst holding the attention of users. Such feats are achieved by exploiting human interest and our propensity for pattern recognition. To this end, much emphasis was placed on the visual codifying of identifiable elements in the Town and context in which they sit. Our goal was to elicit a response which generated an intrinsic motivation to explore the environment and glean meaning, thereby holding attention.

The effectiveness of the Virtual Town required its incorporation into all elements of the Hertfordshire Law School model (Wild, 2017, pp310–312). This provided significant advantages, for instance when using online lectures, the use of an audio-visual medium provided additional variety in a presentation, a multimodal approach that made for a more engaging conveyance of information. When coupled with an integrated MCQ, it could both provide knowledge to students in a novel manner but still be used to test their comprehension. For example, after viewing a short video within a lecture, created using the Virtual

Town tool, a short comprehension exercise followed and data was collected. This data collection could then be used to adjust workshops to focus on areas identified as challenging to students. While the tool was used with online lectures, it could easily be transferred and used in traditional delivery with all the same benefits.

Integration of the Virtual Town into skills sessions and workshops required support from the wider module team. This involved meeting technical prerequisites and ensuring its correct utilisation, the management of which proved to be complex. In addition to the existing cognitive load on staff, a new variable was present, namely to ensure that the Town was used as a tool, and not a gimmick that would merely demonstrate technological skill with limited benefits to the underlying pedagogy. It was decided not to use the technology when teaching leases or mortgages, but to use it when teaching proprietary interests such as covenants, easements, or adverse possession to help illustrate the law in ways that a verbal description might lead to difficulties in comprehension for students. The Town was also used interactively, for instance when asking students to consider the basics of easements such as rights of way, water, light, and support. Students were asked to examine the Virtual Town, projected onto the board, and point out where a potential easement could be and what caselaw they had to support the example that they had chosen.

The Virtual Town was used as a means of posing questions to students in preparation for workshops and allowing them to visualise the scope of a theoretical problem between two neighbours. The audio-visual questions were presented from a first-person perspective, at eye level, as if the student were in practice and walking over the affected area with the client. This approach was particularly effective when teaching the acquisition of easements, an area of English land law that can be complex and difficult to communicate verbally. To ensure the module was balanced for all learners, in addition to the audio-visual presentation of the question, a text-based version was readily available to ensure that different types of learners were supported, in addition to meeting study needs agreements. Finally, the Virtual Town was integrated with the module assessment. For example, an assessment involving a boundary dispute and mediation included photos, plans, and videos of the question. Furthermore, the locations used were referenced during the final examination, meaning the problem-based questions were all set within a familiar landscape.

As with many technologies, the Virtual Town has some limitations when considering its suitability for different contexts. It could not be used for all aspects of the module, especially in relation to leases. In the case of examining interiors, there was insufficient visual fidelity to convey relevant meaning. Most detail was only visible from the outside. Additionally, the time taken to construct such granularity into the Virtual Town was weighed against the benefits for students, deemed to be minimal due to leases having a reduced visual element that most students grasp without detailed visual explanation. The appropriate use of technology is just as important as the technology itself, with this in mind the overuse of the Virtual Town could easily have the effect of becoming a classroom novelty. This is also to say that paying too much attention to a single modality can have diminishing returns when considered in light of student engagement.

Impact of Using the Virtual Town

The success of the Virtual Town tool required a positive impact on student engagement and a positive review from staff teaching on the module, all the evidence for this section of the work is anecdotal so we accept other factors alongside the Town may have played a role in the module's improvement. Our impression was that sessions involving the Virtual Town involved a high level of engagement from teaching staff and students. At the end of the year, in the module feedback questionnaire (MFQ), many comments from the students indicated that the Virtual Town had enhanced their learning and had a positive impact on their learning experience.

An additional, incidental, piece of evidence to support the increasing interest in Land Law was a rise in the quantity of third-year dissertations wishing to explore the subject. Our data from the first year of the use of the Virtual Town also indicates an improvement in student outcomes when embracing the technology, first at the lower end of the marks scheme where the module failure rate dropped 5.8% from the previous year. At the higher end, those achieving firsts (70% plus) increased by 7%. This increase was not at the expense of those achieving 2:1, which remained identical, but a decrease in those receiving 3rds and 2:2 s, pushing the grade bell curve towards the higher end. In the second year, these improvements could not be sustained and while the failure rate increased once more, those who achieved a first-class mark for the module only dropped by 2%: this was still an improvement on the year when no Virtual Town was used. These results suggest a positive impact on student achievement from the ability to visualise concepts. In order to maintain the assessment quality, a rigorous internal and external moderation process was undertaken with audio-visual recordings of assessments being sent to moderators after the assessment. Team members also declared this digital artefact as "useful", noting the improvement in understanding exhibited by students due to having another tool to make such sessions more engaging.

The use of the Virtual Town was generally a success with improved results from across the year group. A more engaged student group emerged, and school staff embraced the use of the Town to develop their own teaching practice.

The Pedagogical Advantages of Teaching with the Virtual Town

Teaching Land Law can be challenging for various reasons. Its underlying concepts and proprietary interests may have little to no point of reference in students' lives, with few having gone beyond entering into a short-term tenancy agreement for their student accommodation. Contrast this awareness arising from the portrayal of Criminal Law through popular culture, the involvement of Contract Law in everyday life, and Public Law's close association with important political events. Land Law, sadly, rarely features in gritty TV legal dramas or murder mystery novels, although we give an honourable mention to the 1927 novel *Unnatural Death* by Dorothy L Sayers, set to the backdrop of the "new" Land Registration Act 1925. The net effect of the failure to produce a drama series in which easement or restrictive covenants are central to the plot is that students often have a very limited idea of the subject prior to the first lecture.

Law teaching is dominated by text, as Haapio notes:

> "In most instances, we communicate our knowledge in written and oral form. Most legal literature is text only, black and white, with no pictures, graphs or examples. We may use charts in our teaching, but when it comes to legal research, memoranda, opinions, textbooks or contracts, most of us tend not to think of visual communication".
>
> (Haapio, 2010, p391; see also King, 2016, p84)

This is particularly so for Land Law, as Weir records:

> "Property lawyers revel in the medieval; the arcane, the convoluted but fundamental concepts that abound in property law. We simply look around us and see property law manifested in the chair we sit on … not to mention the fascination that awaits the next High Court case on native title … A student may not share our enthusiasm".
>
> (Weir, 2007, p107)

In short, a generation of students brought up on a mix of smartphones and highly visual stimuli are taught through black letter text a subject which has no point of reference for them. And yet the use of visual pedagogy (see King, 2016, p91) seems particularly suited to the teaching of Land Law and allows connections to be made with the different rights and responsibilities that attach themselves to land. As Haapio notes: "Visualisation is used in many areas to help reduce complexity and convey information quickly, business managers and engineers commonly use flowcharts, timelines and other visuals to communicate information." (Haapio, 2010, p393). Moreover, Sherwin et al list seven ways in which visual representations can improve legal decision-making and judgement (Sherwin et al, 2006, pp241–245), most importantly in the ability of visual displays to convey more information than words alone, thereby allowing the learner to engage with greater emotional bandwidth (Sherwin et al, 2006, p241). Whilst visual approaches take longer to prepare than traditional text-based modalities, they allow for more opportunities for critical thought and debate, as concepts and legal points are easily conveyed (King, 2016, p91). (See also Weir, 2007, p113 for the suggestion that physical models add interest, but are highly time-consuming to produce and not necessarily the best option when teaching a class of twenty, or more, students.)

The Virtual Town builds on visual pedagogy, with the benefit of a realistic 3D animation giving new views and possibilities to learners and teaching staff. It also complies with Adrian's suggestion that "Legal education needs to keep pace with technology. It is suggested that this is achievable by employing two strategies simultaneously. First, by embracing the concept of law as narrative; and then second, using interactive media to explore that narrative" (Adrian 2010, p257). Further, it meets Hagan's call for innovative development of the legal curriculum with a design-oriented approach focussing on remaining user-centred, experimental, and intentional in how one operates (Hagen, 2019). Within this tool we have embraced these three principles while placing emphasis on Hagan's underlying message of when attempting new ideas, everything should be treated as a prototype. It should remain subject to forces of change, informed by the experience of participants.

The tool itself feeds into a wider approach involving the enhancement of problem-based learning and legal skills for the workplace. In doing so, the use of the Virtual Town goes some way to incorporating and supporting the Knight and York, USEM Model (Knight and Yorke, 2002, pp264–266). It gives the students an understanding of the subject, enhances skills requiring the observation of legal problems and creating arguments using visual media within Land Law. In sum, it encourages efficacy and the student's own recognition of their underlying thought processes in coming to the answers.

The use of the Town can by some within the profession be seen as eroding a traditional teaching modality which places emphasis on knowing the law and cases. We respectfully reject such criticism, as we hold that the teaching of law must move forward, informed by contemporary research, and enabled by diverse skillsets. Our approach to using this tool, both within the classroom and in lectures, brought Land Law concepts alive in a manner not usually seen in the teaching of covenants and other areas. Still, the use of the Virtual Town cannot ensure successful outcomes for students or staff. Students still must put in the hours of work, while staff need adequate support in their use of the technology.

Despite a gradual trend towards a more visual approach, law is still a heavily text-based subject yet the advantages of making a shift towards a more visual delivery are, *increasingly,* too important to continue being ignored. The ability to embrace digital technologies in preparing students for future careers, improving visual literacy skills, and allowing students to learn in a more interactive environment make the use of advanced visualisations vital for the future of Land Law.

Future Readiness in Learning and Teaching Land Law

Future readiness in the teaching of Land Law requires continuous improvement, using technology effectively to enhance learning and teaching. It manifests through the discovery, or development, of methods facilitated by the use of currently available technology. It supports the delivery of a curriculum's constituent elements in an enhanced form, as with the now-common use of digital learning environments across programmes of study, or the use of tools to encourage and promote debate outside of the classroom. This may involve occasional big leaps forward or small incremental improvements.

As Sherwin et al observe, the use of digital and visual communication is changing the methods employed by lawyers; being able to visualise arguments means they will strategise their cases differently. The benefit becomes apparent when cases are prepared in new ways, allowing for a relationship between numerous elements to surface in more emergent fashions. Such discoveries would otherwise remain hidden from traditional (or predictable) modes of cognition (Sherwin et al, 2006, p235). Therefore, for students to become future-ready they will need to cultivate visual literacy as defined by Sherwin et al: "… being able to identify the meanings that pictures leave unsaid and to translate those perceptions into words" (Sherwin et al, 2006, p261).

The adoption of AI technology may impact the legal profession radically (Kairinos, 2019). The potential to reduce the need for extensive legal knowledge is on the horizon, with publicly available databases allowing users to summon obscure legal knowledge with a few clicks of a button. In its place, the future-ready law course will likely be focused on the cultivation of discernment. The acquisition of critical thinking skills while emphasising the examination of law from different perspectives, made possible via the convergence of numerous modalities, is essential. Future readiness is, then, being ready to use new technologies whilst exploring opportunities to adapt and apply them in pursuit of improving the student experience. This, while systematically developing the skills that future lawyers will need as the legal world embraces technology both inside and outside the courtroom.

Digital Empowerment and Future Development of the Virtual Town

Digital empowerment for legal teachers involves employing technology in innovative ways. It means moving beyond the sector-norm of modern university practice to further a student's learning experience and contribute to their legal development. Whether through email or discussion forums, such digital interventions have served to augment social interactions between educators and their students.

It does remain something of an irony that, as we strive for efficiency in our use of technology, it often presents new and unforeseen problems. To address this, it is necessary to turn our attention towards the computer sciences. To understand what is commonly referred to as user experience design (UX) we must decode some subject knowledge in a bid to converge our disciplines. UX, in the context of educational technology, is best understood as establishing best practice as it relates to students' use of technology. It focusses on minimising cognitive load and ensuring that the introduction of new elements does not place additional burden on their studies. Being able to gauge the UX through a faithful interpretation of the student experience may be the most important factor in deciding how one employs technology for teaching.

As discussed throughout this chapter, despite its unfamiliarity to existing land law practitioners, there are numerous affordances attributed to the use of interactive visual media. Its true value, however, becomes evident when exploring the adaptability of computer-generated graphics and its potential to convey content in a manner either photo-realistic or abstract in nature, the latter being defined as a simplified representation of a complex scene. Such abstractions become relevant when considering the potential of other immersive technologies and the manner in which we interface with them. This could be in the form of immersive Virtual Reality (VR), wherein head-mounted displays are used (on which see Chapter 3 in this collection) or as Augmented Reality (AR), which involves the use of what is best described as a looking glass allowing for the real-time annotation of the physical world. Both allow for the control and recreation of physical spaces, re-arranging them to explore hypotheses and communicate ideas. As such technology becomes readily available, so too will baseline digital literacies need to advance in order to exploit them. This might take the form of exploring a remote, inaccessible location to examine living conditions or to experience events from a first-person perspective, revealing new findings.

The 3D visualisations used in the Virtual Town demonstrate the rich potential for embracing technology in the teaching of law. Similar technology could also be harnessed to add value to the greater curriculum, notably in the teaching of the Law of Evidence where it could be used to see if it is possible that a witness could have seen what they claim from a particular viewpoint. While in a Housing Law module the Town could be adapted to explore laws on anti-social behaviour, nuisance and resolving neighbour disputes to just mention a few. A module on Planning Law could utilise the Town to be developed to explore the ideas that regulate and facilitates the use of planning laws, including Local Development Plans (LDP) and also the more sociological aspects of town planning. The scope for the technology within Public International law is most appropriate when exploring dispute settlement concepts, notably countermeasures and land border issues. However, with time and resources to develop the Town, there is no reason that the technology could not be used to illustrate Refugee Law. Finally, the other area that we have considered the development of the Town is Environment Law, here the Town could be redeployed to demonstrate regulatory concepts associated with waste disposal, air pollution, and conservation. In a less modular specific way, the Town could be developed to demonstrate any problem-based questions that have facts within a physically restricted space, for instance in Public Law the Town could be developed to show an irrationality or illegality question confined to a single street.

The above examples are only the ideas that we have considered however the restrictions for its use are only limited by the imagination, the usefulness of being able to demonstrate a legal concept in a virtual environment, and the resources necessary to develop the Town in these new ways.

Furthermore, with the advent in England and Wales of the Solicitors Qualifying Exam (SQE), law schools may embrace the development of an SQE ready LLB style undergraduate degree. This shake-up to legal education would require curriculum changes that embrace not only legal knowledge but enhanced legal skills not usually taught until undertaking an LPC style course. To these ends, new digital tools such as the Virtual Town will be needed to enhance the acquisition of knowledge and concepts, thereby freeing up time within the curriculum to focus on the practical skills required. Finally, the Virtual Town has the potential to bring case law alive by giving students an enriching audio-visual experience in a way that would not be possible when reading from a page.

Conclusion

The Virtual Town has proven itself as a useful tool for the teaching of Land Law, doing so in a way which utilises technology that is available off-the-shelf. It has shown that the module content can be made future-ready by embracing technology as an additional central pillar alongside core subject knowledge, research, and teaching. The use of the digital artefact had benefits for both student and staff experience(s) and made an immediate impact on the grades received by students across the module, moving the class grade profile upwards. It assists students in their development of existing skills in tandem with additional competencies associated with visual literacy, an increasingly important skill for the modern lawyer. The use of the technology has led to suggestions for its potential use in other modules and unlocked the idea of self-learning activities based on the 3D model which a student could access when ready.

The biggest drawback is the time to develop and create 3D models for such sessions which, for those lacking competence, requires greater consideration than simply writing material. Our experience was that it was worth the extra preparation time. Happily, it has also become evident that as familiarity increases, so does the efficiency of the authoring process.

Academics in legal education have a duty to embrace new practices to enhance and support the curriculum. In doing so, they will meet the expectations of students who demand a more innovative and interactive approach to learning. Employers demand a highly competent workforce with skills that are ready from day one and go beyond previous expectations. In order to meet this demand for change, modules need to embrace technology not only in how learning and teaching are delivered but also within the content of the teaching sessions themselves. 3D visualisation is a useful tool in helping to facilitate this change and bring law alive in the classroom.

Bibliography

Adrian, A (2010). The persuasion game: The story of law and legal education. *Entertainment Law Review, 21*(7), 256–262.

Dixon, M (2018). *Modern land law* (11th edition). Milton: Routledge.

Haapio, H (2010). Visualising contracts and legal rules for greater clarity. *The Law Teacher, 44*(3), 391–394.

Hagan, M, Law by design available at http://www.lawbydesign.co/en/ch-6-future-agenda/ accessed 25/10/19.

Kairinos, N, *Here's Why The Legal Sector Is Next In Line For Mass AI Disruption,* lasted updated Jul 16, 2019 as found at: https://www.lawyer-monthly.com/2019/07/heres-why-the-legal-sector-is-next-in-line-for-mass-ai-disruption/

King, F (2016). Visual approaches to property law pedagogy. *International Journal of Law in the Built Environment, 8*(1), 80–94.

Knight, PT, & Yorke, M (2002). Employability through the curriculum. *Tertiary Education and Management,* 8(4), 261–276.

Komedchikov, NN (2005). The general theory of cartography under the aspect of semiotics. In Proceedings of 22nd International Cartographic Conference (pp. 9–16).

Sherwin, RK, Feigenson, N, & Spiesel, C. (2006). Law in the digital age: How visual communication technologies are transforming the practice, theory, and teaching of law. *Boston University Journal of Science & Technology Law, 12*(2), 227.

Weir, M (2007). Ways to make the teaching of property/land law more interesting. *Journal of South Pacific Law, 11*(1), 107–115.

Wild, C (2017). The Flip Side: A case study examining how the refined flipped classroom enhances BAME student performance. *Proceedings of International Academic Conferences 5907143, International Institute of Social and Economic Sciences.* As found at https://ideas.repec.org/p/sek/iacpro/5907143.html

Chapter 3

Using Virtual Reality to Enhance the Law School Curriculum

Emma Jones, Francine Ryan, Hugh McFaul, David Vince, Lawrence Kizilkaya, and Jamie Daniels

Introduction

The tectonic impact of technology on the delivery of legal services is beginning to influence some law schools into re-imagining the use of educational technologies within legal education (Collins, 2016). Virtual simulations in video games offer an innovative teaching method to explore legal and ethical issues using role play in simulated worlds to explore ethical dilemmas without the constraints of real-life consequences (Newbery-Jones, 2016): eg, teaching aspects of international human rights law by adapting a first-person shooter video game into an interactive tool for student learning and assessment (Moffett et al, 2017).

Virtual reality (VR) – a three-dimensional computer simulation – can be used outside gaming (Falconer, 2013); advances in technology and decreasing equipment costs (Barfield & Williams, 2018) allow VR activities within educational settings, and there is already evidence that it can benefit learning (Dede & Richards, 2017). Its use to support law student learning and the development of new skills is being explored (McFaul & FitzGerald, 2019). Its ability to provide an authentic environment, heightening students' sense of immersion and presence (Dede & Richards, 2017) creates forms of experiential learning within a virtual world (Jacobson, 2017).

Reflecting this, The Open University Law School designed and created a VR app for students undertaking its optional clinical legal education (CLE) module. This chapter contextualises the development of this VR app by explaining the importance of skills development within CLE. It then summarises the findings from an initial pilot undertaken with final year undergraduates and ends by exploring how the use of VR can digitally empower law students and enhance their future readiness.

VR and Clinical Legal Education

The experiential nature of VR as a tool for learning and skills development suggests a particular fit within CLE, which allows students to develop a

DOI: 10.4324/9780429351082-3

practical understanding of the law through experience in clinical settings (or simulations) (Grimes, 2020) and encourages students to explore the wider social forces impacting upon law, in contrast to the case method's traditional focus upon law as a form of science (Wizner, 2001). CLE has become increasingly influential within legal education internationally (Bloch, 2010).

Most UK law schools engage in some form of clinical activity, using a variety of forms (Carney et al, 2014); other chapters in this volume reflect its use in, eg, Poland and Australia. Its paradigmatic expression is the law school advice clinic, where students research and draft legal advice for members of the public under the supervision of qualified lawyers. Other examples of practical legal tasks offered to students include policy work, internships in legal charities, and public legal education activities in schools and prisons (Carney et al, 2014).

CLE depends upon students developing and applying practical legal skills and also contextualising their experience of the practical application of the law within wider theoretical, social, and ethical concerns. Its proponents aim to do more than provide practical skills training for students during their academic study: rather they hope to allow students to engage with the law as an open-ended subject with wide-ranging social and ethical implications (Drummond & McKeever, 2015, p12). However, as the development of practical skills remains essential for students to engage in CLE, the remainder of this chapter will explore VR's potential to facilitate the development of these. In particular, it will focus on its ability to provide an authentic and immersive environment for students to develop their presentation skills through repetition and practice, and the generation of appropriate feedback.

The Open University's VR App

The Open University, an open access, distance learning institution, provides online and blended learning, including an LLB. To develop its students' legal and employability skills and provide valuable experience of the practical operation of law, a 30-credit, optional, final year CLE module, W360: Justice in Action was introduced, enabling students to carry out pro bono work, both face-to-face and online, including delivering presentations in a variety of settings. Such oral communication skills, a core component of CLE, commonly feature in employability frameworks and are a key competency within the contemporary legal profession (Cole & Tibby, 2013; Legal Education and Training Review, 2013, para 4.73).

Given the lack of face-to-face contact between students and difficulties in developing students' presentation skills, the authors designed and developed a VR app intended to help students develop the skills and confidence to deliver effective presentations. The VR app runs on students' smartphones and uses a simple headset to allow students to enter a computer-generated school, prison, community, or courtroom setting and give a brief (three to five minute) presentation, which is loaded into the app and is visible to the presenting student.

Students can load and advance presentation slides, read cue cards and take questions from audience avatars (which can be customised by the module team to the topic of the presentation). These avatars will also randomly "heckle" the presenter. There are other potential interruptions, such as a mobile telephone ringing. At the end of the presentation, students receive analytics feedback analysing their technique (eg, the level of eye contact with audience avatars). They are also able to record and playback their performance in-app, to facilitate reflection. Students may repeat the process as many times as they require, in order to develop their skills and confidence.

The Pilot: Research Methodology

Prior to the introduction of the VR app, its use was piloted on a small group of existing final year students whose home address was within a thirty-mile radius of The Open University's Milton Keynes campus, given the need for face to face participation. After email invitations to all current law students within this sample, six volunteered, although one subsequently had to withdraw. The pilot was conducted in August 2017. Each of the five participants was asked to prepare a five-minute presentation (with PowerPoint slides) on a legal topic of their choice, following assurances that the content was not going to be assessed in any way. The presentation slides, created by the students, were uploaded to the VR app simulation ahead of the session.

Each of the participants was interviewed upon arrival on campus by a member of the research team, using a semi-structured approach, focussing on the participant's previous experience of giving presentations, of using VR, and their understanding of the purpose of feedback. They were then individually videoed delivering their presentation in a school setting on the VR app, as well as watching the analytics feedback and in-app playback. Directly after this experience, they were interviewed again by the same research team member who asked them to reflect on how they had found giving a presentation and receiving feedback during the performance and after and the impact of watching their performance on playback. The interviews were recorded and transcribed before a thematic analysis was undertaken (Braun & Clarke, 2006).

The video recording of participants was undertaken to understand if students could undertake five key tasks and identify areas for improvement regarding usability and design of the app. The key tasks were: selecting an avatar to represent the student in the simulation; launching the presentation experience from a carousel menu; receiving a briefing from a teacher avatar; entering the classroom and delivering the presentation; initiating playback mode to view analytics data and re-play a recording of the presentation. Usability concerns the ease of use, and satisfaction, with which users can perform certain tasks to achieve a specified goal. Multiple factors can influence task completion and performance, including factors arising from a user's context, such as prior technology experiences and expectations of how to interact with the technology.

An unfortunate change in internal policy at The Open University led to two videos being deleted. Having only three videos available for analysis is acknowledged as a limitation of the pilot study, as was the small number of participants and the geographically-limited sample size. Nevertheless, the findings of the pilot provided richer and more nuanced insights than from automatically recorded metrics, such as duration of task completion. These insights were useful when refining the VR app, to ensure the technology did not become a barrier to addressing the pedagogical challenge of developing students' legal and employability skills.

Research Findings: The Interviews

The analysis of the interviews provided valuable insight into participants' perceptions of the usability of the VR app and its value as a learning tool. The initial interviews revealed that no participants had significant previous experience with VR, although one mentioned they may have experienced it in a video game or at a cinema. In contrast, there was a significantly varied experience of giving presentations. At one end of the scale, two participants described themselves as giving presentations regularly in a professional capacity and having had relevant training on presentation skills (Participants 1 and 5). On the other end, another participant (Participant 2) described having "Hardly any experience" and no relevant training. The other two had some experience in giving presentations; one had no formal training (Participant 3), and the other had some basic training (Participant 4). These variants in experience may well have influenced participants' feelings prior to using the VR app, with Participant 1 expressing mainly excitement and Participant 2 demonstrating more apprehension about the experience. All participants indicated that they viewed the purpose of feedback as being in some way to improve their skills – "Just to make me better at what I do" (Participant 1).

The interviews following participants' experience of the VR app were generally more expansive in tone, perhaps reflecting a sense of relief or excitement following the VR experience. A key theme was the sense of disorientation or surprise that all participants felt when they initially entered the VR environment:

> I didn't know what to expect, and there was [sic] some things that surprised me. (Participant 2)
>
> When I came out, it's like, wow! It's a big shock for me. (Participant 3)

Interestingly, it was Participant 1 – the most experienced presenter – who expressed the most significant levels of surprise, indicating that "just being in the environment really threw me". Overall, the sense of surprise and disorientation appeared to be caused, at least in part, by having to navigate the unfamiliar technology:

> … I was still sort of coming to grips with the controls … (Participant 5)

The other cause seemed to be the highly immersive nature of the VR environment. Two specific aspects of this were highlighted in interviews. The first was the sense of immersion and becoming absorbed in a new reality. For example, several participants stated they had wanted to lean on the desk in front of them during the presentation (Participants 1 and 5). The second was the use of audience avatars programmed to respond to levels of eye contact during the presentation and to "heckle" at random intervals:

> I probably went into it thinking that this was … a cartoon moving picture in front of me, to give me context, rather than something which was going to be picking up and able to determine if I was looking … (Participant 3)

Overall, this was the most discussed aspect of the VR app and the participants indicated that, after their initial surprise, they found it a valuable part of the experience. The ability to obtain feedback on their performance and watch the in-app playback was also generally agreed to be worthwhile and participants were able to pinpoint areas to work on in future as a result. However, Participants 1 and 2 indicated that they would prefer not to obtain feedback on their initial performance, but instead, practise several times first to familiarise themselves with the VR environment.

When reflecting on the experience as a whole, there were some references to technical issues and limitations, such as the app not sensing arm movements (Participant 1) and the slides being difficult to read (Participant 3), and some general concerns, eg, that the emphasis on eye contact was unrealistic (Participant 4). Despite this, participants were positive about the VR app as a whole and its potential use as a tool to develop presentation skills.

The participants' attitude towards the feedback and in-app playback function suggested that these elements of the app needed support through more general guidance to students on the notion of formative feedback, to ensure that they appreciated the value of receiving feedback at an early stage, not just when they felt their presentation was sufficiently "polished". Huang and Liaw's (2018) study suggests that virtual reality can create rich learning experiences, but an important factor in student engagement with the VR activity is its "perceived usefulness". Therefore, when thinking about the possible uses for VR in legal education, it is important to be realistic about how useful students will consider the app to be and how it effective it will be in achieving the learning outcomes. The VR app's feedback and playback functions were clearly appreciated by participants in the pilot, but would arguably have reduced value if utilised in the way several participants envisaged.

Research Findings: The Video Recordings

Observations of the participants' video recordings generated insights into interactions and methods of control that users intuitively attempted. They form the basis of practical guidance for educators seeking to deploy VR technology in teaching and learning contexts.

The first question considered was whether the participants understood what they needed to do? Without mechanisms to show progress through the experience, some participants were unable to orientate themselves and differentiate between an initial set-up "scene", where they could choose their avatar, and the virtual school setting, where they could practise delivering their presentation. This may have contributed to their sense of disorientation when first entering the setting. Such considerations directly impact the narrative, informing decisions as to whether to utilise avatars to provide instructions to users or to instead rely on visual cues. Designing intuitive mechanisms for users to skip, or go back, are likely to assist with this.

Navigational aids also need to be built into the narrative of a VR experience, so that users can control their progression. Our app utilised gesture, namely gaze, to navigate the VR and interact with menu options. Gestures can be problematic because it's not always apparent what users need to do. Visual cues, such as chevrons were also utilised to encourage participants to reduce the high cognitive load which they might experience. We found that audio instructions and extended prose can easily be ignored by participants. Visual navigation cues were more effective than text at attracting participants' attention towards specific parts of the virtual world or a desired action. More confident participants found that an audio briefing slowed their progress as there was no way of accelerating it.

Where disconnects between real world and virtual actions occurred, participants experienced discomfort. For example, after participants received a briefing from a virtual teacher avatar in a corridor, their avatars began walking down the corridor and into the classroom. Participants experienced this in first-person perspective, while they remained static in the real world. Other navigation mechanisms, such as teleportation instigated by the user, would have enabled freedom of control, providing a more comfortable experience.

After participants had entered the virtual school setting to deliver their presentation, they could rotate 360 degrees. All participants were comfortable with this, and many frequently rotated through 180 degrees to look at their virtual presentation slides and the virtual audience of avatars.

The second question considered through analysis of the video recordings was whether the controls were visible or easy to find? The presentation slides were advanced by holding down a button on a handheld clicker, which displayed a small circle, or reticle, in the centre of the participants' field of vision and a transparent menu. When the circle was hovered over a menu icon for a short period, it would trigger the corresponding action. This allowed participants to advance their slides. Participants soon became familiar with this action. However, educators should consider designing in "shortcuts" to the narrative for repeated features, eg, virtual buttons on a lectern to control the slide deck.

Some participants did not know where to locate guidance, which can be overcome by keeping guidance to a single location regardless of the "scene". A simple "onboarding" process, broken down into chunks, can explain where to locate guidance and minimise decision making efforts for the user.

The third question was whether the participants understood which controls to use? Contextual guidance, or tool tips, around interactions are beneficial. They provide valuable feedback, help avoid distraction, and break otherwise detailed instructions into a series of manageable steps that can easily be accelerated by more confident users. Highlighting interactable objects with an outline is good practice, particularly for users unfamiliar with VR technology: it signposts where users can interact with, or control, the virtual environment, and helps to reinforce where a user is required to undertake an action, accelerating progress through the virtual experience.

Balancing Usability and Realism

Alongside issues particular to the VR app in question, the key theme arising from the pilot project was the need to balance usability and realism. The highly immersive nature of VR enables users to experience a greater sense of presence. In exploiting this, educators may be tempted to create highly realistic virtual environments that closely replicate the real world. However, highly realistic environments may be difficult to navigate because the interface or controls available to the user are not the same as those in real-world contexts. Such usability is arguably particularly important in educational contexts, as student users will need to see the educational value of the technology and are likely to be less forgiving of the technology compared with recreational users, such as gamers, who might enjoy the challenge of difficult interactions and complex virtual environments. For example, our VR app used gesture (gaze), combined with a physical button press, to navigate and make menu selections. VR was a new technology to the participants and such interactions needed to be introduced carefully and scaffolded to avoid the unfamiliarity of the technology or dissatisfaction over its affordances over-riding the value of the VR app as a tool for learning. At the same time, the immersive aspect of the VR experience was viewed as particularly valuable by participants (as demonstrated by the comments generated around the interaction with audience avatars). Therefore, it is important that considerations of usability should facilitate immersion in the VR setting.

Digital Empowerment and Future Readiness

> It is of great importance for individuals to be knowledgeable and educated digital participants having capacity to interpret the world around them

> actively in today's world where digital technologies are an indispensable part of our daily lives.
>
> (Akkoyunlu et al, 2010)

The interviews and video observations of this study's participants largely focused on the primary function of the VR app – as a method to practice, and obtain feedback on, presentation skills. However, it is also important to acknowledge that the participants' interaction with technology has the potential to enhance students' digital empowerment and future readiness, more generally.

As previously discussed, CLE commonly encourages students to explore the wider social forces impacting upon law. Law graduates who proceed into the legal sector are entering a transformed profession where technology is disrupting the delivery of legal services and the administration of justice. Technology and globalisation are changing the practice of law and the pace of change will only accelerate in the next decade (Susskind, 2017). Technology is reshaping the way in which lawyers work, from case management systems, the internet, social media, smartphones to automation, predictive analytics, and machine learning (Lamm & Verrier, 2015, and various chapters in this book). It is vital for students to obtain an insight into, and understanding of, this transformation to enable them to contextualise the traditional substantive legal topics which remain at the heart of the law degree. Using the VR app demonstrates how technology can innovate and transform a traditional 'off-line' experience, allowing students to experience this first-hand.

In more practical terms, the VR app also requires students to develop their digital skills, in order to allow them to successfully engage with it. Such skills and adaptability are vital at a time when many in the legal profession are already struggling to adapt to a radically changing legal world and many in other graduate occupations are likely to experience, or will have already experienced, a similar sense of disruption and transformation.

Conclusion

In The Open University pilot, the VR app was focused on developing the presentation skills of students, with a particular focus on the CLE environment. The pilot results suggest it can do this effectively when an appropriate balance is struck between usability and immersion and where the student experience is scaffolded with appropriate general guidance on formative feedback. However, VR also has potentially much wider uses within the law school. It could be used as a useful tool to develop other legal skills, such as advocacy and interviewing, or as a tool to immerse students in other unfamiliar settings to enhance learning (such as a solicitors' office). In addition, its very inclusion provides law students with the opportunity to identify legal and ethical challenges that arise from technological innovation and critically examine how developments in technology may protect or undermine the rule of law. For example, the increasing commercial potential of VR raises a plethora of new legal issues (Nwaneri, 2018). As costs and capabilities increase, VR is increasingly becoming a viable learning tool for the future.

Legal education is increasingly being required to change and adapt to enable it to produce digitally empowered and future-ready law graduates capable of functioning in this new competitive environment (Lyons, 2015, Susskind, 2017). Students now require digital skills that go beyond ICT skills and are increasingly expected to have an understanding of the technologies underpinning key trends in legal practice and other graduate fields. The incorporation of innovative technology and enhancing student learning and skills is one way in which to successfully meet these demands.

References

Akkoyunlu, B, Yilmaz Soylu, M, & Çağlar, M (2010). A study on developing "digital empowerment scale" for university learners. *Hacettepe University Journal of Education, 39*(39), 10–19.

Barfield, W, & Williams, A (2018). "The law of virtual reality and increasingly smart avatars" In *Research handbook on the law of virtual and augmented reality*, W. Barfield, & M. Blitz (Eds.), pp. 2–43. Edgar Elgar Publishing Limited.

Bloch, FS (2010). *The global clinical movement: Educating lawyers for social justice*. Oxford University Press.

Braun, V, & Clarke, V (2006). Using thematic analysis in psychology. *Qualitative Research in Psychology, 3*(2), 77–101.

Carney, D, Dignan, F, Grimes, R, Kelly, G, & Parker, R (2014). *Lawworks law schools pro bono and clinic report 2014*. LexisNexis UK.

Cole, D, & Tibby, M (2013). *Defining and developing your approach to employability*, Higher Education Authority, https://s3.eu-west-2.amazonaws.com/assets.creode.advancehe-document-manager/documents/hea/private/resources/employability_framework_1568037213.pdf [accessed 2nd November 2019].

Collins, C (2016). Story interface and strategic design for new law curricula. *The Law Teacher*, 50(1), 98–113.

Dede, C, & Richards, J (2017). "Strategic planning for R&D on immersive learning" In *Virtual, augmented, and mixed realities in education*, D. Liu, C. Dede, R. Huang, & J. Richards (Eds.), pp. 237–244. Singapore, Singapore: Springer.

Drummond, O, & McKeever, G (2015). Access to justice through university law clinics.

Falconer, L (2013). Situated learning in accident investigation: A virtual world simulation case study. *International Journal of Learning Technology, 8*(3), 246–262. 10.1504/IJLT.2013.057062.

Frank, J (1933). Why not a clinical lawyer-school?. *University of Pennsylvania Law Review and American Law Register, 81*(8), 907 [Online]. doi:10.2307/3308391.

Giddings, JM (2013). *Promoting justice through clinical legal education*. Justice Press.

Huang, H, & Liaw, S (2018). An analysis of learner's intentions toward virtual reality learning based on a constructivist and technology acceptance approaches. *International Review of Research in Open and Distributed Learning, 19*(1), 91–115.

Jackson, D (2016). Human-centred legal tech: Integrating design in legal education. *The Law Teacher*, 50(1), 82–97.

Jacobson, J (2017). "Authenticity in immersive design for education: Where is the pedagogy?" In *Virtual augmented, and mixed realities in education*, D. Liu, C. Dede, R. Huang, & J. Richards (eds), pp. 237–244. Singapore: Springer.

Kemp, V, Munk, T, & Gower, S (2016). Clinical legal education and experiential learning: looking to the future.

Lamm, C, & Verrier, H (2015). "Large law firms: A business model, a service ethic" In *The relevant lawyer*, Haskins, P (Eds.), pp. 103–112. American Bar Association.

Legal Education and Training Review (2013) *Setting Standards: The future of legal services education and training regulation in England and Wales*. Available at: http://letr.org.uk/the-report/chapter-4/the-ingredients-of-legal-competence/index.html [accessed 2nd November 2019].

Lyons, T (2015) "Legal education: Learning what lawyers need" In *The Relevant Lawyer*, P. Haskins (Eds.), pp. 221–229. American Bar Association.

McFaul, H, & FitzGerald, E (2019). A realist evaluation of student use of a virtual reality smartphone application in undergraduate legal education. *British Journal of Educational Technology*. doi:10.1111/bjet.12850.

Moffett, L, Cubie, D, & Godden, A (2017). Bringing the battlefield into the classroom: using video games to teach and assess international humanitarian law. *Law Teacher, 51*(4), 499–514.

Newbery-Jones, CJ (2016). Ethical experiments with the D-pad: Exploring the potential of video games as a phenomenological tool for experiential legal education. *The Law Teacher, 50*(1), 61–81.

Nwaneri, C (2018). "Starting up in virtual reality: Examining virtual reality as a space for innovation" In *Research handbook on the law of virtual and augmented reality*, W. Barfield, & M. Blitz (Eds.), pp. 44–63. Edgar Elgar Publishing Limited.

Selwyn, N (2017). *Education and technology: Key issues and debates*. Bloomsbury Academic.

Somerland, H, Young, R, Vaughan, S, & Harris-Short, S (2015). "The futures of legal education and the legal profession" In *The futures of legal education and the legal profession*, H. Somerland, R Young, S Vaughan, & S Harris-Short (Eds.), pp. 1–21. Hart Publishing.

Susskind, R (2017). *Tomorrow's lawyers*. Oxford University Press.

Wizner, S (2001). The law school clinic: Legal education in the interests of justice colloquium: what does it mean to practice law in the interests of justice in the twenty-first century. *Fordham Law Review, 70*(5), 1929–1938.

Chapter 4

Twitteryvision: Using Twitter Live Chat to Build Communities of Practice as a Legal Learning Tool

Matthew J Homewood

Introduction

It is to be expected that, as final year examinations draw near, the need for academics to support students with queries and points of clarification increases. As a very visible module leader, principal lecturer and author of the academic text used in the European Union Law module, I found myself as the core contact for a large number of undergraduate law students (n = 932).

There are difficulties in providing revision support for large numbers of students via commonly used response methods. One to one meetings take up significant time, meaning that not all students can be seen, and involve much repetition; this inefficiency is disproportionate to the value to those students for whom meetings could be scheduled. Email also involves repeated questions, and a reply to one student cannot be shared without their consent (as it is a personal communication), and cutting and pasting require various steps to find the relevant earlier e-mail and do the necessary copying and sending. An alternative approach is required.

After exploring a number of solutions, I decided to test the use of the micro-blogging site Twitter as a platform to deliver revision feedback opportunities in light of Junco, Heibergert, and Loken's research (2011) showing the impact that Twitter can have on engagement and performance. The basic premise of the project was to publicise a number of Twitter Revision (TR) sessions, each of 30 minutes duration. The only rule was that a particular hashtag should be used (#eulawrocks) to accompany all queries. The promise was to answer all queries posted within the start and finish time.

The TR sessions had a number of distinct advantages, allowing responses to large numbers of students due to the open nature of the technology and the ability to refer to earlier responses; responses were not "lost" due to the proliferation of third-party apps enabling "stories" to be created against particular hashtags; and given that Twitter is free, all students were able to engage, which they did to varying degrees.

Whilst the original action research of the project focused on engagement and the effect of limiting student queries to 140 characters, an interesting

DOI: 10.4324/9780429351082-4

development saw students respond to queries from other students, changing my role to that of moderator, stepping in at appropriate times to confirm and consolidate understanding, recognising the need for active teacher engagement in facilitating and supporting this collaborative learning aspect (Brindley, Blaschke, & Walti, 2009).

As such, the activity changed from one of dialogue between student and tutor which was viewable by all to something bearing the hallmarks of a Community of Practice (Lave & Wenger 1991, Wenger 1998), which involves a more social constructivist approach to learning than the assumed individual approach that higher education has often operated upon (Hodgkinson-Willliams et al, 2008). Communities of Practice have three key characteristics (Wenger 1998) identifiable from Wenger's definition, "Communities of practice are groups of people who share a concern or a passion for something they do and learn how to do it better as they interact regularly". From this, the characteristics required are a domain (namely a shared interest, concern or passion), a practice (something that is done and learned to be done better through discussion, activity and sharing with members, who are in some sense practitioners and so bring a different dimension to conversations between random persons) and a community (ie, going beyond a forum which allows interaction and actually sharing information, discussing, interacting, and helping to learn).

Whether it was a Community of Practice was important, given that the well-documented benefits of such could be enjoyed. Members can engage in a process of collective learning through interaction and shared concern or passion, providing an opportunity to engage in an enriching learning experience, in this case through the use of technology. In addition to learning gains, if Twitter could be used in this way there are implications for the higher education sector in effective utilisation of staff time and worthwhile investment in the development of digital literacies given the limited input required from academics.

If however what was created fell short of a Community of Practice, the value of the activity is arguably less easy to support with reference to the literature and its place within the range of academic support available to students is less certain from a pedagogic perspective. This being true, the other recognised benefits and economies of scale set out above are still of value.

This led to two linked research questions (for which ethical approval was given by Lancaster University):

RQ1: Did the Twitter revision sessions develop a Community of Practice within the relevant cohort?

If so,

RQ2: How does the use of Twitter, facilitate learning in such a community?

Short Literature Review

Although a structured approach to searching for relevant literature was adopted, involving the use of specific and inclusive search strings and with an awareness of the variability in terminology, it became clear that little research exists on the use of Twitter in developing Communities of Practice. Some studies have looked at Twitter more widely in relation to educational benefits and Communities of Practice but little was discovered in relation to using Twitter with students within a Community of Practice.

Whilst early research on the use of Twitter (Al-Khalifa, 2010) indicated scepticism of its use as a learning tool within higher education or academia more widely, a number of potential benefits of the micro-blogging site on educational experiences are now generally accepted including developing Professional Learning Networks (Grosseck & Holotescu, 2008) and interaction and collaboration between students (Dunlap & Lowenthal, 2009).

In answering calls in earlier studies asking how Twitter can be used for learning (Grosseck & Holotescu, 2008), Ebner et al, (2010) identified a number of educational applications including synchronous and asynchronous activities such as instant feedback in lectures to a space for "beyond the lecture" discussion. Of course, some research has drawn attention to the limitations of the platform including its potential for distraction (Grosseck & Holotescu, 2008) and restrictions on the number of characters allowed (Luo, Sickel & Cheng, 2017), though in relation to the latter concern Dunlap and Lowenthal (2009) concluded that this has the potential to encourage precision.

Luo, Sickel, and Cheng's study reported on Twitter as a live chat tool and the positive experiences of students in engaging with it. The preference for synchronous tools has been recognised in providing "a direct and interactive environment in which students reacted and responded to the topic at hand, chitchatted, and immediately make supportive comments to each other" (Davidson-Shivers et al, 2001).

Lewis and Rush (2013) reported on the development of Twitter-based Communities of Practice within higher education, demonstrating its role in building networks which underpin the development of learning professionals. However, their focus was on practitioners promoting the use of digital technologies within their institutions, and on a very intentional use of the technology in creating a personal network of practice and analysing the network developed.

Rosell-Aguilar (2018) concluded that a group of language teachers using a particular hashtag (#MFLtwitterati) could be described as a Community of Practice with reference to Wenger's research. That was the perception of the group as expressed through a direct messaging survey. Indeed, 10 out of the 11 interviewees considered the #MFLtwiterrati a Community of Practice. Murillo's (2008) work shares some similarities with this empirical study albeit using different technology, through the analysis of discussion groups against Wenger's characteristics of a Community of Practice, identifying a number of virtual communities emerging spontaneously in the social areas of the internet.

This short literature review informed the research design through a desire to fill the lacuna identified. It is clear that such micro-blogging sites have the potential for educational benefits but less clear in a Higher Educational environment how such benefits are realised and whether this aligns with a social constructivist approach.

Ontology and Epistemology, Methodology

This piece of research is grounded in social constructivist theories of learning and aligns with Vygotsky's (1980) three themes regarding social interaction, the more knowledgeable other, and the zone of proximal development. Thus, learning is a social process with social interaction and social processes playing a fundamental role in cognitive development. In particular, it draws upon the importance of social interaction to cognitive development, resting on the premise that learning is enhanced through engagement achieved through interaction and collaborative learning opportunities (Vygotsky, 1986).

Determining whether activity within the TR project led to a Community of Practice is most closely aligned to the research methodology of documentary research (Cohen et al, 2011) in that the data already existed in the form of hashtag organised tweets which were not produced for the research.

Data Collection and Analysis

All comments attached to the relevant hashtag and submitted during the relevant times were analysed against Wenger's key considerations. Contributions to the revision session were transcribed and coded using Nvivo software to distinguish between the nature of those contributions. This was done within overlapping categories of content, conversation (both meaningful and non-meaningful) and notes of thanks informed by the C4P framework (content, conversation, connections, context, and purpose) developed by Hoadley and Kilner (2005) with reference to technology-enhanced learning as a model of how learning takes place in such a community, positing that the greater any one of the five elements present within a community, the "more likely and effective the knowledge generation and transfer will be". All five elements in this non-linear framework are important to effective knowledge building and they "feed off and reinforce each other" (Figure 4.1).

Content is foundational and has four purposes: it attracts and socialises members, and provides a basis and motivation for interaction; conversation has

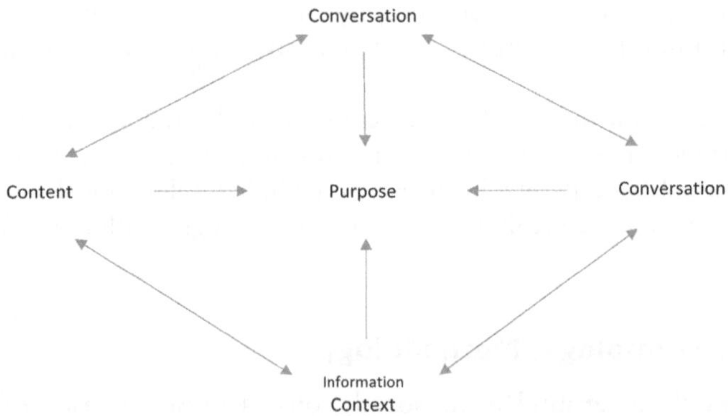

Figure 4.1 Hoadley and Kilner's (2005) C4P Framework for Communities of Practice.

to be meaningful and towards the shared endeavour, rather than being for the sake of it; connections are the "lifeblood of knowledge-building community" (Hoadley & Kilner, 2005) without which online spaces are merely chatrooms or repositories of content; the information context is the background for understanding a knowledge object (such as where it has come from or a previous application of it). The sense of a shared purpose helps to drive the community: if the purpose is not stated, it may emerge.

The Design for Distributed Cognition Framework

A further framework used, the design for a distributed cognition framework (Hutchins, 1991), was developed by reviewing successful examples of the use of technology in various learning environments in a number of domains. In essence, it focusses on "what works" for individuals and groups and identifies three specific advantages that technology can bring to learning, namely (i) representational support, ie, being able to represent information in a number of different forms, (ii) process support, ie, the capacity for technology to scaffold tasks and procedure, and (iii) social context support, ie, advantageous changes to the social context in which learning occurs.

Validity and Reliability

The data collected was produced independently from the focus of the research, which supports its validity and reliability. Whilst the underlying research project was aimed at students within Nottingham Law School, Nottingham Trent University (NTU), some contributions may well have come from other universities: but the inclusion of such data may enhance the consideration of Communities of Practice.

Analysis and Discussion

RQ1: Did the Twitter Revision Sessions Develop a Community of Practice within the Relevant Cohort?

It is clear that the TR project did create a Community of Practice aligned with the characteristics set out in Wenger's research. The shared domain was easily identifiable both from the purpose of the activity and the content of the interactions, namely understanding of European Union law relevant to the module learning outcomes. Indeed, 86% of interactions coded and analysed explicitly linked to the domain. The practice element was also easily identifiable, namely legal study, in which the academics and students were practitioners due to their expertise, understanding and knowledge of EU law (albeit at differing levels). The community was evident through the extensive interactions between the members consisting of questions and answers, development of understanding by building upon the material of others and the creation and sharing of learning resources within the community.

The members of this community shared an interest in developing and consolidating their understanding of a specific subject area in anticipation of impending assessments. The discussion and interaction between the members provided a space for learning to develop in a way that would not have been done in the absence of such interaction. Of course, what is particularly interesting is that that this was an unintended consequence of what was originally an idea to simply enable a tutor to efficiently provide students with a means to receive feedback on revision queries.

The positive answer to the first research question means that the second question becomes relevant.

RQ2: How does the use of Twitter, Facilitate Learning in Such a Community?

It is clear that the use of Twitter had a number of advantages in supporting learning within the Community of Practice with reference to the C4P and distributed cognition frameworks. As to the former and its five elements, (i) the content of the interactions and the resources developed were central; because members could see it "working" and the content was building, others joined in, often in unexpected ways such as developing answers already given by peers. (ii) As to conversation and the need for it to be meaningful regarding the shared endeavour rather than being for the mere sake of it, assessing this was a challenge. About half of interactions did not amount to "meaningful conversation", with flippant comments or asides proving common (such as "I hate part a it hurts my brain: (still worried about cheeky essay questions", "okay fair enough ha.. Do you take bribes", and "you make me sick with this eulawrocks hashtag"). However, the remaining interactions did amount to meaningful conversation.

(iii) The connections within the TR project were clear in that almost all of the members had the connection of being a law student and studying EU law; other connections related to myself as a member and other academic staff colleagues. (iv) The information context within the TR project was vital, being informed about the knowledge provider(s). Students understood the context within which the knowledge was generated, shared and developed through the clarity of the guidance that was provided as to the purpose of the project. This encouraged greater interaction as students recognised the context of other students' contributions and developed them further. Within my own role as a member of the community, this context was also important in my own contributions, especially when errors of understanding required intervention.

(v) As to the purpose, the original shared stated purpose was to provide feedback on student understanding. However, that purpose developed further into a shared purpose of greater understanding of aspects of the subject (for example, recognising links between topic areas and nuances in application) rather than just answers to specific and often more simple questions (such as "would you need to mention EU law supremacy and case law for a problem question on direct effect etc?" and the like).

Turning to the distributed cognition framework, the data from the TR project showed that Twitter provided representational support with the use of quizzes, infographics, and direct links to additional content such as interactive flashcards. It enabled students in various locations and institutions to interact, converse and access content which could be represented in a number of ways. As academic profiles and some members were known within the community, the information context was addressed enabling members to better interpret and understand postings.

There was process support through quick links to external resources such as Prezis and online diagnostic assessments, which supported the content being explored through the common purpose. Thus, discussions relating to certain subject areas led to links to external resources providing detail simply not possible within (the then) 140 character limit. Third-party apps allowed for subsequent management and ordering of created content and custom widgets embedding the Twitter stream into the University LMS were exploited.

There was also social context support in that the TR sessions widened and varied the context for learning by including students in a variety of courses including full-time, part-time, and distance learning and across a number of different levels including Framework for Higher Education Qualifications (FHEQ) levels 4, 5, and 6. It is very difficult to imagine such connections and conversations occurring without the use of technology. Indeed, a number of the distance learning students who were members of the community had not attended a classroom during their studies and had not met and discussed the areas that formed the content of the community beyond their own Course boundaries.

Conclusion

It is clear that Twitter can provide a useful technological solution to support student learning. For the busy academic, it is an efficient tool in developing a Community of Practice and brings with it a number of advantages to encourage learning aligned to the C4P framework which would arguably be less easy to realise in the absence of the technology, certainly at least at scale. This has great potential for impact within higher education given the ease, and low comparative resource costs. Furthermore, it has potential benefits in building a sense of belonging and providing further value to those who study in non-traditional ways. Using Twitter in this way also has scope for the creation of extensive Communities of Practice which could exist across institutions, across disciplines and indeed, across continents. Imagine a course on comparative competition law with Twitter being used to develop a Community of Practice which includes members in the UK sharing content on domestic law, European members sharing content on EU competition law, and US members sharing content on North American anti-trust law. The scope for Twitter to develop Communities of Practice at such a scale is truly exciting.

However, there are some limitations which should be noted. Twitter is largely an anonymous environment which makes it challenging with reference to the information context to build confidence in the development of content. It is limited by its restrictions on characters which may limit the quality of the interactions. Whilst it is true that external resources can be linked, it doesn't provide a natural means by which to store artefacts or a meaningful way to file them, meaning that members are reliant on a variety of third-party apps. Furthermore, whilst it is submitted that limited digital competencies are required to support the development of such communities, there is a cost to developing academics and resistance may well be met.

The use of Twitter as seen in this research could be seen to have had a positive impact on the way students use technology for educational purposes. As academics have navigated the challenges of increased online teaching through the Covid-19 pandemic, greater use has been made of discussion boards and forums, virtual walls, and chat functions within online meeting environments such as Zoom or Microsoft Teams. Such spaces can surely be seen as Communities of Practice in themselves with the approach taken through micro-blogging site communications, being entirely appropriate and suited to such spaces.

This research adds to the existing body of knowledge on Communities of Practice and the use of social media to support student learning. However, it is limited by not exploring the views and thoughts of the members of the community and the impact on their learning. It is submitted that further research would be valuable in interviewing members of such communities as in Rosell-Aguilar's (2018) research, to explore their perceptions and reflections on the experience and to establish a mechanism so far as is possible to record tangible learning gains; and, in so doing, seeking to address the accusation that educational technologies frequently fail in this regard (Amiel & Reeves, 2008).

The research undertaken provides a useful and engaging example of how technology can enable student learning to occur. However, it is important to recognise that it is not the technology, in this case, Twitter, that delivers the learning gains. Rather the technology is the mechanism by which established forms of learning are facilitated. In this way, it can be seen that Twitter is no more than a tool to be used, along with "traditional" technology (such as whiteboards for example) in the toolbox that educators have available to enable student learning. Understanding how they enable this provides a useful insight to inform tool selection. As new tools emerge, educators should be open to the opportunities presented whilst also being mindful of the limitations.

Postscript: Whilst a change of role for the author to a senior management position with limited direct teaching responsibilities led to the ending of activity with the hashtag, the author intends to build upon this work at scale from a strategic perspective given the positive impacts identified.

References

Al-Khalifa, HS (2010). Finding a place for Twitter in higher education. *eLearn*, *5*(6). Retrieved from https://elearnmag.acm.org/archive.cfm?aid=1821980

Amiel, T, & Reeves, TC (2008). Design-based research and educational technology: Rethinking technology and the research agenda. *Journal of Educational Technology & Society*, *11*(4), 29–40. Retrieved from https://www.learntechlib.org/p/75072/

Aramo-Immonen, H, Jussila, J, & Huhtamäki, J (2015). Exploring co-learning behavior of conference participants with visual network analysis of Twitter data. *Computers in Human Behavior*, *51*, 1154–1162. 10.1016/j.chb.2015.02.033

Aramo-Immonen, H, Kärkkäinen, H, Jussila, JJ, Joel-Edgar, S, & Huhtamäki, J (2016). Visualizing informal learning behavior from conference participants' Twitter data with the Ostinato Model. *Computers in Human Behavior*, *55*, 584–595. 10.1016/j.chb.2015.09.043

Brindley, J, Blaschke, LM, & Walti, C (2009). Creating effective collaborative learning groups in an online environment *The International Review of Research in Open and Distributed Learning*, *10*(3). Retrieved from http://www.irrodl.org/index.php/irrodl/article/view/675

Cohen, L, Manion, L, & Morrison, K (2011). *Research Methods in Education* (7th ed.). London: Routledge.

Davidson-Shivers, GV, Muilenburg, LY, & Tanner EJ (2001). How do students participate in synchronous and asynchronous online discussions? *Journal of Educational Computing Research*, 25(4), 351–366.

Dunlap, JC, & Lowenthal, PR (2009). Tweeting the night away: Using Twitter to enhance social presence. *Journal of Information Systems Education*, *20*(2).

Ebner, M., Lienhardt, C., Rohs, M., & Meyer, I. (2010). Microblogs in Higher Education – A chance to facilitate informal and process-oriented learning? *Computers & Education*, In Press, Accepted Manuscript, Available online 4 January 2010, ISSN 0360-1315, DOI: 10.1016/j.compedu.2009.12.006

elearn Magazine: Finding a Place for Twitter in Higher Education. (n.d.). Retrieved September 28, 2018, from https://elearnmag.acm.org/archive.cfm?aid=1821980

Gilbert, S (2016). Learning in a Twitter-based community of practice: An exploration of knowledge exchange as a motivation for participation in #hcsmca. *Information, Communication & Society*, *19*(9), 1214–1232. 10.1080/1369118X.2016.1186715

Grosseck, G, & Holotescu, C 2008. "Can We Use Twitter in Educational Activities?".

Hoadley, C, & Kim, DE (2003). "Learning, design, and technology: Creation of a design studio for educational innovation" In *Proceedings of the IADIS International Conference e-Society 2003*, A Palma dos Reis, & P Isaís (Eds.), pp. 510–519. Lisbon, Portugal: International Association for the Development of the Information Society IADIS.

Hoadley, C, & Kilner, PG (2005). Using technology to transform communities of practice into knowledge-building communities. *SIGGROUP Bulletin*, *25*(1), 31–40.

Hodgkinson-Williams, C, Slay, H, & Siebörger, I (2008). Developing communities of practice within and outside higher education institutions. *British Journal of Educational Technology*, *39*(3), 433–442. 10.1111/j.1467-8535.2008.00841.x

Hutchins, E (1991). "The social organization of distributed cognition" In *Perspectives on socially shared cognition*, LB Resnick, JM Levine, & SD Teasley (Eds.), pp. 283–307. Washington, DC, US: American Psychological Association.

Information Technology - Data Analytics; Researchers from Free University Discuss Findings in Data Analytics (Twitter data analysis for studying communities of practice in the media industry). (2018, March 1). *Computers, networks & communications; Atlanta*, p. 500. Retrieved from https://search.proquest.com/docview/2007576142/citation/C3DA02CC0454471EPQ/1

Introduction to communities of practice | Wenger-Trayner. (n.d.). Retrieved from http://wenger-trayner.com/introduction-to-communities-of-practice/

Junco, R, Heiberger, G, & Loken, E (2011). The effect of Twitter on college student engagement and grades. *Journal of Computer Assisted Learning*, *27*(2), 119–132. 10.1111/j.1365-2729.2010.00387.x

Komorowski, M, Huu, TD, & Deligiannis, N (2018). Twitter data analysis for studying communities of practice in the media industry. *Telematics and Informatics*, *35*(1), 195–212. 10.1016/j.tele.2017.11.001

Lave, J, & Wenger, E (1991). *Situated learning: Legitimate peripheral participation*. Cambridge University Press. 10.1017/CBO9780511815355

Lewis, B, & Rush, D (2013). Experience of developing Twitter-based communities of practice in higher education. *Research in Learning Technology*, *21*(0). 10.3402/rlt.v21i0.18598

Luo, T, Sickel, J & Cheng, L 2017. Preservice teachers' participation and perceptions of Twitter live chats as personal learning networks. *TechTrends*, 61(3), 226–235. DOI: 10.1007/s11528-016-0137-1

Mills, KA, & Chandra, V (n.d.). Microblogging as a literacy practice for educational communities. *Journal of Adolescent & Adult Literacy*, *55*(1), 35–45.

Murillo, E 2008. Searching usenet for virtual communities of practice: Using mixed methods to identify the constructs of Wenger's theory. *Information Research*, v13, n4 Retrieved from https://files.eric.ed.gov/fulltext/EJ837276.pdf

Novakovich, J, Miah, S, & Shaw, S (2017). Designing curriculum to shape professional social media skills and identity in virtual communities of practice. *Computers & Education*, *104*, 65–90. 10.1016/j.compedu.2016.11.002

Rosell-Aguilar, F (2018). Twitter: A professional development and community of practice tool for teachers. *Journal of Interactive Media in Education, 2018*(1). 10.5334/jime.452

Vygotsky, LS (1980). *Mind in society: The development of higher psychological processes*. Harvard University Press.

Vygotsky, LS (1986). *Thought and language*. Cambridge, MA: MIT Press.

Wenger, E (1998). *Communities of practice: Learning, meaning, and identity*. Cambridge University Press.

Wesely, PM (2013). Investigating the community of practice of world language educators on Twitter. *Journal of Teacher Education, 64*(4), 305–318. 10.1177/0022487113489032

Chapter 5

Innovative Opportunities in Technology and the Law: The Virtual Legal Clinic

Jacqueline Weinberg and Jeff Giddings

Introduction

The COVID-19 pandemic has hastened the shift to digital learning. Universities are making dramatic changes to their operations, especially to how they engage with students. Law schools that have relied on conventional classroom-based teaching are now moving to new forms of delivery. This chapter examines how clinical legal education (CLE) can best adapt to this rapidly changing environment.

CLE is generally recognised as having dual foci: social justice – with a community focus – and integration of substantive law with legal practice. There is strong complementarity between these purposes. Ashford and McKeown's collation of examples from various countries allowed them to describe CLE as a key instrument in bringing the "social justice agenda to life in law schools and in communities around the world" (Ashford & McKeown, 2018, p1).

A common form of CLE is the university law clinic, where students undertake CLE to learn how laws affect community members and what lawyers actually do in practice. Students engage with real-life clients and manage their matters, learning practical legal skills under the supervision of qualified legal practitioners ("clinical supervisors"). In addition, students learn about the various technical, ethical and procedural obligations that lawyers must meet.

Technological advancements in legal practice present a challenge for law schools and legal educators to ensure they are educating students to respond effectively to current and future changes. The dynamics of modern professional life and legal practice make it imperative that students master a range of new technologies and communications methods. Clients wish to be more involved in the legal provision process, which necessitates changes in the lawyers' approach and attitude towards their clients, their management of client matters and their professional relationships with courts and other professionals (Giddings & Weinberg, 2020). Lawyers need to take a client-focused approach to communication, persuasion, and relationship-building to develop and convey the best possible options to clients. The idea behind this is to offer

DOI: 10.4324/9780429351082-5

effective legal services in new, less costly, more client-friendly ways. This may mean using virtually-delivered legal services better suited to the client's needs.

Machines are becoming increasingly capable and lawyers need to consider technology and the internet in ways that not only automate but also innovate current work practices (Susskind, 2013). Online systems will become more commonplace in helping clients to recognise when they need legal help and to select the best sources of advice at a cost they can afford (Susskind, 2013). Graduating law students, as "future lawyers" soon to enter legal practice, should be provided with opportunities to use unfamiliar technological applications to ensure they develop skills and gain confidence in their use (Thanaraj, 2017).

In this chapter, we will show that the Monash Clinical Program has built on 45 years of CLE experience in developing the Virtual Legal Clinic (VLC), which provides opportunities for students to learn the skills needed to make the law available to people who would otherwise have no affordable sources of legal help. We address how a VLC within a CLE setting presents distinctive opportunities for expanding legal education. We show how the VLC provides an opportunity to implement technological systems to assist clients to access justice. We also consider how the VLC adds value to educating students about technological advances in legal practice, equipping them with frameworks for the knowledge, skills, and attributes to be technologically proficient legal practitioners of the future.

We focus on issues that need to be addressed to prepare students to use technology effectively in assisting and building trust with clients, including developing communication skills for interacting with clients via technology. The implementation of a VLC adheres to the educational aims of CLE: to provide legal education to students that enhances 21st-century legal practice and to assist the broader community by utilising technology to extend legal services delivery to people whose needs would not otherwise be met. Although this discussion focuses on the Australian context, we argue it also applies to other jurisdictions.

We begin by looking more closely at Australian CLE. We focus on how a VLC can form part of CLE and contribute to preparing the "new lawyer" for changes in legal practice while at the same time enhancing access to justice.

Clinical Legal Education in Australia

Recognising the value of "learning by doing and reflecting", various writers, academics, and commentators have called for legal education to teach students what lawyers actually do in practice. A strong practice-oriented trend of legal education has developed in Australia (Giddings, 2017). As described in the *Best practices: Australian clinical legal education* report:

> "Clinic" or clinical legal education (CLE) is a premier method of learning and teaching. CLE places law students in close contact with the realities,

> demands and compromises of legal practice. In so doing, CLE provides students with real-life reference points for learning the law. CLE also invites students to see the wider context and everyday realities of accessing an imperfect legal system.
>
> (Evans et al, 2013, p4)

Clinical pedagogy directs clinicians to teach students to focus on the importance of listening to each client and treating them as a person, not just a legal problem, reflecting social justice values, such as people's dignity and right to equality (Evans et al, 2013). Clinical educators should view skills teaching as truly complementary to a clinic's social justice mission, enabling students to suspend judgement, communicate, and listen across differences, and explore solutions creatively (Evans et al, 2013). The aims and outcomes of CLE build on students' problem-solving skills, reflective thinking about legal culture and lawyering goals, learning how to both behave and think like a lawyer, and understanding the issues of access to justice and social justice (Evans et al, 2013).

The pedagogic value of clinics derives from students having the opportunity to experience the practice of law, thereby coming to appreciate how it functions in a practical real-world setting (Evans et al, 2013, p5) A clinical setting provides opportunities for students to see, analyse, reflect on, and deal with the various ways in which law actually manifests in people's lives, and to consider the need for law reform (Evans et al, 2013, p15). These skills encompass several aspects that are generally captured under the umbrella term "social justice". As will be shown later in this chapter, virtual service delivery fits comfortably within the framework of clinical pedagogy.

The most recognised model of CLE, the "live client" clinic, involves working with real clients. (Evans & Hyams, 2015, p6). This model develops key understandings and skills – such as structuring and conducting interviews, preparing for and conducting negotiations, and reflecting on personal performance – and allows students to extrapolate and generalise from their experiences (Giddings, 2013, p76). Further, working with real clients in this learning context provides particular opportunities for students to develop their understanding of the lawyer–client relationship and to refine their legal practice-related skills (Giddings, 2013, p94).

Most Australian law school clinical programmes are established within, or closely connected to, community legal centres (CLCs) (Kingsford Legal Centre, 2019). This relationship aligns with the longstanding mission of CLE as "having its origins in the fight against poverty, injustice and underrepresentation of minority interests in the legal process" (Bloch, 2011, p159). CLCs are independent, non-profit, community-based organisations that provide free and accessible legal and related services to everyday people, including people experiencing discrimination and disadvantage. CLCs mostly provide legal assistance with tenancy, credit and debt, administrative law, social security, criminal law matters, and family/domestic violence. These are all areas of work that have an affinity with issues of social justice.

This close association between CLCs and CLE exposes students to social issues and the role that the legal system can play in improving social justice (Evans et al, 2017). Students become aware of the reality of their clients' circumstances, and how important legal representation is to the resolution of their clients' problems, heightening their awareness of their responsibilities to their clients (Wizner, 2002). Aligned with the pedagogy of CLE, the VLC provides a forum for enhancing clients' access to justice while at the same time educating students to become practice ready for the 21st century.

Virtual Delivery Within a Clinical Legal Education Framework

Accessing justice is a global issue, made difficult because of cost (expense of accessing legal assistance), time (significant delays in resolving matters), and complexity (difficulties with understanding the legal system) (Winkelmann, 2015). In addition, access may be affected by whether the individual recognises the legal dimensions of their problem, their capacity to engage with the justice system and the types of legal problems that they face.

One option to improve access to justice is to use technology in ways that increase opportunities for people to access legal assistance and to provide community-based services that are sufficiently flexible to respond to emerging needs. A VLC within a community setting can provide user-focused services to address client needs and assist those who would not otherwise be able to access justice.

Essentially, the VLC focuses on providing legal services to those who cannot attend community services in person, eg, because they live in regional or remote areas or because of disadvantage and marginalisation. With improvement in internet access, the use of video conferencing is a growing trend in communication. As of January 2019, there were 21.74 million internet users in Australia, constituting 87% of the Australian population. For many, video conferencing is becoming the norm in everyday communication, especially in the context of the COVID-19 pandemic; thus, implementing video conferencing for legal service delivery mirrors the broader changes occurring in global communications. Access to and use of video conferencing applications such as Skype, Zoom, FaceTime, and Google Hangouts is predicted to continue to increase. However, it is important to note that in Australia, limited internet access is likely to indicate levels of disadvantage and could be related to socio-economic factors, such as age or geographical isolation. Access to legal assistance via video-conferencing will not be suitable for everyone; in that case, legal advice may be provided using other virtual means, such as via telephone.

The Virtual Legal Clinic Process at Monash Law Clinics

The Monash University clinical program maintains a strong community service focus while also developing significant aspects of clinical teaching, particularly in relation to professionalism and values (Giddings & Weinberg, 2020). With this heritage in mind, the VLC was established at Monash Law Clinics (MLC), aimed at blending the clinical and the digital. This clinic involved identifying ways in which to adapt existing models to expand practice-based learning opportunities for clients to access justice.

The VLC operates in a similar way to more conventional services, while also incorporating digital technology to make appointments, assess potential conflicts of interest, and provide documents and information that prepare the client for their "virtual appointment". Clients are made aware of the availability of the VLC, with further information on the MLC website (https://www.monashlawclinics.com.au/). The success of the VLC depends on the preparation of all participants. Clients are provided with sufficient information about the VLC, students are trained regarding interaction with clients, and administrative staff and supervisors are informed about procedures and protocols to ensure that appropriate processes are followed by all participating students and supervisors.

The VLC process can be simplified into six essential steps:

Step 1 The client contacts the clinic by telephone to book an appointment. The client is informed about how the VLC operates, and staff confirm the client's eligibility for the VLC. This screening process is conducted following the protocols for administrative staff. Most importantly, clients are required to have access to a reliable internet service to engage with the clinic. If the client does not have reliable internet, they are offered telephone advice or a face-to-face appointment. Clients are informed that a telephone interpreter will be provided, if required.

Step 2 Once a virtual clinic appointment has been made, clients are provided with information to prepare for the appointment. Staff explain that the client will be sent an email confirming the appointment date and time, a link for submitting documents required for the appointment, and information about how to prepare for the appointment. Further, staff inform clients that if they encounter difficulties, such as accessing the email or link, they should contact MLC and staff will assist them through the process. In the event that clients do not respond within 2–3 days, staff follow up with clients to offer their assistance.

Step 3 In preparation for their appointment, the client completes and submits information online via Google Forms, including the Client Agreement and Authority to Act. The client is able to upload relevant documents ahead of their appointment which are stored digitally.

Step 4 On the day of the interview, the student logs into the dedicated virtual clinic email. They check that the client has completed the forms correctly and peruse these forms and attachments in preparation for the interview.

Step 5 At MLC, the Zoom digital platform, which is supported by Monash University, is used for client interviews. Zoom is generally used for video conferencing. Importantly, its features include capacity for screen sharing with others, while at the same time maintaining eye contact with the other person through the camera function. This enables more active client participation in the interview. Other digital platforms that can be used include Skype, Microsoft Teams, and Webex. Skype is simple and user-friendly. Microsoft Teams is an application developed to be integrated with other Microsoft applications. Users of Microsoft Teams can share documents with ease, communicate through the chat feature, and conduct video conferences with multiple parties. These applications are also available on smart devices. Webex, a video-conferencing application with comprehensive security features, is another means by which to communicate with clients in an audiovisual manner.

At the appointment time, the student logs into the Zoom website and sends a Zoom invitation to the client so that the appointment can begin. The interview rooms at the clinic are designed to enable technology-based service delivery. The student communicates with the client via a desktop computer or laptop from the interview room, and the client uses their own computer at an offsite location.

Step 6 The student interviews the client and takes instructions. The student pauses the interview when seeking advice from the supervisor. The student requests the client to stay near their computer and mutes the microphone. After consulting the supervisor, the student returns to the interview room, unmutes the microphone, and conveys the advice to the client.

Challenges to Implementing the Virtual Legal Clinic

Although there are many noted benefits and opportunities for implementing a VLC, there are some challenges related to video conferencing. Barriers include:

- Transmission quality: Online video conferencing is dependent on a stable high-speed internet connection (at least 500 kbps). A poor connection will result in poor quality audio and/or video. When scheduling a virtual

appointment, the client should be advised to have Internet access of sufficient power and speed during the scheduled time period.
- Ease of use: Good usability and client familiarity with particular software will facilitate efficient and successful virtual conferencing. Utilising software that is simple and user-friendly reduces the potential risk of clients being unable to use the software effectively. Clients can be provided with step-by-step guidance on how to set up their computers and use the software for the virtual appointment.

Zoom conferencing software is used at MLC as it satisfies legal practice security and confidentiality requirements, including locking a Zoom session that has already started so that no one else can join and using host controls to maintain control of the screen. Users need to be aware of these security features to ensure interviews are kept secure. It is stressed to students that virtual appointments should not be recorded and client confidentiality must be guaranteed.

Student and Supervisor Interaction in the Virtual Legal Clinic

The design and delivery of the VLC have been informed by best practice protocols with learning outcomes intended to expose students to the "realities, demands, and compromises of legal practice" (Evans et al, 2013, p6). All Monash University clinical supervisors have been trained to support students to take a client-centred approach to deliver legal services and develop reflective practices. Supervision is structured, ensuring consistency and continuity, and responsive to the issues raised by individual students. The VLC broadens clinical best practice to include virtual service delivery, educating students to provide advice to clients via technological means on a variety of legal matters. In line with best practice, seminars are delivered to students to support their learning in reflective practice and legal ethics (Evans et al, 2017, p90). Students are attuned to issues of social justice, including the reasons clients are unable to, or prefer not to, access our onsite legal services. These insights provide them with opportunities to analyse and reflect on the relationship between law and access to justice, and the contributions that lawyers make.

At MLC, simulations are used to prepare students for the VLC process. Students engage in simulated virtual interviews before talking with "real" clients. As technology is critical to the delivery of the clinic, students need time to become familiar with and practise using the tools before they engage with clients (Long & Meglich, 2013). It is important not to make assumptions about students' skill levels; the ability to use social media applications does not mean students can adopt new technologies easily (Long & Meglich, 2013). The principal advantage of using simulation as a clinical teaching method is that it provides a safe environment within which students can learn. Because simulations are not real, "the learner can take risks which might produce disastrous results for a client in the real world and learn from them without causing harm" (Giddings, 2013, p85). During simulations, no client confidentiality concerns need to be safeguarded, making it easier to provide students with scaffolds to support them as they continue to engage with the issues and interests raised by particular legal situations (Giddings, 2018). In this way, students are better prepared for their later contact with real clients, particularly in terms of interviewing skills (Maranville, 2000).

Client-centred Approach and Communication

The VLC directs students to tailor their communication and advice to the situation and context of each client as part of a client-centred approach. When providing advice through the VLC, students need to be focused on developing those skills that will enhance digital communication and client centredness, such as self-awareness and responsibility. As students become aware of the reality of their clients' circumstances and how important legal representation is to the resolution of their clients' problems, they become more aware of their responsibility (Wizner, 2002). Students' social consciousness is raised as they realise that, in all likelihood, their clients would not have access to legal advice but for their assistance. (Wizner, 2002, p1931).

By participating in the VLC, students learn that access to justice issues affects almost every client. Students can reflect on why the legal needs of clients and communities are not being met, or how they can be better met. Thus, the VLC is not only a valuable educational opportunity for students but also assists clients to receive the legal help that they require. During the COVID-19 pandemic, clients were unable to access legal services face to face but rather did so through virtual technology. Students who partake in the VLC will be better prepared for the challenges that this climate presents. Similarly, clients who engaged with lawyers through technological means during COVID-19 may wish to continue using such platforms in the future as they seek more flexible, cost-effective means of accessing legal advice. As such, it is imperative that students master a range of new technologies and communication methods. The challenges extend beyond "how" to communicate with clients; students need to communicate "meaningfully" with clients to maintain and build constructive relationships. The VLC provides an opportunity for students to develop and showcase their technological skills and their adaptability not only to implement technological systems to assist clients to access justice but also to become adept with technological advances in legal practice. Students are equipped with frameworks for the knowledge, skills, and attributes to become more technologically proficient and "employment ready" for their roles as legal practitioners of the future (Giddings, 2018; Weinberg, 2018).

The VLC teaches students to utilise video-conferencing platforms to manage and build relationships, using empathy and compassion so that clients feel valued and understood. Students learn that technology need not be a barrier to communicating with clients, but that it is important to take proactive steps to communicate in meaningful ways with clients – learning about their values and goals.

Clinic students who engage with clients through virtual technology develop the emotional intelligence to become attuned to their clients' needs when clients are not face-to-face. Students learn that law cannot be practised in a vacuum; they need to view their clients holistically to develop an increased awareness of their clients' circumstances and expectations. This should enhance their ability to build trust with their clients and maintain and build relationships.

The Value of the Virtual Legal Clinic

This chapter has outlined how a VLC within a clinical setting not only provides legal services to a far wider network of clients but also teaches students how to use technology to provide clients with better access to legal services. While face-to-face clinics will continue to be an indispensable part of CLE, emerging technologies provide opportunities to apply clinical pedagogy in new contexts. If clients have access to reliable technology that they know how to use, they may prefer to make use of a VLC. Others may prefer to interact with their lawyers face-to-face to ensure they build a trusting relationship with their advisors.

The potential of VLCs became clearer during the COVID-19 pandemic when legal practitioners were required to utilise technology to provide clients with enhanced access to legal processes. The continuing development of virtual delivery of legal services requires practitioners to become adept with new skills and competencies. In particular, they need "to learn to communicate differently, to gain mastery of the data in their disciplines, to establish new working relationships with their machines, and to diversify" (Susskind & Susskind, 2015, p114). More generally, they need to be flexible and adaptable as new roles and tasks arise.

At a rudimentary level, the VLC aligns with the notion that professionals need to become more versatile users of technology by building new forms of relationships with technologies that "demand fresh skills and an open mind" (Susskind & Susskind, 2015, p117). Similarly, clinical students participating in a VLC need to understand how machines and systems can support their practice. Although these relationships seem daunting to some professionals, they are unavoidable in a world where "information technology and the internet have combined to transform the information-creating, information-seeking and information dissemination habit of human beings" (Susskind & Susskind, 2015, p116).

The COVID-19 crisis showed clearly how practitioners were able to utilise technology to provide services that enhanced their clients' access to justice, whether they were in private practice, working in an in-house legal department, for government or in a community setting. These circumstances enabled practitioners to appreciate that they can "exploit new technologies to enable them to be more efficient and to organise and make available their collective knowledge and expertise in society" (Susskind & Susskind, 2015, p153). Likewise, we posit that in the future, the VLC will continue to provide innovative opportunities for harnessing technology to deliver efficient, affordable, and widely available legal services, while also preparing law students for 21st-century practice that embraces ongoing technological change.

References

Access to Justice Taskforce, Attorney-General's Department. (2009, September). *A strategic framework for access to justice in the federal civil justice system. Report by the Access to Justice Taskforce Attorney-General's Department.*

Ashford, C, & McKeown, P (Eds.). (2018). *Social justice and legal education.* Cambridge Scholars Publishing.

Barry, M (2007, July). Clinical legal education in the law university: Goals and challenges. *Journal of Clinical Legal Education*, 27–50. 10.19164/ijcle.v11i0.76

Bloch, FS (Ed.). (2011). *The global clinical movement: Educating lawyers for social justice.* Oxford University Press.

Bloch, FS, & Noone, MA (2011). "Legal aid origins of clinical legal education" In *The global clinical movement: Educating lawyers for social justice*, F. S. Bloch (Ed.), pp. 153–166. Oxford University Press.

Boersig, J, Marshall, J, & Seaton, G (2002). Teaching law and legal practice in a live client clinic. *Newcastle Law Review*, *6*(2), 51–68.

Brayne, H, Duncan, N, & Grimes, R (1998). *Clinical legal education: Active learning in your law school.* Blackstone Press.

Carter, C, Spence, C, & Muzio, D (2015). Scoping an agenda for future research into the professions. *Accounting, Auditing & Accountability Journal*, *28*(8), 1198–1216. 10.1108/AAAJ-09-2015-2235

Cody, A, & Schatz, B (2011). "Community law clinics: Teaching students, working with disadvantaged communities" In *The global clinical movement: Educating lawyers for social justice*, F. S. Bloch (Ed.), pp. 167–182. Oxford University Press.

Department of Justice and Regulation, Victorian Government (2016). *Access to justice review: Summary report August 2016.*

Evans, A, Cody, A, Copeland, A, Giddings, J, Noone, MA, & Rice, S (2017). *Australian clinical legal education: Designing and operating a best practice clinical program in an Australian law school.* ANU Press.

Evans, A, Cody, A, Copeland, A, Giddings, J, Noone, MA, & Rice, S (2013). *Best practices: Australian clinical legal education.* Office for Learning & Teaching.

Evans, AH, & Hyams, RL (2015). Specialist legal clinics: Their pedagogy, risks and payoffs as externships. *International Journal of Clinical Legal Education*, *22*(2), 147–180. 10.19164/ijcle.v22i2.426

Giddings, J (2013). *Promoting justice through clinical legal education.* Justice Press.

Giddings, J (2017). "Clinics and Australian law schools approaching 2020" In *Australian clinical legal education: Designing and operating a best practice clinical program in an Australian law school*, A Evans, A Cody, A Copeland, J Giddings, P Joy, MA Noone, & S Rice (Eds.), pp. 11–39. ANU Press.

Giddings, J (2018). "It's more than a site: Supporting social justice through student supervision practices" In *Social justice and legal education*, C. Ashford, & P. McKeown (Eds.), pp. 43–64. Cambridge Scholars.

Giddings, J, & McNamara, M (2014). Preparing future generations of lawyers for legal practice: What's supervision got to do with it? *University of New South Wales Law Journal, 37*(3), 1226–1262. 10.2139/ssrn.2740209

Giddings, J, & Weinberg, J (2020). "Experiential legal education: Stepping back to see the future" In *Modernising legal education*, C Denvir (Ed.), pp. 38–56. Cambridge University Press.

Gold, N (2015). Clinic is the basis for a complete legal education: Quality assurance, learning outcomes and the clinical method. *International Journal of Clinical Legal Education, 22*(1), 84–141. 10.19164/ijcle.v22i1.406

Goodman, C (2019). Impacts of artificial intelligence in lawyer-client relationships. *Oklahoma Law Review, 72*(1), 149–184.

Horrigan, B (2019). Designing and implementing an enhanced clinical program in the age of disruption. Part One: The environment for clinic. *International Journal of Clinical Legal Education, 26*(2), 75–104. 10.19164/ijcle.v26i2.851

Horrigan, B (2020). Designing and implementing an enhanced clinical program in the age of disruption. Part Two: Clinical activities. *International Journal of Clinical Legal Education, 27*(1), 204–230. 10.19164/ijcle.v27i1.916

Hyams, R (1995). The teaching of skills: Rebuilding, not just tinkering around the edges. *Journal of Professional Legal Education, 13*(1), 63–80.

Hyams, R (2008, December). On teaching students to 'act like a lawyer': What sort of lawyer? *Journal of Clinical Legal Education, 13*, 21–32. 10.19164/ijcle.v13i0.65

Hyams, R, Campbell, S, & Evans, A (2014). *Practical legal skills* (4th ed.). Oxford University Press.

Johri, A (2014). "Engineering knowledge in the digital workplace: Aligning materiality and sociality through action" In *Reconceptualising professional learning: Sociomaterial knowledge, practices and responsibilities*, T Fenwick, & M Nerland (Eds.), pp. X–X. Routledge.

Kingsford Legal Centre (2019). Clinical Legal Education Guide: Your guide to CLE courses offered by Australian universities in 2019/20.

Long, LK, & Meglich, PA (2013). Preparing students to collaborate in the virtual work world. *Higher Education, Skills and Work-based Learning, 3*(1), 6–16. 10.1108/20423891311294948

MacFarlane, J (2008). *The new lawyer: How settlement is transforming the practice of law*. UBC Press.

Maranville, D (2000). Passion, Context and Lawyering Skills: Choosing Among Simulated and Real Clinical Experiences, *Clinical Law Review*, 7, 123.

Marson, J, Wilson, A, & Van Hoorebeek, M (2005, August). The necessity of clinical legal education in university law schools: A UK perspective. *Journal of Legal Education*, 7, 29–43.

Noone, MA, & Dickson, J (2004). Teaching towards a new professionalism: Challenging law students to become ethical lawyers. *Legal Ethics, 4*(2), 127–145. 10.1080/1460728X.2001.11424148

Pistone, M (2015). Law schools and technology: Where we are and where we are heading. *Journal of Legal Education, 64*(4), 586–604.

Ryan, F (2019). A virtual law clinic: A realist evaluation of what works for whom, why, how and in what circumstances? *The Law Teacher, 54*(2), 237–248. 10.1080/03069400.2019.1651550

Sourdin, T (2015). Justice and technological innovation. *Journal of Judicial Administration, 25*(2), 96–105.

Spencer, R (2012). Holding up the mirror: A theoretical and practical analysis of the role of reflection in clinical legal education. *International Journal of Clinical Legal Education, 18*, 181–216. 10.19164/ijcle.v18i0.6

Stickley, A (2011). Providing a law degree for the 'real world': Perspective of an Australian law school. *The Law Teacher, 45*(1), 63–86. 10.1080/03069400.2011.546966

Sullivan, WM, Colby, A, Wegner, JW, Bond, L, & Shulman, LS (2007). *Educating lawyers: Preparation for the profession of law*. Jossey-Bass [John Wiley, distributor].

Susskind, R (2013). *Tomorrow's lawyers*. Oxford University Press.

Susskind, R, & Susskind, D (2015). *The future of the professions: How technology will transform the work of human experts*. Oxford University Press.

Thanaraj, A (2017). The proficient lawyer: Identifying students' perspectives on learning gained from working in a virtual law clinic. *US-China Law Review, 14*(3), 137–167. 10.17265/1548-6605/2017.03.002

Weinberg, J (2018). Keeping up with change: No alternative to teaching ADR in clinic. An Australian perspective. *International Journal of Clinical Legal Education, 25*(1), 35–78. 10.19164/ijcle.v25i1.694

Winkelmann, H (2015). Access to justice: Who needs lawyers? *The Judicial Review, 12*(3), 341–357.

Wizner, S (2002). The law school clinic: Legal education in the interests of justice. *Fordham Law Review, 70*(5), 1929–1937.

Chapter 6

Developing a 21st-century Legal 'APP'titude: Observations from a Postgraduate Legal Technology Unit

Kate Offer and Alex Cook

Introduction

As is evident from the subject matter of this book, there is flux in legal practice, including from the impact of technology. Law Schools must equip graduates with the skills for the current and emerging changes, as even though there is significant uncertainty as to how technology will cause the profession to evolve, it is clear that success in legal practice increasingly requires lawyers who are able to engage and collaborate with technology.

The Law Society of New South Wales dedicated a chapter to legal education in its Future of Law and Innovation in the Profession (FLIP) Report of 2017. It pointed to the need both for graduates to be equipped with skills in "technology" and also non-technological skills such as business skills, "soft" skills such as the ability to communicate effectively and to work as part of a team, as well as "project management" skills (FLIP Report, 2017).

The challenge of meeting the valuable aim of incorporating all these skills into an already content-heavy curriculum is particularly difficult in Australia where the Priestly Eleven, a group of eleven subjects which must be successfully completed for a law graduate to be eligible for admission, governs core curriculum (Skead & Offer). It is remarkably prescriptive at both the broader and more granular levels and has been described as "a 'dead hand' which purports to provide law students with the essential content for something which really no longer exists—a career as a solicitor in general practice" (Rees, 2015). At the University of Western Australia (UWA), where the Law degree is a 24 unit postgraduate Juris Doctor, core curriculum currently accounts for 17 units. In this chapter, we describe a unit we developed that aimed to secure the concurrent development of both technological and "soft skills", a combination made necessary by the constraints of the university calendar. It involved the creation of "apps" for community organisations.

DOI: 10.4324/9780429351082-6

Objectives

The intersection of law and technology is a crowded and ever-evolving space, ranging from relatively established technologies through to emerging solutions predicated on advanced analytics, such as eDiscovery services. However, one established and significant impact of artificial intelligence technology on legal practice is through the creation and use of expert systems, which allow for the automation of an expert's decision-making processes in the form of a decision tree. The technology is customised to ask a series of questions of the user, with a document, advice, database, or some other output generated as a result (Guihot & Bennett Moses, 2020). Expert systems, which usually exist in the form of a legal application (known as an "app"), can streamline both the internal processes of an organisation as well as the external client-facing delivery of legal services. An app is created through no-code software, which is a comparatively straightforward task and something that is generally achievable in a relatively short period of time. Although opinions vary on whether lawyers should be learning to code (Susskind, 2018; Legal Economy, 2016), we took the view that, given the fact that the applications could be easily created using a no-code method, as well as the compressed 12-week nature of the university calendar, this was not an area we needed to engage with. Consequently, we opted not to formally collaborate with computer science academics at UWA. However, consistent with the course's aims, we provided students with access to external computer science and legal technology experts through informal talks and networking opportunities.

Our primary aim of contributing to the development of technically competent law graduates was supplemented by two additional goals. Firstly, we determined that the unit would have a client-focused nature to allow for the development of as many of the Juris Doctor Threshold Learning Outcomes (TLO) skills as possible. Discipline standards were developed nationally by the Australian government-funded Learning and Teaching Academic Standards project in 2012. The six TLOs prescribed for law degrees (both JD and LLB) are knowledge (TLO 1); ethics and professional responsibility (TLO 2); thinking skills (TLO 3); research skills (TLO 4); communication and collaboration, (TLO 5); and self-management (TLO 6) ('Juris Doctor Threshold Learning Outcomes' (2012)).

Second, we wanted to ensure that the community-driven selection of clients involved in the unit provided an opportunity for students to give back to the community and broaden their horizons beyond the confines of the university. Whilst technological skills could be acquired through the development of apps for hypothetical clients with pre-determined issues, incorporating "live clients" from the not-for-profit sector allowed students to develop legal apps whilst simultaneously addressing community needs. The constructivist theory of education has driven the push for experiential learning for many years (Piaget, 1976; Dewey, 1998) and, although working with real clients to design a solution to an existing problem is more challenging from both an educational and logistical perspective, we wished to provide a practical and meaningful contribution to the community, given that the opportunities for experiential learning projects in Law School are often sadly lacking. Work-integrated learning (WIL) and service-learning expose students to the workforce and can facilitate "transformative learning experiences" (Valencia-Forrester et al, 2019) and a broadening of the university curriculum beyond purely academics and into the development of civic values (Seider & Butin, 2012). As Furco notes, critical to the development of civic values is that the "service learning itself is designed in such a way to provide equal benefits to the provider and recipient of the service and place equal emphasis on service provision and learning" (Furco, 1996). By incorporating clients from the not-for-profit sector, students have the opportunity to address human and community needs together in a structured environment which has the additional benefit of promoting their own learning and development (Jacoby, 1996).

The Unit

Background

A 2017 pilot programme allowed us to review and refine content, curriculum design and learning outcomes and most importantly, see what a realistic goal might be for a 12 week period. The pilot involved the use of fictional clients (roleplayed by various members of academic staff) and focused narrowly on the development of technical skills. Through this process, we realised quite quickly that we were at risk of missing a great opportunity – the inclusion of real-life clients would allow students to obtain a much richer experience, consistent with the broader set of aims discussed above.

Following the successful completion of the pilot, Legal APPtitude was included in the Juris Doctor elective unit offerings for 2018. Not-for-profit organisations, predominantly community legal centres, were engaged as participants, and the Perth office of national law firm Corrs Chambers Westgarth agreed to sponsor the unit with legal technology vendor Checkbox providing the software. Financial costs related to the unit were modest; the involvement of a national law firm was primarily motivated by providing the students with practical input from, and exposure to, the profession.

Whilst content relating to more advanced and emerging forms of legal technology are incorporated into the unit through lectures, guest presentations, and in the research students undertake in order to write a mid-semester assignment, the student projects are deliberately limited to expert systems, for reasons noted above, using a commercially available no-code platform for the creation of expert-system based apps which we found relatively straightforward and simpler to use than other options. We wanted to ensure that the output could be maintained by the client partner at the conclusion of the unit:

limited technical knowledge and resources, as well as the broader deficit of time and money in the sector, precludes overly complex solutions.

Structure

Legal APPtitude is run over the course of the 12 week semester. Numbers are capped at twenty-eight students, who are neither required nor expected to have any technical skill or anything beyond very basic digital literacy. Students are required to express their interest in writing, with a first-come first-enroled system in place, though final year students are prioritised over other students to ensure they have an opportunity to complete the unit. We operate a waiting list in case of any last-minute dropouts from students, although, given the popularity of the unit, this is a relatively rare occurrence. Prior to the start of each semester, the two unit co-ordinators meet with community sector organisations to determine what type of app will assist them. At the beginning of the semester, students are allocated to their client in teams of either three, four or five, based on their stated interests and choice of collaborators. Students are generally able to get either their first or second preference. Students are told at the outset that, although they may obtain guidance from the unit coordinators when needed, they are primarily responsible for management of the project, including navigating client relationships as well as the design and development of their legal app. On several occasions throughout the semester, lawyers from Corrs Chambers Westgarth attend to provide mentoring and practical advice to the student groups.

Student groups are expected to coordinate their efforts outside of class time, and we have observed that most student groups communicate digitally every week and met in person at least every second week. Student groups are also expected to meet with their clients outside of class time. Again, these meetings happen in a variety of ways – digitally, at the University, at the client's office, etc. We provide no administrative or logistical support to students regarding these meetings, other than assisting with coordination for the initial introductory meeting.

Assessment Items

Given the various aims of the unit, we have several components of assessment. Firstly, there is a participation mark, worth 20%, half of which is based on both attendance and participation in class and team work; the other half is from an 800-word journal, reflecting on their experiences throughout the semester and more specifically, what they have learned working with both the client and the other members of their group whilst creating the app. Students are encouraged to specifically discuss any difficulties they encountered, steps they took in response and what they learned as a result.

Second, 30% is given for a written assignment on a question or statement regarding legal technology, examples including whether criticism of the legal profession for moving too slowly to adopt innovation is fair or whether statistics which show a dramatic increase in the number of legal technology start-ups are indicative of a coming revolution in the practice of law. The aim of this assessment piece is to give the students an opportunity to think about the broader themes underpinning the unit, as well as the broader structural changes currently taking place in the legal sector.

The final 50% of the final mark is allocated to the creation of the app, but with three components in the form of (i) two short online quizzes on the Checkbox instructional materials, each worth 5% (and so 10% overall), marked individually, to ensure that all students have a minimum level of competency in the relevant legal technology prior to commencing work on the legal apps (ii) 30% App Creation (a group mark, and the maximum permitted under university policy); and (iii) 10% Presentation, marked individually, and based on students presenting their legal app to their peers, the not for profit organisations, the UWA Law School, and the broader WA legal community at an evening event in the final week of the semester. While the presentation is marked individually, the students in each group are required to co-ordinate their respective content, to both ensure a cohesive narrative and avoid repetition. Clients are not formally involved in the marking process – both to minimise their workload and to ensure that marking is conducted in a manner consistent with university protocols. However, informal feedback is sought from clients across the entire unit. Just as a student's constitutional law paper is assessed by academics with sufficient understanding of constitutional law to appropriately review the work, the students' work in this unit is assessed by academics with an appropriate background in software development, project management, and legal technology.

With the exception of the 800-word journal, the assessment structure has remained constant across the unit's iterations. The 800-word journal was added after the unit's first iteration, in response to student feedback that a more structured process of reflection would prove beneficial.

Outcomes for Students

When we initially conceived of the idea for this unit, our primary goal was for students to develop skills in relation to legal technology. As we ran the pilot programme and began to move forward with the creation of the unit we realised that we would be able to incorporate a far wider set of skills. From our observations throughout the three iterations of this unit, we are gratified at the wide collection of capabilities our students develop and can take with them into the workplace and beyond.

Technical Literacy

The primary outcome for students was enhanced technical literacy, relating both to the app creation software and a more general familiarity with technological concepts – including the constant state of development – and appreciation of technology's utility in legal practice. The latter arises as the written assignment gives them an opportunity to think about technology's broader role in the legal profession and guest lecturers from the legal profession and legal technology start-ups ensure that students can develop an understanding of general technical concepts, such as algorithmic processing, basic analytics, and the degree to which existing manual or human-driven processes can be sped-up, replaced, or otherwise augmented. We acknowledge the limitations for students of focussing on a particular piece of software, although there are skills they develop that are transferable. One such skill is the ability to break legal questions down into decision trees which, by making them "reverse engineer" a problem, can encourage a deeper understanding of the law (Rostain et al, 2013). Students are also exposed to some of the less glamorous but perhaps more realistic aspects of technical development, such as iterative development, whereby a product, particularly software, is created, developed and tested in continual cycles. At the beginning of the semester, students receive training in agile development methodology from the Innovation Quarter (IQ) team at UWA. Agile development means that development is not a linear process, but rather one where 'short feedback-loops are necessary to achieve the desired outcome' (Dingsøyr, Dybå & Moe, 2010). Consequently, the unit does not have interim goals; rather, students must have produced an app by the last week of the semester. Throughout the semester, students get regular feedback from their clients on various iterations of the app until it is fully functional. Dealing with the realities and frustrations of the iterative development process helps prepare students for potential participation in real-world software development.

Of course, in 2020, the COVID-19 pandemic required a sudden response from education providers. Western Australia has been extremely fortunate in its experience with COVID-19 due to the state government's implementation of a hard border, which effectively stopped community transmission of the virus. Since Legal APPtitude is run in second semester (from late July to late October) when internal restrictions had already been lifted, the 2020 class was only minimally affected. Lockdowns were not in place during the teaching period and we were able to procure rooms that facilitated appropriate social distancing. However, both students and academics had experienced teaching and working during the early 2020 lockdown in Western Australia and we observed an increase in both awareness and enthusiasm about the need for technology-enabled legal practice and education. Student groups were more flexible in their willingness to meet with each other and their clients via telephone and video conference, and we were able to source a number of guest speakers from the eastern states, who appeared via video link in the classroom.

Client Management/Communication Skills

Exposure to the realities of working with clients is generally limited in Law Schools. Students can complete a law degree without any exposure to the reality of how difficult it can sometimes be to obtain information from a client in regard to their legal issue, without learning how to communicate concisely and effectively with a client in a real-world environment, how to develop a good working relationship with a client or ultimately provide them with a solution to their problem. In contrast, Legal APPtitude incorporates largely unsupervised client interaction from the first day of the semester. While clients are typically not-for-profit or community legal organisations, rather than the corporate entities and/or individuals as clients that students may be more likely to be exposed to after graduation, students nonetheless still experience exposure to the real-world complexity of client management. Example issues that students confront throughout the course of the semester include mismatched expectations, delays in communication, and changing stakeholders. With appropriate supervisory intervention where required, students are encouraged to solve these problems within their groups.

TLO 5(a) provides that JD graduates will be able to communicate in ways that are effective, appropriate, and persuasive for legal and non-legal audiences. This skill is central to how well a legal practitioner performs their role. Fundamental to communicating effectively is the ability to listen "carefully and critically and to observe and interpret verbal, vocal and visual cues and messages" (Skead & Offer, 2016). Arguably the key skills developed when working closely with clients relate to communication; students in the Legal APPtitude unit quickly learn that clarity is key when working with clients; not only in what they say but in interpreting what the client is asking of them.

Presentation Skills

At the UWA Law School, students do have the opportunity to make oral presentations in moots and case study presentations but these are usually confined to the more theoretical aspects of law. In contrast, the Legal APPtitude presentation, given to clients and others, requires students to present in a much more commercial manner as they are essentially 'pitching' their solution to the legal community. This type of presentation, as per TLO 5(a), requires a level of pragmatism and commercial nous similar to the type of presentations that students are frequently required to do, should they pursue a commercial career in the law. There is only one primary opportunity to do this in the final presentation: however, throughout the semester, students are required to give more informal updates to the class each week.

Team Work

TLO 5(b) provides that JD graduates will be able to collaborate effectively and collaboration and the ability to work as a part of a team are particularly crucial skills in the modern workplace. In Legal APPtitude, students work with their project teams across the entire semester and are expected to be present each week in class, as well as available for additional work with their group when needed outside of class hours. They are encouraged to view their project group as their primary support network for the unit, albeit with oversight and intervention from the unit coordinators as required. Students gain significant benefits from opportunities for group work, where they can "learn from each other and navigate the complexities of working as part of a team" (Ryan, 2020). Working as a team is not easy and there are sometimes conflicts between group members, although to date there have been no significant issues that have required mediation by unit co-ordinators. This may well have something to do with the fact that students are able to choose one member of the class with whom they would like to be paired and so already know that they can work well with that person. This is not necessarily something that would be replicated in a workplace.

Project Management

Project management skills ensure that a project is undertaken as effectively and efficiently as possible. We have informally observed that demand for project management skills in the legal profession is growing. As law firms increasingly face both an actual and perceived threat of external disruption, an increase in internal innovation projects has been a major catalyst for this change. Simultaneously, as clients expect greater efficiency and transparency in the provision of legal services, as legal services increasingly become "unbundled" and as different service providers become involved in the running of litigation, the ability to apply processes that ensure oversight over workflow and that different services are integrated correctly is crucial (Galloway, Offer & Skead, 2017). Skills required include setting objectives and defining a scope to the work, identifying and scheduling activities, assigning tasks and managing the team and managing the budget. Although students in Legal APPtitude obviously do not need to concern themselves with budgeting, they are entirely responsible for running their project over the course of the semester. With this level of autonomy, the students are meeting the aims of TLO 6(a): Self-management, which expects JD graduates to be able to learn and work with a high level of autonomy, accountability and professionalism.

Reflection Skills

Most academic commentators agree that reflective journaling encourages the development of critical thinking skills (Spiker, 2014) and TLO 6(b) provides that JD graduates will be able to "reflect on and assess their own capabilities and performance, and make use of feedback as appropriate, to support personal and professional development". Self-reflection or "personal literacy", to use the term coined by Rust and Froud, is "literally, the ability to read oneself, to be critically self-aware" (Rust and Froud, 2011). Personal literacy is of particular use to lawyers, especially ones entering the profession at a time of great change. In the reflective journal, students were assessed on how proficiently they demonstrated reflection and deep thinking of acquired knowledge and concepts, how well they were able to integrate that into different issues from a wide range of perspectives as well as any creative solutions and critical thinking skills demonstrated in the writing.

Creativity and Innovation Skills

Creativity is considered the most important leadership quality for managing the complexities of a global and technologically transformed world (Ryan, 2020). TLO 3(d) provides that JD graduates will be able to demonstrate sophisticated cognitive and creative skills in approaching legal issues and generating appropriate responses and the ability to engage in creative thinking is essential to problem solving. Problem solving is, of course, the essence of what lawyers do (Weinstein and Morton, 2003).

In the unit, the students are presented with their clients' problems. The client does not know what is or is not possible or what will solve the problem; it is entirely up to the students, working with the client, to devise a solution that is smart, customised, and innovative. Similarly, the software itself has constraints that students are required to get around. For example, there are limitations on the degree to which the user interface can be customised, which sometimes leads to students having to rework or revise to get to their end goal. An unintended consequence of requiring students to actively problem-solve around software limitations is that it makes their experience more realistic – and more akin to the realities of actual software development in a legal environment or, indeed, dealing with clients in general.

Conclusion

Today's law students enter a workforce that has shifted dramatically from what it once was and equipping students with the myriad skills they need to succeed in this environment is of vital importance. Whilst technological skills are undoubtedly important in this new world, the timeless skills of listening carefully, communicating clearly, and thinking creatively remain essential for any graduate. These "soft" skills often prove very hard to learn, as Muriel Pénicaud, France's Minister of Labour observed at the World Economic Forum held in Davos, Switzerland, at the beginning of 2020. Discussing the skills most crucial for the workforce, she noted:

> First, I think it's soft skills – probably the most difficult to learn, but probably the most decisive for the long term. And second, it's learn, learn, learn. It means curiosity. People will have a range of skills that will be unique to each person tomorrow, because they will learn AI, but also cooking, and also soft skills. This cocktail of skills will make the difference over time.

Students enroled in Legal APPtitude are given opportunities to develop soft skills, become familiar with new technologies transforming legal practice, and create something meaningful and useful for the community. All three are extremely valuable learning experiences, but it is unfortunately not guaranteed that all students will have these opportunities before completing their legal studies, and certainly vary rare to encounter all three simultaneously. Legal APPtitude serves up a "cocktail of skills" that will give students an edge in the workplace but lets them make a positive difference in the community before they have even graduated.

And, whilst Legal APPtitude was one of the first forays into legal technology at UWA Law School, it is now just one part of a broader strategy of engagement with legal technology; the questions it raises, the challenges it presents, and both pedagogical and efficiency-related innovations it offers. Many units now include some degree of focus on legal technology – whether that be the impact of smart contracts on traditional contract law, artificial intelligence on professional ethics, or a host of other concerns. We are conscious that our unit is only one small part of what is required in developing a 21st-century Legal 'APP'titude in our students.

References

Berry, W (1987). The loss of the university. In *Home economics*. San Francisco, CA: North Point Press 1987.

Council of Australian Law Deans (March 2012). Juris doctor threshold learning outcomes https://cald.asn.au/wp-content/uploads/2017/11/Threhold-Learning-Outcomes-JD.pdf

Dewey, J (1998). *Experience and education* (60th anniversary edition). Simon & Schuster.

Dingsøyr T, Dybå T, & Moe NB (2010). "Agile software development: An introduction and overview" In *Agile software development*, T. Dingsøyr, T. Dybå, & N. Moe (eds). Berlin, Heidelberg: Springer, doi: 10.1007/978-3-642-12575-1_1

Furco, A (1996). "Service-learning: A balanced approach to experiential education" In *Expanding boundaries: Serving and learning*, A. Furco (Eds), pp. 2–6. Washington DC: Corporation for National Service.

Galloway, K, Offer, K, & Skead N (2017). Disrupting legal education. *Brief (East Fremantle, W.A.)*, *44*(10), 10–11.

Guihot, B, & Bennett Moses, L (2020). *Artificial intelligence, robots and the law*. LexisNexis Butterworths.

Inhelder, B, Chipman, H, Zwingmann, C, & Piaget, J (1976). *Piaget and his school: A reader in developmental psychology*. Springer-Verlag.

Jacoby, B (1996). *Service-learning in higher education: Concepts and practices*. San Fransisco, CA: Jossey-Bass.

Law Society of New South Wales. (2017, March). The FLIP report future of law and innovation in the profession https://www.lawsociety.com.au/sites/default/files/2018-03/1272952.pdf

Legal Economy (2016, August 22, updated 2017, December 12) https://legaleconomy.com.au/blog/2016/08/22/should-lawyers-learn-code-maybe-not/

Mabry, JB (1998). Pedagogical variations in service-learning and student outcomes: How time, contact and reflection matter. *Michigan Journal of Community Service Learning, 5*, 32–47.

Piaget, J (1976). Piaget sampler: an introduction to Jean Piaget through his own words, Wiley.

Rees, N (2015). *I look ahead: Sir Ninian Stephen Lecture 2015*. The University of Newcastle.

Rostain, T, Skalbeck, R, & Mulcahy, KG (2013). Thinking like a lawyer, designing like an architect: Preparing students for the 21st century practice. *88 Chicago-Kent Law Review*, 743, 746.

Rust, C, & Froud, L (2011). 'Personal literacy': The vital, yet often overlooked, graduate attribute [online]. *Journal of Teaching and Learning for Graduate Employability, 2*(1), 2011, 28–40.

Ryan, F (2020). Rage against the machine? Incorporating legal tech into legal education. *Law Teacher*, 1–13. 10.1080/03069400.2020.1805927

Seider, SC, & Butin, DW (2012). Introduction to special issue on "the future of community engagement in higher education". *Journal of College and Character, 13*(1).

Skead, N, & Offer, K (2016). Learning law through a lens: Using visual media to support student learning and skills development in law. *Alternative Law Journal, 41*(3), 186–190. 10.1177/1037969X1604100310

Spiker, A. (2014). Don't waste my time; exploring the reflective journaling requirement in the student teaching experience. *Networks: An Online Journal for Teacher Research, 512*, 16(1).

Susskind, R (2018). *Tomorrows lawyers an introduction to your future* (Second edition.). Oxford University Press.

Valencia-Forrester, P, Patrick, CJ, Webb, F, & Backhaus, B (2019). Practical aspects of service learning make work-integrated learning wise practice for inclusive education in Australia. *International Journal of Work – Integrated Learning, 20*(1).

Weinstein, J, & Morton, L (2003). Stuck in a rut: The role of creative thinking in problem solving and legal education. *9 Clinical L. Rev, 835*.

Chapter 7

Online Digital Platforms For Teaching Law

Vernon Rive

Introduction

Following tentative forays into digital innovation in the late 1980s and 1990s, many learning institutions, including higher education institutions (and specifically law schools), have embraced deeper changes to pedagogy in the 2000s and 2010s, often – although not always – centred around online platforms. The evolution in teaching practice has been accompanied by a growing body of analytical and reflective commentary from educational psychologists (Chen & Catrambone, 2015), learning technologists (Cochrane in Cochrane et al, 2017) and, of course, academics. (Galloway, 2017; Castan & Hyams, 2017; Thanaraj & Sales, 2015; Levy, 2015).

Commentary on technology in education involves three broad positions within a range of perspectives. The first is an enthusiastic embrace of digital technology, applauding the advantages ("affordances") of efficiency, equity and enhanced student engagement (Corbin & Bugden, 2018). The contrasting second group display marked scepticism towards the professed benefits of digital technology, calling for caution before conventional non-digital pedagogies are jettisoned for the latest digital fad (Cuban, 1986). Members of a third group have feet in both camps, recognising both the benefits of digital techniques in education and its "afflictions" (Watermeyer et al, 2020); some call for renewed appreciation of, and engagement in, time-honoured conventional approaches in legal teaching, alongside the targeted use of virtual platforms and digital technology (Levy, 2015, p305).

As I was writing a reflective account of an incremental adoption of aspects of online teaching and learning of public and environmental law, including pilot online learning platforms, using e-books to supplement traditional textbooks, teacher, and student-curated standalone websites with interactive features, online marking, and in-class use of mobile digital technology (building on a brief discussion in Cochrane et al, 2017), COVID-19 struck. In March 2020, with less than a week's notice, all New Zealand tertiary institutions were ordered to cease on-campus activities. After a brief pause, all teaching and learning moved to online platforms, as happened in most parts of

DOI: 10.4324/9780429351082-7

the world, leading to the wholesale rollout of what US law professor Aaron Saiger memorably described as a set of "jury-rigged virtual education systems of 2020" (Saiger, 2020, p2). Given his apt observation that for a person writing during the disruption of 2020 it would be "both impossible and foolhardy to try to survey, much less assess, the ... impacts of throwing all the nation's schools into the deep end of virtual education" (Saiger, 2020, p2), I limit myself to some preliminary observations on my and colleagues' experiences of the turmoil, including thoughts on the medium and longer-term impacts of these unplanned but largely wholesale moves to online platforms.

As with similar studies (Castan & Hyams, 2017), my reflections follow an "auto-ethnographic" approach – "a qualitative research method that utilises data about self and its context to gain an understanding of the connectivity between self and others within the same context" (Ngunjiri et al, 2010). I acknowledge the limitations in this methodology which flow from the absence of control groups or formal survey methods. The preliminary assessments outlined here may be useful in informing future research programmes.

Exploring Different Pedagogical Approaches to Teaching and Learning Public Law

Setting the Context

I teach at AUT Law School, a relatively new law school (established in 2009) within the Faculty of Business, Economics and Law in New Zealand's second-largest university – which attained university status in 2000 – in its largest city, Auckland (population around 1.6 million). In 2020, AUT Law School had some 840 undergraduate students (far fewer than the other law school in Auckland). 98% are domestic enrolments; just over 65% are aged 20–30 years and 15% are aged 30–40; as at other law schools in New Zealand, female enrolments outnumber males (New Zealand Law Society, 2018, p46), at AUT by more than 2:1. In percentage order, ethnic groups include: European (31%); Asian (25%); Pasifika (22%); Māori (13%), with "Other" or "non-declared" contributing 9%. We have a relatively high number of part-time students: 52% in 2019.

The structure (and to some extent, method of delivery and assessment) of five compulsory elements of the LLB in New Zealand (contracts, torts, criminal law, property law, public law) is subject to regulatory oversight by an independent statutory body constituted under the Lawyers and Conveyancers Act 2006, the Council of Legal Education (CLE). Law schools can make other courses compulsory, and AUT requires students to complete courses on legal reasoning and writing, legal system, personal property, company law, trusts, advanced private law, public international law, and ethics during the four year LLB programme. Other courses are available as electives.

During the period discussed, public law involved two separate but connected courses: constitutional law (offered in the second year) and judicial review of administrative action (judicial review) (from 2018, a third-year course), taught through a combination of large lectures and small-group workshops. In 2018, pedagogical and resourcing issues led to judicial review workshops moving online.

Are Public Lawyers Born or Moulded?

Australian law academic Graeme Orr has wryly observed that "the typical law student is not by birth a public law 'junkie'" (Orr, 2015, p309; for similar sentiments relating to the USA, see Mark Seidenfeld, 2010, p293). As Elliot notes in the English context:

> Especially in its more abstract, institutional and conceptual guises, the subject can be off-putting to students – not least because it fails to adhere to the black-letter paradigms with which students begin to identify early in their academic careers.
>
> (Elliott, 2013)

Although "[r]ecent and detailed information on New Zealand law student experiences is sparse" (Taylor et al, 2017, p21), a 2014–2015 study of first and second-year law student experiences at the universities of Auckland, Canterbury, and Waikato provides some material (Taylor et al, 2015). A survey of 224 first-year law students in 2014 reported 32.7% of respondents as having "an interest" in public law, well below criminal justice (59.7%), international law (49.9%), commercial and company law (43.2%), and family law (41.9%), but higher than property law (26.7%). The second phase of the study, relating to second-year studies, when most law students begin to take the compulsory CLE-mandated courses, reported no findings specific to public law (Taylor et al, 2017).

My impressions from a decade of teaching public law at AUT echo aspects of Orr's, Seidenfeld's and Elliott's observations. Fully-formed student public law "junkies" are indeed rare. However, I have observed a higher level of genuine interest in public law issues than some of the more pessimistic observations in the literature. Many law students from Māori or Pasifika backgrounds are *intensely* interested in aspects of New Zealand's constitutional and public law framework and practice on matters such as the contemporary relevance and application of the Treaty of Waitangi. Some part-time law students already in law-related employment have remarked on the direct application of administrative law concepts to their existing or anticipated future practice in areas such as immigration, local government, and financial regulation. And some have drawn connections between current events with obvious public law dimensions, and have remarked – sometimes with self-professed surprise – at their high levels of interest in the application of public law concepts and principles to contemporary affairs, even changing work plans to include public law as a practice area (this echoes Elliott, 2013).

Accessibility of Public Law Scholarship and Materials

A common theme from students is the inaccessibility of many textbooks on public law. Reasons for this may include a reduced appetite among younger generations for reading longer textbooks. Castan and Hyams (2017, p154) report "typical responses" from law students to the use of visual technology over textbooks as including "Videos were less confronting than reading large sections of books and cases" (for a spirited challenge to that position, see Levy, 2015, p291). Cost, too, is a factor for a reasonable proportion of AUT law students.

Up until 2016, we produced and distributed hard copy casebooks, which in 2015 included over 100 decisions in four volumes. It was not always apparent that each case was read, and piles of uncollected casebooks remained each year. As an academic in the third group noted above, receptive to the benefits of digital platforms in legal education but enthusiastic for perseverance with non-digital media in appropriate settings – recognising, for example, that the core skill of effective lawyers is the ability to wade through large volumes of documentation and words to distil and analyse the key elements and propositions – I was interested to explore making the material more accessible for students.

iBooks and ePubs for Judicial Review

An early project involved providing judicial review course materials through mobile-accessible multi-media content uploaded to the student Learning Management System in an "iMaterials" folder. Initially, in 2014, there were chapters for the Apple iBook platform containing the relevant week's reading materials including embedded PDF copies of judicial decisions, text, and video commentary links to dynamic online content such as law blogs and law commentary websites together with an introductory video podcast from the lecturer. The materials were also available in PDF for students without Apple devices. In 2015, the pilot was extended to cover approximately three-quarters of the course content, using a generic e-book platform accessible via all mobile devices in light of student feedback and informal surveys on device ownership which confirmed that many more students used non-Apple devices.

Around the same time, I piloted the use of digital platforms in an elective course for third and fourth-year students, international environmental law, which covers theories of international environmental law, including concepts of state sovereignty, and jurisdiction and liability in the area of international environmental protection. Topics include the international law framework for climate change, law of the sea, biodiversity protection, nuclear testing and international trade, and environment. These inherently global subjects lent themselves particularly well to student-led online research platforms, where fellow class members and members of the international environmental community alike are able to interact online, exchanging information and views through social media platforms. Students were able to develop online research websites as part of the compulsory research component, which approximately 75% of the class chose to do: this also allowed a much greater degree of interaction between students on their self-selected research topics.

In 2016, encouraged by my university's Learning Technology Team and reflecting on the feasibility of updating and reformatting annual versions of the electronic books used in the two courses, despite positive student feedback, I moved to a website format. Although websites at that time lacked some of the aesthetic appeal and convenience of an iBook or ePub (which could be used without an active Internet connection once downloaded), the benefits of ease of editing and updating (which I could do without technical assistance) outweighed this. Also, by 2016 and 2017, mobile data facilities were improving in New Zealand. The ePub books were transferred to two WordPress websites, https://autjr.wordpress.com and https://autlawiel.wordpress.com.

Impact on Students

Based on course surveys and my impressions, students in both classes responded very well to the initiatives. Judicial review students reported ease in using the website, and there was an increased understanding and level of engagement in the (sometimes challenging) course content, which was also reflected in higher and more informed participation in class discussions. Students in international environmental law demonstrated an impressive degree of initiative and creativity in presenting material relevant to their chosen research topics on their websites. The online platforms also allowed more interaction, which supported course learning objectives.

Impact on Pedagogy

Positive impacts on pedagogy arose from both initiatives. The development of digitally-based course content for judicial review forced me to distill complex and wide-ranging materials (such as lengthy judicial decisions and jargon-laden legal commentary) into clear and succinct summaries, benefiting both students and me in and outside of the classroom. For international environmental law, the need to model website structure and content for students using a WordPress website allowed me to share the experience of dynamic online interaction on the topic through regular Twitter activity as well as commentary on class websites.

The Great Migration: Online Public law Teaching and Learning Strategies during the COVID-19 Pandemic

In 2020, I assumed leadership of the second-year compulsory constitutional law course. This normally involves a weekly two-hour lecture for 12 weeks to

215 students at our two campuses and fortnightly interactive workshops of up to 25 students. After four weeks of face-to-face teaching, New Zealand moved into "lockdown" on 23 March 2020 in response to the COVID-19 pandemic, which precluded in-person teaching. After a pause and an early Easter break, lectures and workshops resumed through online platforms for the remaining eight weeks of the course, largely following the existing timetable, with some truncation of content in light of the disrupted term.

The lockdown arrangements were designed to allow students to continue their studies with as much continuity as possible whilst recognising and attempting to accommodate the very challenging circumstances arising including childcare responsibilities – students with children now needed to actively manage their presence at home; employment responsibilities, particularly pressing for our many students who also work; and general financial and other stresses, including dealing with the negative impacts of social and family isolation. Many of our students relied heavily on access to on-campus library and other facilities for study, with low levels of textbook ownership and limited residential internet access, and in some cases, computers shared among family members, if the family had one at all.

In the Australian rural context, Karen Yager has noted that "online learning [has] exposed more than ever the inequity and rural remote gap where many students did not have access to technology or good internet coverage". This directly reflects AUT's lockdown experience, to which the University responded by loaning laptops and funding broadband internet packages.

Online Lectures

As many students were unable to reliably commit to participating in the previously timetabled lecture and workshop slots, the decision was that compulsory papers with workshops would combine *asynchronous* recorded lectures, supplemented by scheduled *synchronous* workshops (with some recording of these for students unable to participate at the scheduled time).

As there had been widespread media coverage of the pandemic and some infections in New Zealand (28 as of 19 March 2020), and so some students might not wish to attend in person, I had posted an audio recording of the week four in-person lecture (of 20 March 2020), together with a PDF of the slides used. After campus closure, for lectures, I used both videoed "talking head" lectures and recording an audio commentary over a set of slides which I exported to a combined video file, using the Apple Keynote application, which was posted on Youtube as an unlisted upload on a dedicated channel (with a link sent to students) and also placed on the University Learning Management System. This approach was influenced by two principles: ease of access (through the variety of methods) and presence. The latter was aimed to retain an element of personal connection with students. (On the role and impact of instructor "presence" in online learning and teaching, see Corbin & Bugden, 2018, pp18–20).

On the basis of tracking data (such as view counts and other analytics for the posted video lectures), the level of engagement with the asynchronous online lectures was, in my assessment, around 10% lower than the typical attendance rate at in-person lectures. A number of the video lectures had view counts over double the number of students enroled in the course; however, the Youtube analytics also reported lower numbers of individual viewers and that the average "percentage viewed" for videos was between 50% and 60%, which indicates that a reasonable number of students started, but did not complete, viewing of the entire lecture.

The New Zealand government's response to the pandemic faced various public law challenges, as did other governments (see, for example, Tomlinson et al, 2020 in the UK context). They included critical academic commentary and judicial review proceedings challenging the legal basis for some of the actions taken (Knight & McLay, 2020). Discussion of these matters was included in the lectures.

Online Discussion Boards

Prior to the migration of lectures to online delivery, we had created online discussion boards on our LMS platform. Initially, there were three different aspects of the course: the 40% in-course written assignment; workshops; and a "Constitutional law topics for discussion" which invited students to post questions, topics for discussion or comments on current cases/articles relating to constitutional law. After "lockdown", we added two more discussion boards: one headed "Student Feedback on Online Lecture delivery"; and another for queries on the final time-constrained assessment. The written assignment and general constitutional law topics discussion boards had modest levels of student participation – with between 5% and 10% of students posting. Students visited the other discussion boards even less. I discuss strategies for encouraging better use of discussion boards below.

Online Workshops

The fortnightly 50-minute online workshops were delivered synchronously via the LMS. Workshop materials were made available digitally. In addition to allowing students to put into practice concepts and principles covered in lectures, and engage in discussions with the workshop coordinator in a smaller group setting, they had a pastoral dimension as workshop facilitators could receive information on progress and challenges faced. However, on average, no more than a quarter of the students logged in to workshops. Those who did tended to take a more passive than active role, despite best efforts in creating opportunities for student participation. This was the experience of colleagues doing workshops in other subjects: students rarely appeared by video or indeed audio, with most using chat functions. I suspect that this was influenced by noise in the house (including from children), bandwidth problems, and shyness (the latter probably also affecting discussion board use).

Assessment

Usually, assessment for constitutional law would involve a compulsory 40% written assignment and 60% three-hour final examination, the latter being a CLE requirement. All students were given an additional two weeks to complete their assignment, with more for those able to demonstrate extraordinary challenges or disruption. All assignments were assessed and returned to students online with detailed written feedback, marked up electronically using "Dragon" voice-dictation software. Instead of supervised exams, which the closure of campuses precluded, students were required to complete a take-home exam in a limited time. The assessment was released to students at 6 am on the scheduled day, with a requirement to upload answers by no later than 9 pm that day. The timing was to allow students with child-care or other duties to allocate what was expected to be three–four hours to complete the task.

Student Experiences During the COVID-19 Disruptions

Unsurprisingly, a number of students commented on the difficulties from the unplanned migration to an online platform, end-of-course anonymous feedback including reference to the stress and time taken from learning, and the content being more difficult without a class environment. However, many students either were relatively unfazed by the move to online or *preferred* it to a traditional lecture format. Students noted the ease of pausing to write notes, the ability to watch or listen again for revision, or the combination of videos, audio files, and slideshows allowing the choice of the resource that worked for them, including for example downloading files to listen to them whilst driving or exercising. Students also responded well to the inclusion in lectures (and indeed in the assessment) of topical material relating to the government's response to the pandemic, demonstrating the relevance of the subject.

Academics' Experiences During the COVID-19 Disruptions

The short-notice migration onto online platforms in the context of a global pandemic also provoked emotions and reactions among academics. Initial reactions of colleagues included adrenaline-fuelled energy that comes from responding to emergency situations and a sense of achievement in being able to overcome technical challenges and (largely) successfully reconstruct courses online under urgency. A heightened perception of solidarity may have arisen, not only among academics but also with the student body – a recognition that "we are all in this together". Inevitably, this dissipated, and my ability and willingness to devote eight hours to the production of a one-hour video lecture became more of a struggle. It is fair to say that towards the end of the 12 week teaching semester, my energy levels were lower than they were at week five.

Reflections

The first set of initiatives described above involved reasonably well-planned pilot projects aimed at facilitating greater engagement by law students in legal material, often (but not always) regarded as confronting and challenging to people with little or no legal background, by using ePub and then website-based materials. These platforms were not intended (and *are* not intended) to replace either law textbooks or cases and commentary books, whether in hard copy or digital form. Instead, their purpose was to function as scaffolding resources, through a combination of text, video and other digital media to provide a more accessible and more easily digestible entrée (for undergraduate students) into more advanced doctrinal and theoretical material.

A risk with such introductory platforms is that some students will not go beyond them, resting on the bridge, without pushing on to more challenging and rewarding destinations. To an extent that risk always exists in an educational context, however the material is presented, and however learning activities are created.

One way of mitigating the risk is by teachers consistently emphasising the role of these introductory platforms as a stepping stone to other material. Another strategy is to create material incentives for students through assessment structures which include, as a marking criterion, students' ability to demonstrate familiarity with material beyond the introductory platforms. This might be done in different ways, such as setting research tasks which build on concepts introduced in an ePub or course website but which cannot be adequately answered by reference to that material alone. The strategy is most effective where course leaders *explicitly* signal to students (including in study guides or course documentation) that reference to material beyond the website or lectures will be an assessment criterion.

The second set of initiatives was associated with the unplanned migration online as a result of the COVID-19 global pandemic. Three points come to mind from reflecting on my experiences in teaching law at AUT during New Zealand's 2020 lockdown.

First, the rapid migration online highlighted existing gaps between wealthier and less wealthy sections of society (Hall et al, 2020). Household income impacts on various factors relevant to success in higher education, but our experiences at AUT have highlighted socio-economic disparities affecting access to the core educational "tools" of functioning computers, laptops, reliable broadband internet connections, and spaces to work away from the university. While AUT and other universities took steps to address those gaps by assisting with equipment and internet, a material proportion of students are, and will remain, disadvantaged by a wholesale move to online teaching.

Second, there is a range of levels of confidence and performance among students. Sometimes, existing disparities in confidence and performance may be exacerbated by migration to online platforms, though not always because the feedback (and my own observations) shows that some students who might have been seen as lower performing under pre-COVID-19 conditions found it *easier* to study through online platforms because of the ability to pause, go back, listen again to recorded lectures and workshops.

At the same time, lower-performing students are disadvantaged in important aspects of the on-campus experience in lectures (and more so in interactive workshops), including from reduced opportunities for students to ask questions and engage in activities which reveal skills and knowledge gaps which can be immediately recognised by the lecturer and steps taken to address them. Online platforms allow for interventions, whether in response to proactive student requests for help or if an attentive teacher is able to detect gaps or misunderstandings through remote observation of performance. But my experience was that in the majority of cases, the poor performance of struggling students was consolidated rather than alleviated by even fewer opportunities to check and intervene.

Third, there are opportunities and advantages with online platforms. One academic has described the global pandemic in 2020 as having "accelerated the use of technology in education by at least a decade in a very short time" (Yager, 2020, p16). That might be overstating it a little, but the requirement to migrate teaching and learning activities to online platforms in 2020 has opened eyes to possibilities in legal education that may not have been taken up as rapidly, or at all, without the imperative of a global emergency.

For all of these reasons, the events and experiences of 2020 have confirmed my instinctual alignment with the third group of scholars mentioned in the introduction to this chapter: attentive to the demonstrated benefits of aspects of online delivery, but with a renewed appreciation of, and commitment to, maintaining non-digital, in-person dimensions of law teaching where that can be done safely and appropriately.

As noted by several commentators, effective online learning and teaching must do more than simply replicate conventional pedagogical approaches on online platforms (Corbin & Bugden, 2018). There is a risk that potentially flawed (or at least inadequate) teaching models created with very little preparation or deep thinking about pedagogy will, through inertia or institutional pressure, become the default foundation for future arrangements. In this regard, particular focuses for me would include a careful analysis of the course's assessment structure. I doubt that assessment models designed for in-person class-based attendance will necessarily be appropriate for an all-online delivery format. I intend to explore alternate assessment structures which encourage active rather than passive engagement online, such as assigning a percentage of an overall grade to student activity online (for example, posting queries and comments on discussion forums; oral or other participation in online class activities). Similarly, if required to deliver interactive workshops online, I would reflect on the need for techniques which make it easier (or even necessary) for students to participate, such as pre-assigned roles as discussants or contributors on particular issues.

It is impossible to know what the future holds, but it seems likely that at the very least, online arrangements will be a part of the COVID-19-affected legal education landscape for a number of years. Beyond the pandemic's lifespan, more far-reaching changes to legal education in which digital technology and online platforms feature heavily seem inevitable. It is incumbent on academics to take stock (and for their institutions to give them appropriate time and resources to do so) and to reflect deeply on the appropriate use of digital technology in legal education, in order to get the best out of the opportunities which 2020's challenges have begun to reveal.

References

Bowcott, O (2020, July 2). High court hears legal challenge to England's lockdown restrictions. *The Guardian.* http://www.theguardian.com/world/2020/jul/02/high-court-hears-legal-challenge-to-englands-lockdown-restrictions

Castan, M, & Hyams, R (2017). Blended learning in the law classroom: Design, implementation and evaluation of an intervention in the first year curriculum design special topic – legal education active research network. *Legal Education Review, 27*, 143–162.

Chen, D-W, & Catrambone, R (2015). Paper vs. screen: Effects on reading comprehension, metacognition, and reader behavior. *Proceedings of the Human Factors and Ergonomics Society Annual Meeting, 59*(1), 332–336. 10.1177/1541931215591069

Cochrane, T, Antonczak, L, Guinibert, M, Mulrennan, D, Rive, V, & Withell, A (2017). "A framework for designing transformative mobile learning" In *Mobile learning in higher education in the Asia-Pacific region*, A. Murphy, H. Farley, L. E. Dyson, & H. Jones (Eds.), (Vol. 40). Springer Singapore. 10.1007/978-981-10-4944-6_2

Corbin, L, & Bugden, L (2018). Online teaching: The importance of pedagogy, place and presence in legal education. *Legal Education Review, 28*, 22.

Cuban, L (1986). *Teachers and machines: The classroom use of technology since 1920.* Teachers College Press.

Elliott, M (2013, June 22). Teaching public law: Topicality—a blessing or a curse? *Public law for everyone.* https://publiclawforeveryone.com/2013/06/22/teaching-public-law-topicality-a-blessing-or-a-curse/

Galloway, K (2017). A rationale and framework for digital literacies in legal education special topic—legal education active research network. *Legal Education Review, 27*, 117–142.

Hall, KH, Doolan-Noble, F, McKinlay, E, Currie, O, Gray, B, Gray, L, Richard, L, Stubbe, M, & Jaye, C (2020). Ethics and equity in the time of coronavirus. *Journal of Primary Health Care, 12*(2), 102. 10.1071/HCv12n2_ED2

Knight, D, & McLay, G (2020, May 11). Is New Zealand's Covid-19 lockdown lawful? – An alternative view. *UK Constitutional Law Association.* https://ukconstitutionallaw.org/2020/05/11/dean-r-knight-and-geoff-mclay-is-new-zealands-covid-19-lockdown-lawful-an-alternative-view/

Levy, JB (2015). Teaching the digital caveman: Rethinking the use of classroom technology in law school. *Chapman Law Review*. http://papers.ssrn.com/sol3/papers.cfm?abstract_id=2604350

New Zealand Law Society (2018). *Snapshot of the profession*. New Zealand Law Society.

Ngunjiri, FW, Hernandez, K-AC, & Chang, H (2010). Living autoethnography: Connecting life and research. *Journal of Research Practice*, *6*(1), 17.

Orr, G (2015). Teaching public law: Content, context and coherence special issue – teaching public law. *Legal Education Review*, *25*, 299–316.

Saiger, A (2020). "Education in virtual environments" In *The Oxford Handbook of U.S. Education Law*, KL Bowman (Ed.). Oxford University Press. http://oxfordhandbooks.com/view/10.1093/oxfordhb/9780190697402.001.0001/oxfordhb-9780190697402-e-37

Seidenfeld, M (2010). Challenge of teaching administrative law, the [comments]. *Brandeis Law Journal*, *293*. Stats NZ Tātauranga Aotearoa 2018 at https://www.stats.govt.nz

Taylor, L, Cheer, U, Baird, N, Caldwell, J, & Wilson, D (2015). *The making of lawyers: Expectations and experiences of first year New Zealand law students*. AKO Aotearoa National Centre for Tertiary Teaching Excellence and the University of Canterbury.

Taylor, L, Brogt, E, Cheer, U, Baird, N, Caldwell, J, & Wilson, D (2017). The student experience in second year programmes in New Zealand law schools. *Legal Education Review*, *27*(1), 21.

Thanaraj, A, & Sales, M (2015). Lawyering in a digital age: A practice report introducing the virtual law clinic at Cumbria Practice Report: Teaching and learning in clinic. *International Journal of Clinical Legal Education*, *22*, [ci]–[cxxix].

Times Higher Education. (2020, June 24). Best young universities: Millennials. *Times Higher Education (THE)*. https://www.timeshighereducation.com/student/best-universities/best-young-universities-millennials

Tomlinson, J, Maxwell, J, Hynes, J, & Marshall, E (2020, June 1). Judicial review during the COVID-19 pandemic (Part II). UKAJI. https://ukaji.org/2020/06/01/judicial-review-during-the-covid-19-pandemic-part-ii/

Watermeyer, R, Crick, T, Knight, C, & Goodall, J (2020). COVID-19 and digital disruption in UK universities: Afflictions and affordances of emergency online migration. *Higher Education*. 10.1007/s10734-020-00561-y

Yager, K (2020). Lessons from the online world of teaching and learning. *METAphor (English Teachers Association of NSW)*, *2*, 4.

Chapter 8

A Blueprint for Designing Creativity into Learning Design

Ann Thanaraj, Paul Durston, and Sam Elkington

Introduction

The World Economic Forum (2016) describes our present era as "The Fourth Industrial Revolution" (4IR) – the exponential growth of technology, all-encompassing, shaping, mediating, and altering every aspect of our lives. Against such a background, where educators are unable to confidently answer what makes a particular profession or industry, we need to assess how Higher Education can equip students with the skills, knowledge, and abilities necessary to meet the demands of a global and digital workplace.

Legal education is operating in this evolving and disruptive landscape (Surden, 2014; McGinnis and Pearce, 2014), leaving legal educators unable to confidently answer what makes the legal profession or how the law degree can be designed to be relevant in the changing professional landscape (World Economic Forum, 2016). The complexity is enhanced because legal education operates within a multiplicity of conflicting but coexisting narratives about the past, present, and future telos and axiology of law degrees (Bradney, 2000, 2003, 2011). Law schools are questioning their role and identity in addressing the demand for different and to some extent unknown knowledge and skills (Nedelkoska and Quintini, 2018).

It is now time to have a serious conversation around the telos, the aim, and axiology, the value, of a law degree. The law degree finds itself in a restless position of being a versatile academic course with a deep and wide variety of knowledge and skills appreciated and valued by a variety of professions and industries, affording a variety of career opportunities; and now, in England and Wales, the law degree or the law conversion course is no longer a pre-requisite to becoming a solicitor (though remaining a pre-requisite for those wishing to become barristers). As such, what opportunities lie in reimagining how we prepare our future lawyers?

Even prior to the Covid-19 pandemic, this debate was ongoing and law schools were developing roadmaps towards digitally transforming their curriculum and methods of delivery, using technological solutions for efficiency in delivery and to help students experience digital learning to prepare them for

DOI: 10.4324/9780429351082-8

the tech-focused new world of work. Including and beyond legal education, learning and teaching practices are recognising the need for academic practices to embrace the seamless integration of digital and physical learning ecosystems, where students engage with digital fluency and practical subject and professional skills through the use of various tools. This seamless flow between digital and physical learning experiences should cultivate creativity in learners.

Other chapters in this book give examples of creative uses of technology in legal education, establishing evidence-informed practices of developing future-ready law students and allowing students to develop original ideas, to be inventive and agile – which is vital to navigate change, complexities, and challenges and become future-ready. For example, in chapter 13, Rebecca and Václav, describe and reflect on their practice-oriented Oxford LawTech Education Programme and the academically-oriented Law and Computer Science programme, demonstrating that collaborative interdisciplinary approaches prepare students to be future-ready. Their reflections and findings identify gaps within legal education, and they advocate for a curriculum that develops an interdisciplinary mindset, one that is focused on the use of data and design-thinking, with robust ethical grounding, to the use of technology for lawyering. In chapter 12, Rónán shares a real-world experiential initiative, Law and Innovation at the National University of Ireland, Galway, in which students worked on real-world app projects, developing their ability to critically assess the suitability of digital solutions to address practical legal and social issues, and to work across disciplines to develop a systems solution through design-thinking approaches, including assessing the legal implications. His work has led to the development of an influential perspective on the purpose of legal education, focusing more on high-level skills and understanding, and on efficiently and effectively engaging in repeated behaviours or actions.

The shift in legal practice includes the introduction of alternative business providers, has legal technology underpinning the delivery of legal services and recognises the value that non-lawyers or subject matter experts can bring, precisely because they think differently. As such, creativity is the foundation for future-ready, digitally-empowered law students. It affords opportunities to think differently and innovate, drawing on the experiences of technology and classroom-based practices demonstrated in other chapters.

In this chapter, we present the development of the Digital Learning Design Framework and Toolkit, a Teesside University project supported by Jisc UK (Thanaraj et al, 2021). Our ambition is to support course teams across learning organisations to develop a vision of how they can integrate digital solutions to future-proofing learning and teaching experience. Through the use of the toolkit, we anticipate that course teams will begin to reimagine their academic practice and teaching. The key learning design principles of the toolkit will allow courses to be designed to embed creativity, resilience, and adaptability into subject disciplines and by reimagining how assessments are designed, this will help prepare students to tackle grand challenges in the world through a broad curriculum, supported by personalised learning opportunities through digital tools and adaptive assessments and feedback.

Developing learning opportunities that harness these learning design principles also allows course teams to continually invest in their own professional development. The toolkit offers course teams a step-by-step process to provide a deep, analytical, and robust design tool for thoughtful and meaningfully designed courses with the student journey in the heart of the learning design. It also offers a benchmark to develop and maintain an academic quality offer that is rigorous and high-quality. This brings out the best digital learning experiences for students – a learner journey that is clear, logical, systematic, and one designed with a rich pedagogic rationale that is relevant to the subject discipline. It also encourages the avoidance of practices which resulted in the Virtual Learning Environment becoming a ground for simply transferring what happens on campus to online or as a repository of all things that would be covered on campus to online, without carefully planning and designing for the student-centeredness of a design principle. The toolkit has been shaped and influenced by a Teesside University student who has worked with us throughout this collaboration. As a full-time student, Archana had experienced student life during the pandemic when the campus was functioning in a hybrid system and later completely online. Archana's journey with as a student at the University enabled us to add a unique student voice to the project.

We advocate for learning that is designed with a focus on developing creativity in law students through an ability to take ownership of knowledge and learning and approaching these in new ways, empowering them to use their creativity, skills, and knowledge confidently in familiar and unfamiliar circumstances, contextualising and adapting knowledge and skills based on ongoing experience and learning.

We believe that an approach such as this will allow students to put their learning to work in ways that enable them to adapt to and thrive in different situations and scenarios. In chapters 6, 11, and 14, the authors discuss the value of studying law through interdisciplinary approaches, affording the use of knowledge in creativity and novel ways to find and solve problems through collaboration and critical use of learning and experiences. Kate and Alex share the development of innovation at the University of Western Australia where students created apps for community organisations. The apps aided decision-making processes through a series of questions, accompanied by associated documents and advice. The module was supplemented with guest talks and access to external computer science and legal technology experts. Lucia, Alan, Kim, and Andy discuss their interdisciplinary and collaborative approach to introducing students to lawtech to aid students' development of new literacies in data, technology and humanities, communication, and design. Their module was created with an emphasis on access to justice and legal design, a key future-ready skill for law students to address diverse client needs by breaking down legal solutions into a set of simple rules brought to life by technological solutions. The module develops new ways of thinking in both law students and computer science students. Similarly, Cemile shares her experience of designing and teaching a Masters in Legal Technology to empower lawyers for the digital age through an in-depth study of how technologies are changing the legal sector, incorporating STEM subjects into the study of law and developing design-thinking in lawyers and law graduates.

In this chapter, our views are framed around creativity and resilience as being core to realising authentic future-facing learning and as setting the context for many of the wider capabilities and complex learning we seek to develop through our courses and modules (WEF, 2018; Gibson, 2010). It is how, through the curriculum, we empower our students and graduates to develop the self-awareness and wide-ranging qualities, abilities, and behaviours to prepare for the future and sustain rewarding professional lives (Egan et al, 2017), particularly where there are significant changes in the process of qualifying for the vast array of established and new roles in the legal profession. This may mean a combination of graduate attributes, skills, knowledge, and experiences inculcated throughout the learning experience and beyond. It may mean aptitude and a mindset beyond graduate attributes, potentially contributing towards humans and automations working together and facing the as-yet-undefined workings of a global economy.

We are faced with a vast array of challenging questions to which there is no answer that can adequately address these wicked problems of how will students be learning in an unknown future. How can we retain the momentum of creativity right through assessment? What new perspectives are needed? How can we leverage the many digital tools we now have at our disposal meaningfully to offer authentic experiences? Similarly, how do we ensure that curricula remain relevant and responsive to contextual challenges and to student needs? What competencies do future graduates need and how do we anticipate these? How do we prepare graduates to be future-ready in a constantly changing digital world, and for the challenges of artificial intelligence? As the needs of students change, so do those of academics. How will professional development look in the future? What is the role of the scholarship of teaching and learning in propagating a future-ready mindset?

Three Principles for Planning a Built-for-Digital Academic Experience of the Academic Learner Journey

Our role as educators is to devise pedagogic strategies that allow problem-focused learning, learner agency and engagement, and that value learners' creative contributions. This involves creating opportunities for meaningful development of self-efficacy and encouraging risk-taking in safe environments where learners engage with messy and unpredictable situations which have several plausible outcomes. This requires meaningful ways for students to approach how they identify problems and find innovative solutions. Implementing this in compelling ways that meet the needs of the audience creates an environment of learning that focuses on:

- Creating authentic and creative learning experiences and assessments.
- Inculcating future readiness and digital empowerment in learners.
- Embedding digital literacies contextualised to the needs of the discipline and profession within the curriculum and learning design.

Creating Authentic and Creative Learning Experiences and Assessments

In a technologically rich and constantly evolving knowledge economy, a sense emerges that knowledge cannot, by itself, provide the core of an authentically future-facing higher education. What works depends on the types of thinking and learning we want to encourage at any particular moment in the students' learning journey. It is also heavily dependent on the learner and their progress. Students need sufficient time and space in the curriculum to allow them to develop their creativity: so teachers need to provide incremental opportunities for students to develop confidence in their ability to explore and experiment.

Where assessment is intentionally designed to allow for outcomes which are not narrowly predetermined or fixed, this emphasises assessment of 'process' to draw together and apply learning throughout a module or course and provide important opportunities to demonstrate creativity. This means students are given the autonomy to choose to work in new and interesting ways, enabling all students to be creative in ways appropriate to their own experiences and learning situations. Students are supported to manage their own learning strategies by providing flexibility and choice in the kinds of work they engage with and produce and encouraging and valuing their efforts to be creative. Through this, students are challenged through authentic, demanding, and meaningful work, encouraging them to embrace unfamiliar tasks and working practices, be open to new ideas and perspectives and recognise opportunities to create new and build on existing knowledge and insight in real-world learning situations. This affords a learning environment that encourages active engagement, reflection, and personal development, supporting students to collaborate with others, communicate their ideas, showcase their abilities and make cognitive, relational, and cultural connections.

Some points for the course designer to reflect on are the extent to which you are:

- Providing opportunities for students to confidently practise and apply their learning in creative ways that reflect and respond to their changing learning needs, motivations, and preferences?

- Providing flexibility and choice in the kinds of approaches and work students can engage with and produce throughout your module or course?
- Requiring students to put forward and showcase their own ideas about and solutions to problems they themselves have researched and defined in meaningful ways?
- Providing students a variety of opportunities for meaningful and productive disciplinary, interdisciplinary and professional collaborations?

Inculcating Future Readiness and Digital Empowerment in Learners

To nurture the core skills of creativity and resilience requires curriculum and learning designs that move beyond an emphasis on the "acquisition" of knowledge and understanding to favour more engaged, creative, authentic, and collaborative learning. Enabling creative learning in this way helps students to appreciate new insights and confidently put their learning to work in ways that enable them to adapt to and thrive in different situations and scenarios.

The future-readiness of a law student working towards becoming a digitally proficient professional is less about the tech itself and more about understanding what technology works best in a given situation and how to optimise and work in ways which are augmented by technology and legal expertise. Within the context of the legal profession, this means that the digitally proficient lawyer understands a legal or business problem, is able to appreciate the transcending boundaries of their client's problem across the physical and digital worlds, and has innovative ideas about how to solve it through the medium of technological tools and solutions where appropriate. This is where old legal problems can be approached in new ways by working out which tasks are repetitive or time-intensive, which require express legal knowledge, and which are most important to the client. Using a blend of legal and interdisciplinary knowledge and methodologies beyond the components of subjects and modules that make up a law degree will help the student to thrive in legal practice. The future-ready law graduate will be prepared with the art and science of lawyering, and the needs of legal practice focusing on the digital transformation of practice, delivery, and user experience.

Their digital fluency will be captured through their deep understanding of core technologies, their features and functionalities, how they are being utilised and the impact of these technologies on the role of legal professionals. Equipped with understanding the gaps in the profession and the opportunities to merge law with technology towards creating hybrid professions within the legal sector, they can confidently explore the limitations and gaps in legislation. For example, in the UK, the House of Lords Select Committee on Communications has been consulting widely to develop new legislation around how regulation of the Internet should be improved, and whether online platforms have sufficient accountability and transparency. This requires a multi-layered and multidisciplinary foundation to consider the necessity, scope, proportionality, and legitimacy over something with prevalent influence on society (House of Lords, Regulating the Digital World). Similarly, the House of Lords examined amendments to what became the Domestic Abuse Act 2021 relating to directing the use of data analytics to tackle domestic violence and other crimes by police forces in England and Wales, and to help decision-making using analytics and algorithms that are in fact accurate, fair and ethically obtained, with a broader consideration on human rights and other legal implications (Domestic Abuse Bill 2019-21:2019–2021: Progress of the Bill April 2021). This needs an understanding of the technology itself and how it operates, the data it uses, and its capabilities to analyse and produce results. Addressing gaps in such legislation will require collaborations between lawyers, economists, business scholars, social scientists, architects, computer scientists, engineers, and students to collectively provide a genuine holistic approach to these difficulties and come up with clear recommendations. The opportunities for law schools and their students to contribute and create new knowledge in these areas not only help to shape key policy making at the highest level but also enhance the real-world learning experience for students.

The future-ready law student is also an emerging leader, equipped with the leadership skills and confidence to shape the conversation around regulating in the digital age, capturing the physical and digital worlds and the intersection between technology, law, and society. This will involve using new and existing laws and the episteme of the rule of law to shape the (digital) transformation of social, economic, democratic, political, and ethical structures which are being reimagined in the 4IR landscape. Drawing on their solid legal knowledge, the law student will be able to frame discussions about technologies, innovation, and law around the use and impact of technology in legal services, grounded in one's values, ethics, and professional responsibilities in a rapidly evolving legal profession and practice.

We need to consider how to create learning experiences within the curriculum and course design which help students develop flexible and creative ways of thinking and working that empower and prepare them for their future. Simultaneously, we will need to consider how these attributes are delivered across levels on the course and the extent to which this builds developmentally as students progress. The following features may help in course design that has nurturing creativity in learners at its heart:

- Setting (and mapping) the scene: making the opportunities for creativity clear within the modules to help students understand the role they play is a prerequisite for creative student learning.
- A focus on personal development: equipping students with a range of practical and reflective tools and encouraging them to use and adapt these tools to align with their own goals, motivations and decision-making processes will allow students to develop self-awareness and a capacity for

reflection that enables them to recognise their own learning as it emerges and to make claims of understanding and achievement at different points in their learning development.

- Flexible learning: this requires openness to and scaffolding for learner choice and agency, utilising flexible and adaptable approaches that facilitate students' decision-making, practising problems and situations that they themselves choose/identify.
- Enterprise and originality: requiring students to consider or seek out new concepts and fresh perspectives or draw from their own learning in several modules and/or tasks, whilst encouraging them to judge for themselves appropriate response(s), will promote and develop their ability to confidently and effectively move between a generative way of thinking (developing new ideas, topics, and associations) and an analytical one (focused, structured, and evaluative).
- Crossing boundaries: encouraging the ability to use knowledge, skill and behaviours developed in one context and apply these in another context is important for developing creative learning and requires situations and tasks that are experienced as authentic and novel to learners but are achievable (realistic) using the skills and behaviours students are developing.
- Learning-focused assessment: strategies that require and enable students to draw together and apply their learning throughout a course and/or module provide important opportunities for students to demonstrate their creativity and reveal their understanding of how they have acquired key learning outcomes from a course.

Embedding Digital Literacies Contextualised to the Needs of the Discipline and Profession within the Curriculum and Learning Design

Digital literacies are core to the knowledge and skills students need to thrive in the 4IR, particularly where professions, industries, and sectors are evolving through automation, requiring creative skills that cannot be automated. Digital literacies are the awareness, active, confident, and fluent choice and use of digital solutions for intended outcomes – such as communicating, storytelling, conveying to a variety of audiences in impactful ways, creating new ideas, problem finding, analysis, and problem solving. Designing digital literacies into a module or course is complex and rewarding, requiring them to be grounded in the disciplinary and professional needs of the course, making them relevant to the nature of what and how students are studying and the intended outcomes of their studies. To incrementally develop students' digital literacies from awareness to fluency requires incremental steps to experiment and build opportunities to confidently articulate their creativity. The use of tools gives students the opportunity to be impactful in their future readiness.

Inculcating digital literacies into course design and student learning requires more than the use of tech tools and software; it must involve demonstrating a wide variety of transferable skills contextualised within professional and disciplinary knowledge and practice. The ability to think and work creatively is widely recognised as a catalyst for innovation, adaption, and resilience in all modern professional contexts. It includes, for example, confidently and fluently making the choice and using the most appropriate tools for communication, critical thinking, finding, and solving problems and working with resilience and adaptability.

Therefore, the main question for us as educators is the meaning of digital literacies in our subject discipline and the likely range of professions to which our students are heading. How will you equip your students with the necessary knowledge, skills, and future readiness to thrive in these professions – and how do digital solutions enable you to achieve this? Within the context of legal education, drawing on Dworkin's theory which suggests that legal propositions as a set of logical, self-sustaining, and predictable rules alone are inadequate to solve legal disputes (Dworkin, 1986), it is argued that the need for legal expertise in the form of judgement, interpretation, contextualisation, and reasoning refutes attempts at automation. Further, as everything that cannot be digitised and automated becomes extremely valuable, it is to be noted that it is still impossible to frame rules to anticipate and provide for every possible combination of circumstances which the future may bring, and datasets need to evolve with interpretations and social norms (Velsberg, 2019). It further affords the argument that the law is indeed constructivist in its episteme (MacCormick, 2007, Twining, 2018) because, whilst legal precedents are used to bind future decisions of courts, interpretation, reasoning, and judgements are analysed for relevance and currency. Therefore, the design of the study of law should strive to embrace its interpretive flexibility, in its episteme of a "living instrument" (Theil, 2017, Letsas, 2012) so that the law can speak to the realities of the world.

However, the construct of creativity within the design of legal education is fraught with challenges. There are ongoing contentions around the lack of balance between the syllabus and intended learning outcomes stipulated by the professional regulators and the space within this model of learning for digital literacies and preparing for the 4IR as the legal profession evolves. In this context, the focus on digital skills is not foregrounded in disciplinary and professional identity but more so towards the use of tools, and the focus on an arbitrary set of legal propositions and the method of objective testing via the vocational stage of education for prospective lawyers in England flies in the face of the ontology of the evolving nature of knowledge and the fluidity to adapt to changes over time to demonstrate the legal validity and truth between knowledge and reality (Leiter, 2010, Douglas et al, 2012). All of these challenges could be argued as factors which contribute towards the inadequacy of the current legal education system in preparing students for future readiness.

We propose some questions relevant to considering how to embed digital literacies within legal education:

- What would a law degree look like if underpinned by digital literacies/competencies for equipping students for the changing needs of the legal profession, taking into consideration that roles are evolving and new careers within the legal profession are emerging?
- How do we equip law students with the resilience to navigate the digital transformation of the legal services industry and profession?
- How will you determine a course design that allows students to demonstrate their legal knowledge, drawing on interdisciplinary methodologies and solutions to problem solve, including the ability to compellingly communicate their actions?
- What do digital literacies mean to legal education and the profession?
- What does creativity mean within a law degree?
- Crafting and embedding digital literacies into your course and module design requires going beyond the technical use of tools – so, what are the other dimensions of learning that you would like your students to be able to articulate and showcase?
- What kinds of pedagogic practices and environments are best suited to nurturing creative learners?

Practical Considerations for Designing Creativity in Learning Designs

We argue for a holistic, complex appreciation of the affordances of a law degree through systematic design which looks beyond preparing for legal practice, but instead, drawing on the episteme of law and law degrees uses legal knowledge and skills to shape the changing world. By foregrounding our work in nurturing creativity in learners, a student's development of a "sense of being" is the cornerstone of creativity, as it mediates their emerging personal and professional identities (Solomonides et al, 2012). To seek to develop creative learning is to seek a greater sense of authorship and authenticity in day-to-day working practices that, in turn, shift focus from knowledge and "knowing" (existing understandings of the world) to a sense of "coming-to-know" and "becoming" – characterised by a willingness to engage, to have a go, and learn; a preparedness to listen, explore, and an openness to new experiences and perspectives; and a determination to keep improving and moving forwards.

The modelling of a "tolerance for uncertainty" where the educator can develop the student's capacity for working productively within uncertain conditions is encapsulated in the concept of becoming future-ready (Orr and Shreeve, 2018). This is about recognising the discomfort that can arise in the face of uncertainty and supporting students to develop the disposition, the ability, and the strategies to deal with the unknown and the ambiguous – and in doing so, learn how to persevere and navigate their way through it in productive and meaningful ways.

Deciding How You Want to Teach

Naturally, teachers are subject matter experts. You may well also have detailed knowledge about the needs of your students and how best they learn and the professional needs of the discipline. This should allow you to bring an informed mind when taking the important steps of designing a course for optimal learning outcomes. Naturally, your choices will be limited to whatever is the learning ecosystem and tools in your institution. However, there are some key themes to consider.

Constructivism, a learning approach where students discover and construct knowledge and have the opportunity to apply knowledge, can lead students into developing a broad range of creative and critical skills. Constructivism requires:

- A clearly designed learning path for students to follow that is clear, logical, and systematic.
- High-quality teaching that engages with students and provides clear steering in the construction of learning.

Online learning is *not* putting course materials online and allowing students to learn in their own time. On the contrary, active learning online requires significant engagement by tutors to support students to scaffold their learning and develop a deep and critical understanding of the subject area, just as much as face-to-face teaching. Teaching online redefines what it means to be an academic into a contemporary, agile, flexible, and multifaceted academic role (Atkinson, 2020). Steps such as moderating conversations in forums and opening new threads, posting videos of helpful guides and reading materials, recording summaries, and providing feedback to students are essential to develop and sustain the success of the online community and keep students engaged and on track with their learning. This in turn means that managing the workload, for the tutor and the students, is critical, so that adequate time can be afforded to the activities without being overburdened by the volume of tasks and feedback.

Some matters to consider in this context:

- The significance of the academic in affording the best academic experience when teaching online and the role(s) they play in the different learning activities in a module (and what are the roles in a campus-taught module and how they differ).
- The pragmatic need to manage and deliver effectively and in a timely manner independent learning and creativity and impactful tutor-led interventions.

- Is my role in learning to help learners to acquire the ability to question, analyse and apply information or knowledge?
- Is learning a peer and collaborative activity between students, guided by the tutor?
- Is there a combination of approaches suitable for my course or module?
- Does my subject discipline have examples of successful seamless integration of digital technologies and practices which I could adopt?
- How do my teaching methods help me and my students meet the learning outcomes?

Think about Boundary-Crossing Ecosystems of Learning

The way in which we design our courses and modules contributes to and influences how students experience, engage, and consequently learn. The best learning experiences are designed from a student journey perspective. Instead of attempting simply to replicate what happens in the classroom, which could lead to missed opportunities arising from the flexibility of digital tools, a number of key features contribute to successful integration of digital technologies in course and module design.

How you use your learning ecosystem – the classroom and the Virtual Learning Environment – affords a variety of innovative opportunities to transform the learning experience. The best digital learning experiences for students require learning designs that create a learner journey that is clear, logical, systematic, supported by a rich pedagogic rationale that is relevant to the subject discipline, and brought to life by a learning environment that encourages active engagement through collaboration and communication, reflection, and knowledge development. By seeing the VLE as part of the learning ecosystem, it ceases to be the location for simply transferring what happens on campus to online or a repository of all things that would be covered on campus, and becomes a tool to achieve successful learner engagement before, during, and after a planned activity (whether campus-based or online).

Making full use of the features and functionalities of a VLE is pivotal for learning. Understanding some key principles will help teaching staff to maximise the affordances of ecosystems of learning, allowing alignment with the professional world where fluencies to work in different ways, expertly using different skills and creativity is key:

- The VLE, a boundary-crossing ecosystem of learning and student engagement, is an extension of a campus learning experience and environment.
- It allows the reimagination of module delivery, drawing on seamless integration of the best elements of online and face-to-face practice, considered during the course or module design.
- It provides a one-stop hub for the student's academic journey which is designed into the heart of a module and course.

- It affords space to enable and nurture creativity in learners through collaboration, communication, and construction of knowledge beyond conventional spaces.
- Together with the campus delivery of a module, the VLE brings out the best learning experiences for students based on a purposeful pedagogical underpinning and systematic learning design principles.

As such, you should consider:

- What innovative elements of your existing use of the VLE would you like to keep in the design of your module?
- How do you plan to integrate the seamless flow of learning by enabling learning, thinking and conversation across multiple spaces and over time?
- Do all the different elements that make up a topic/module flow coherently from classroom-based initiatives to online initiatives?
- Is there an adequate blend of synchronous and asynchronous learning throughout the module? Is this based on pedagogic rationales, learning outcomes, and the assessment strategy for the module?
- What risk factors have you identified from synchronous and asynchronous learning and how will this be mitigated and addressed in the design of your module?

Designing the Student Journey into Course Design

Designing the student journey – which is akin to laying a building's foundation – allows consideration of how students are going to engage in and succeed in your module. Learning from a student-centeredness perspective should be designed as a clearly laid out pathway for students to take and as a tool to develop and maintain an academic quality offer that is rigorous and high-quality.

The following matters should be considered:

- How to balance the design of the module, the expectations on yourself, and the expectations on students.
- How to communicate all of this to your students.
- How to scaffold and interweave content and meaningful tasks, with clear instructions that help students make sense of the purpose of the content and consolidate the knowledge and understanding developed during earlier sessions.
- How to help students understand why online communities of learning matter, including how to collaborate online and contribute to online discussions and how you as the tutor will be working with students collaboratively. Much of the research into student retention and attainment identifies that being part of an engaging and well-managed online

community has a positive impact on student achievement and retention (Kahn et al, 2017; Bawa, 2016).

- What will your role be in a multi-modal learning ecosystem (in the classroom and the VLE)? Will you play an active role in scaffolding and feed-forward in collaboration tasks?
- How learning and teaching activities on your course or module develop creative attributes to enable students to confidently navigate changing professional industry contexts and respond positively in challenging scenarios.

Designing Student Engagement

High-quality active learning, whether on campus or remotely, can nurture creativity. However, defining "Engagement" is as complex as defining "Success" or "Excellence" in learning and teaching. Engagement can be reflected in the time and energy students invest in their learning and the effort course designers and academics invest into creating meaningful and effective learning that encourages a student (Kuh et al, 2006). How do we keep our students motivated and actively learning? What constitutes excellence in student engagement in quality online learning?

Since individual creativity will thrive best when people are part of a larger creative "system", through which different ideas, attitudes, and perspectives can come together in new and interesting ways, curriculum design should encourage learners to actively engage with new and unfamiliar ideas and viewpoints and to collaborate in their mutual development (Belluigi, 2013). Creativity in learning is characterised by two interconnected abilities: creative thinking and creative performance (Lin, 2011).

Creative thinking involves the capacity to generate and connect ideas and create frameworks to judge the worth of ideas and potential solutions; it is akin to higher-order academic skills and capabilities. Creative performance requires a positive motivational outlook and personal commitment, evidenced by perseverance and willingness to take calculated risks, experiment, and make things happen (Belluigi, 2013). The conditions generally recognised as facilitating students' creativity in educational settings include:

- Providing incremental opportunities for students to develop confidence in their ability to explore and experiment, take risks in "safe" environments, and initiate work in different situations.
- Having activities and working situations sufficiently varied and diverse to enable all students to be creative in ways appropriate to their own experiences and learning situations.
- Giving students autonomy to choose to work in new and interesting ways, providing flexibility and choice in the kinds of work they engage with and produce and encouraging and valuing their efforts to be creative.

- Challenging students through authentic, demanding, and meaningful work and through unfamiliar tasks and working practices to be open to new ideas and perspectives, and to recognise opportunities to create new and build on existing knowledge and insight in real-world learning situations.
- Designing assessment to allow for outcomes which are not narrowly predetermined or fixed, through flexible and integrated assessment designs, that emphasise the assessment of "process" (Conrad and Donaldson, 2004).

Some approaches that might secure these aims include:

- Regular opportunities for students to develop confidence in their ability to explore and experiment with new ideas, perspectives, and practices in their learning through the academic, practical and experiential components of the law degree.
- Opportunities for students to focus on, practise, and apply their learning in creative ways, using various mediums to narrate in compelling ways they see as meaningfully reaching their audience. This space to be creative also allows students to reflect and respond to their changing learning needs, motivations, and preferences.
- Within modules outside of the mandated professional body syllabus, developing the flexibility and choice in the kinds of approaches and work students can engage with and produce throughout your module or course.
- Opportunities to create new knowledge and build on existing knowledge and insight in real-world learning situations, particularly when collaborating with students from other disciplines and industries, drawing on the strengths of two bodies of knowledge to creatively problem find and solve, and in that journey develop creative and critical thinking skills.
- Allowing students to put forward and showcase their own ideas about and solutions to problems they themselves have researched and defined, particularly in areas of law which still require resolution or in areas that are emerging such in the intersection between innovation and regulations.
- Opportunities for students to demonstrate their creativity through assessment of "process", supporting students to draw together and apply their learning throughout a module or course in meaningful ways. This is where the art of reflection and learning as a continual and gradual development process applies and is relevant in professional skills modules in particular.

Choice and Flex in Assessments for Personalised and Inclusive Learning

It is "Time to rethink assessment and feedback processes" (Brown and Sambell, 2020) because of:

- A lack of relevance to students' future lives.
- A limited range of assessment types and formats.
- Feedback often an afterthought in assessment design.

Assessment methods are powerful pedagogic tools (Elkington, 2016), lynchpins towards the coherence and connectedness of teaching, support, and experience towards attainment of learning outcomes. Assessment designs need to recognise that, as our world changes, so too our learning, teaching and assessment practices must find new forms to help support learners not just react to current trends or repeat dominant patterns of thinking, but be capable of constructively reappraising their approaches and pursue divergent futures through their learning choices. Assessments should aim to foster the kinds of attitudes and dispositions, as well as the knowledge and skills, that learners need for the variety of situations they will be confronted with during their studies and throughout their lives.

Yet, within legal education we adopt conservative practices of written examinations focusing on knowledge recall and application, affording little flexibility and choice in how students demonstrate their learning. A key factor for the lack of flex and creativity in how learning is assessed and how assessments are designed was the regulatory framework in law. In New Zealand, for example, the regulatory framework requires final exams for core subjects because that is what the legal profession has made a pre-requisite (New Zealand Council of Legal Education) In other jurisdictions, such as in Ireland (Bar of Ireland and Law Society of Ireland), Hong Kong (Bar Association and Law Society), England and Wales (Bar Standards Board and Solicitors Regulation Authority) where the legal professions have an entrance exam, it is a practical necessity to have training to answer exams as part of the assessment process. Yet large volumes of law graduates with law degrees don't always enter the legal profession, instead, using their law degrees in other careers. As such, in a continually changing graduate environment, there are calls to develop "flexible" assessment that shifts priorities from formulaic approaches of content learning to tasks that focus on the process of learning and that are sensitive to the needs of students, giving them more control over assessment processes (Boud and Soler, 2016).

Balancing the desire to introduce creativity, innovation, and flex into assessments and the need to prepare students to answer entrance examinations in the interest of regulating the standard competency offered to the public, is a fine and fair balance towards bringing change to how law students demonstrate their learning.

For some law schools, professional centralised examinations post-law degree mean that they have the space to be creative and to design curricula that may be interdisciplinary and innovative, whilst others are incorporating competency-based methodologies into their learning and assessments. The impact of a competency-based method of assessment by way of objective testing possesses, as proposed by the Solicitors Qualifying Examination (SQE) in England and Wales, risks teaching through the "banking" (Freire, 2000) method whereby students receive knowledge as a given rule or principle, and in a mechanical way learn to logically "apply" the rules and principles of law in order to determine the "correct" legal answer. A key risk is students coming to believe that in every situation there is one correct legal answer, creating a hierarchy of propositional and doctrinal knowledge as a single source of truth. Instead, in preparing students for competency in using the law, rather than privileging a universal notion of truth, reflecting the contested and complex reality resonates with the episteme of law, one that is open to interpretation, argument and reasoning within specific context and facts. The complexities and abilities of justification and judgement of a learner which are essential skills of a lawyer remain unverified through this process (Hall, 2017).

Shifting our focus to sustainable approaches and designs that are sensitive to the needs and circumstances of students, giving them more control and ownership over assessment processes with no learning deficit is key to reflecting the future readiness of law graduates. This view of flexibility extends to choices students make about assessment methods and formats, as well as the extent to which they have an active role in shaping the assessment approaches and processes they are involved in (Irwin and Hepplestone, 2012). This means students choose how to assess and students choose what to assess (Jones-Devitt, 2020).

The key principles for designing assessments that nurture students with the creativity needed for the changing world of work include:

- Personalising learning: Using a variety of assessments rather than relying on one or two signature (high-stakes) assessment methods (ie, written exams), and this includes, where possible, shifting from an arbitrary list of competencies, fields of substantive law (Guth and Ashford, 2014) and the mandated use of objective testing methodology to assess this acquisition.
- Diversify approaches: Consider how combinations of different assessment methods and tasks might meet the learning needs and preferences of diverse student groups. Further, the continued compartmentalisation of legal knowledge continues to carve an unrealistic expectation of the sorts of challenges a prospective lawyer will need to address for their clients flies in the face of the complex landscape of 4IR.
- Allowing choice: Provide students with the opportunity for negotiated and managed choice between an accepted range of 'alternative' assessment methods.
- Embedding agency: Students are gradually introduced to the idea of flexible assessment at a module level, where early low-stakes (formative) assessment tasks are broken-down to afford a degree of choice.
- Be realistic: Do not assume all students have the same access to technology or have had the same experience. Remove limiting conditions that are not necessary for making accurate judgements on student work. The opportunity

for interpretive freedom, intellectual creativity and curiosity are features of human character that cannot be digitised and automated. Together with legal expertise and the art of lawyering requiring human creativity, flair, and knowledge, they will become extremely valuable in the digital age. The opportunity for interpretive freedom can become neglected in assessments (Twining, 1997; Hart, 1997), and revised approaches allow law to be studied within the realities of practice, societal needs, and the lived realities of today's changing world.

- Be accessible: Flexible assessment arrangements 'work' across a spectrum of settings and device specifications whilst still meeting key learning outcomes.
- Embedding digital literacies and confidence: Giving students the space to experiment and express their creativity in new and different ways using a variety of tools to problem find and problem solve

Here are some design tips to consider:

Using a variety of assessment approaches/methods:

- Does assessment on your module provide every student with an equal opportunity to demonstrate their achievement?
- To what extent are students encouraged to bring their own backgrounds and experiences to bear on assessment tasks?

Incorporating choice and flexibility into assessment design.

- To what extent do students have choice in the topics, methods, and criteria, of assessment tasks on your course/module?
- To what extent are you providing students with opportunities for regular formative feedback as a way of checking for individual understanding and progress?

Nurturing Future Readiness and Digital Empowerment through Course Design

The ideas above focus on embedding principles of creativity into course design through the use of digital technologies to create authentic and creative learning experiences and assessments and ensure that digital literacies are part of the curriculum. This sets the foundation towards preparing students to become future-ready and digitally empowered in the face of technological change.

The need to balance consistency of outcomes and standards and flexibility in delivery and in enabling student choice and agency through curriculum design is crucial. Enshrined in the concept of nurturing creativity, the concepts of future readiness and digital empowerment are far-reaching and overlapping. They consist of shifting attributes which are intricately connected, yet, are complex concepts which can have profound implications on course designs and students' academic experience. While different disciplines in higher education may recognise and value different forms of creativity, the ability to think and work creatively is widely recognised as a catalyst for innovation, adaption, and resilience in modern professional contexts (Menkel-Meadow, 2001). As educators, it is for us to decide the role creativity plays within our courses and modules in preparing our students for increasingly uncertain future professional lives. But how do we do this? What kinds of pedagogic practices and environments are best suited to nurturing creative learners? This chapter offers a systematic course design model, intertwined within which is a means to engage meaningfully with such questions, providing actionable insight into the ways academic colleagues might embed and nurture creativity through curriculum and learning design.

Digital empowerment is far-reaching, complex and multifaceted, particularly when paired with creating readiness for the changing and uncertain and unknown future of our personal and professional lives. The concept of empowerment becomes one that affords the capability to act in a way that would enable multi-dimensional self-determination and autonomy. We argue that making a difference comes from the conscious and knowledgeable confidence and agency to create, shape and influence something in a responsible and impactful way. A certain level of digital competency to allow the person to fulfil their responsibilities is necessary. Within HE research, deciphering digital empowerment typically sits within the realm of frameworks of digital literacies (JISC, 2014; Hague and Payton, 2010; Beetham, 2017; Belshaw, 2015) and competencies (Brown, 2017). Digital literacies and competencies can be broadly defined, from the technical know-how of using technology to the cognitive skills of digital literacy, developing critical thinking, understanding and utilising information, and the functional competencies needed to confidentially and flexibly adopt the use of technologies.

Competency is typically framed around the ability to adapt flexibly (Ferrari, 2012) and is strongly related to professional expertise (Spante et al, 2018). We take a broader view. We look towards empowerment as the nature of the relationship of individuals to society to effect change. This means the ability to use knowledge, experience, and skills to contribute and shape the way technology is used, regulated, and capable of influencing a wide range of elements of our social, cultural, political, and economic life, including its ability to mediate and shape our experience in the world. As such, we argue that empowerment goes further than literacies and competencies, and towards a process that is characterised by knowledge, confidence and agency, and being accountable for this. As such, this confidence or empowerment is whereby one is able to use skill and knowledge levels to navigate other digital domains in a "transferable" manner, knowing the informed basis of one's choices and actions, coupled with accountability. To be accountable involves awareness and understanding of ethical issues and concerns; ensuring security and privacy;

understanding the impact of our digital activities. See further, Chapter 15, in which Ann argues for an interdisciplinary model of law degree to prepare students to become future-ready and digitally empowered.

Conclusion

In this chapter, we have sought to highlight the very real challenges involved in designing creativity into course design when learning is set against a rapidly changing educational, professional and technological environment.

We argue for a more holistic, complex appreciation of the affordances of a law degree through its systematic design, which calls for looking beyond preparing for legal practice, but instead, drawing on the episteme of law and law degrees, to using legal knowledge and skills to shape the changing world. Both empowerment through the use and critical understanding of technology and the readiness for the changing and uncertain and unknown future, both professionally and in our personal lives, are enshrined in what we advocate as creativity in self and agency. To do this, we must also find ways of valuing the role of "relative failure" as an integral part of the creative learning process, since initial mistakes will eventually allow for improved outcomes. The acceptance of failure and experimentation, as much as the reward for success, plays a key part in developing individual resilience and offers an incentive for innovation. What works from a learning design perspective depends on the types of thinking and learning we want to encourage at any particular moment in the students' learning journey. It is also heavily dependent on the learner and their progress, aided by scaffolded and timely support. To prepare our students for the technologically advancing world of work, for them to be future-ready and digitally empowered, is largely dependent on the digital competencies and dispositions of academics, in ensuring that the tools can be most effectively employed for meaningful use (Thanaraj and Durston, March 2020). As technology evolves and brings changes to all facets of work and life, digital empowerment becomes a critical goal and one that is a lifelong learning skill.

From this perspective, the function of a future-facing higher education is reconceptualized as the building of human capital, supporting the development of each individual learner's creative capabilities to seek out and face everyday problems, as well as enhance their capacities for future success. As such, an empowered and future-ready graduate will possess a broad range of attributes including:

- Authenticity: learners are encouraged to take ownership of initiatives and tasks by actively constructing and making judgements on their own knowledge and understanding of concepts and relationships relevant to real-world contexts.
- Curiosity: the ability to elicit, analyse, refine and evaluate existing knowledge to create unique and cogent ideas and artefacts.

- Receptivity: response to learning tasks and situations that require an openness to new and different knowledge, ideas and perspectives and the ability to connect and work with others, communicate ideas, and be responsive to multiple sources of feedback.
- Proactivity: a capacity to take measured risks, an ability to perceive and create development opportunities and the resourcefulness to pursue novel perspectives on and solutions to problems.
- Personal flexibility: in response to unpredictable situations that require the self-awareness and confidence to embrace and navigate change and the capacity to put learning to work in a variety of ways and settings.
- Resilience: adaptive behaviour to overcome obstacles and deal with uncertain situations and outcomes, requiring a tolerance for ambiguity, a positive motivational outlook, and a proclivity for solving relatively complex problems.

It is important to acknowledge that different disciplinary epistemic frames from pure law degrees, law degrees which incorporate the vocational stages of preparing to become a lawyer and interdisciplinary models of law degrees will recognise and value different forms and combinations of these attributes; the context of practice is, therefore, vital to the interpretation and meaning of creative learning in curriculum and learning design.

Bibliography

Alencar, EM, Fleith, DDS, & Pereira, N (2017). Creativity in higher education: Challenges and facilitating factors. Temas em Psicologia, *25*(2), 553–561.

Attewell, S, Iosad, A, & Pauli, M (May 2020) JISC: Assessment rebooted https://www.jisc.ac.uk/reports/assessment-rebooted

Barnett, R, & Jackson, N (2019). *Ecologies of learning and practice*. London: Routledge.

Bawa, P (2016) *Retention in online courses: Exploring issues and solutions—a literature review*. Sage Open, accessible via: doi: 10.1177/2158244015621777

Beetham, H (2015). Revisiting digital capability for 2015. *JISC Digital Capability Codesign Challenge Blog*, https://digitalcapability.jiscinvolve.org/wp/2015/06/11/revisiting-digital-capability-for-2015/

Beetham, H (2017; 9th March). Digital capability framework: An update. *Blog post in Jisc Digital Capability Codesign Challenge*. Available at https://digitalcapability.jiscinvolve.org/wp/2017/03/09/digital-capabilities-framework-an-update

Belshaw, D (2015). *The essential elements of digital literacies*. [Self-published through Gumroad Inc]. Available at https://dougbelshaw.com/blog/2016/01/02/digilit-ebook-199/

Belluigi, DZ (2013). A proposed schema for the conditions of creativity in fine arts studio practice. *International Journal of Education in the Arts*, *14*(19), 1–22.

BlackBoard Academy, 6 Core Competencies to Enhance Digital Teaching and Learning https://www.hepi.ac.uk/2020/05/13/online-learning-are-we-asking-the-right-questions/

Bradney, A (Winter 2000). Society of public law teachers. *Reporter, 21*.

Bradney, A (2003). *Conversations, choices and chances: the liberal law school in the twenty-first century*. Hart Publication.
Bradney, A (2011). How to live: Aristocratic values, the liberal university law school and the modern lawyer", 2 Web JCLI http://webjcli.ncl.ac.uk/2011/issue2/bradney2.html
Bratman, B (2015). Improving the performance of the performance test: The key to meaningful bar exam reform. Vol.83 UMKC Law Review, p.565 https://papers.ssrn.com/sol3/papers.cfm?abstract_id=2520042
Brown, M (9th November 2017). The challenge of digital literacy: Beyond narrow skills to critical mindsets, available at: https://www.linkedin.com/pulse/challenge-digital-literacy-beyond-narrow-skills-critical-mark-brown
Brown, S, & Sambell, K (2020). Changing assessment for good: A major opportunity for educational developers. *Post-Covid19 SEDA Educational Developments Special issue*. London: SEDA.
Boud, D, & Soler, R (2016). Sustainable assessment revisited. *Assessment & Evaluation in Higher Education, 41*(3), 400–413.
Clay, J (21 May 2020). Hybrid - eLearning stuff, accessible via: https://elearningstuff.net/2020/05/21/hybrid/
Clay, J (21 May 2020). Lost in translation - eLearning stuff, accessible via: https://elearningstuff.net/lost-in-translation
COFAonlineUNSW (2011). Teacher presence, motivation of learners. *Engaging and motivating students*, accessible via: https://www.youtube.com/watch?v=DvJuzE-g7OM
Conrad, R, & Donaldson, A (2004). *Engaging the online learner: Activities and resources for creative instruction*. Wiley & Sons, Accessible via: http://eltandtech.pbworks.com/f/engaging+the+online+learner.pdf
Davies, M (2018). Changes to the training of English and Welsh lawyers: Implications for the future of university law schools Vol. 52 The Law Teacher.
Dearing, R (1997). Report of the national committee of inquiry into higher education: (http://www.leeds.ac.uk/educol/ncihe/)
Douglas, M, Wilson, J, & Ennis, S (2012). Multiple-choice question tests: a convenient, flexible and effective learning tool? *A case study, Innovations in Education and Teaching International, 49*(2), 111–121.
Dworkin, R. (1986) *Law's Empire*. Harvard University Press.
European Political Strategy Centre EPSC (2016). The future of work: Skills and resilience for a world of change: https://ec.europa.eu/epsc/publications/strategic-notes/future-work_en)
Egan, A, Maguire, R, Christophers, L, & Rooney, B (2017). Developing creativity in higher education for 21st century learners: A protocol for a scoping review. *International Journal of Educational Research. 82*, 21–27 (p. 21).
Elkington, S, Westwood, D & C Nerantzi (Eds.) (2019). Creativity for student engagement: Purpose, process and product. *Special Issue of the Student Engagement in Higher Education Journal*. Available at: https://sehej.raise-network.com/raise/issue/view/72
Elkington, S (2020). *Transforming Assessment in Higher Education Guide. Advance HE Student Success Framework Series*. York: Advance HE: https://www.advance-he.ac.uk/knowledge-hub/essential-frameworks-enhancing-student-success-transforming-assessment
Elkington, S (2016). The case for transforming assessment in higher education, HEA Viewpoint https://www.heacademy.ac.uk/system/files/downloads/assessment_viewpoint_aug16.pdf
Ferrari, A (2012). *Digital competence in practice: An analysis of frameworks JRC technical reports*. Luxembourg: European Commission, http://ftp.jrc.es/EURdoc/JRC68116.pdf

Freire, P (2000). *Pedagogy of the oppressed* (30th anniversary ed.). New York: Continuum http://www.msu.ac.zw/elearning/material/1335344125freire_pedagogy_of_the_oppresed.pdf

Garrison, DR, Anderson, T, & Archer, W (2000) Critical inquiry in a text-based environment: computer conferencing in higher education. *The Internet and Higher Education, 2*, 87–105.

Gibson, R (2010). The 'art' of creative teaching: Implications for higher education. *Teaching in Higher Education, 15*(5), 607–613.

Guth, J, & Ashford, C (2014). The legal education and training review: Regulating socio-legal and liberal education?. *48*(1) The Law Teacher 5–19 http://nrl.northumbria.ac.uk/20961/1/Guth_and_Ashford_LETR_article_final_submitted.pdf

Hague, C, & S Payton (2010). 'Digital literacy across the Curriculum'. Slough, Futurelab, available at: http://www2.futurelab.org.uk/resources/documents/handbooks/digital_literacy.pdf

Hall, E (2017) Notes on the SRA report of the consultation on the solicitors qualifying exam: "Comment is free, but facts are sacred", *51*(1) The Law Teacher 364.

Harris, A (2014). *The creative turn: Toward a new aesthetic imaginary*. Rotterdam: Sense Publishers.

Hart, HLA (1997). *The concept of law, Clarendon law series*, 2nd Ed., Oxford University Press, pp. 150–170.

House of Lords Select Committee on Communications published a parliamentary report titled 'Regulating the Digital World' https://publications.parliament.uk/pa/ld201719/ldselect/ldcomuni/299/299.pdf

Ihde, D (1990). *Technology and the lifeworld: From garden to earth*. Indiana University Press, pp. 38–41.

Institute for the Advancement of the American Legal System, 'The whole lawyer and the character quotient' available online at http://iaals.du.edu/foundations/reports/whole-lawyer-and-character-quotient

International Bar Association, Presidential task force on the future of legal services, drivers for change in the legal profession: https://www.ibanet.org/Task-Force-on-the-Future-of-Legal-Services.aspx

Irwin, B, & Hepplestone, S (2012). Examining increased flexibility in assessment formats. Assessment & Evaluation in Higher Education, *37*(7), 773–785. http://shura.shu.ac.uk/6529/

Jackson, N (2020). Exploring learning ecologies. Chalk Mountain Press. *Networks: The Creative Academic Network: a global network of people interested in creativity and committed to enabling students'* creative development: https://creativehecommunity.wordpress.com/

Jahnke, I (2011). How to foster creativity in technology enhanced learning. In B White, I King, & P Tsang (Eds.), Social Media Tools and Platforms in Learning Environments: Present and Future: 95-116. Jackson, Norman. "Developing students' creativity through a higher education." Available at: http://www.normanjackson.co.uk/creativity-in-highereducation.html

JISC (2014) *Developing students' digital literacy*, http://www.jisc.ac.uk/guides/developing-students-digital-literacy

Jones-Devitt, S (27 April 2020) Flexible learning comes of age. Accessible via: https://www.advance-he.ac.uk/news-and-views/flexible-learning-comes-age

Jones-Devitt, S (2020). Essential frameworks for enhancing student success: Flexible learning https://www.advance-he.ac.uk/knowledge-hub/essential-frameworks-enhancing-student-success-flexible-learning

Jones-Devitt, S, Lawton, M, & Mayne, W (2016). *HEA Patchwork Assessment Practice Guide.* https://www.heacademy.ac.uk/knowledge-hub/patchwork-assessment-practice-guide

Kahn, P, Everington, L, Kelm, K et al. (2017). Understanding student engagement in online learning environments: The role of reflexivity. *Education Tech Research Dev, 65*, 203–218, accessible via: https://link.springer.com/article/10.1007/s11423-016-9484-z#citeas

Krook, J (21st June 2018). Teaching law students creative skills could save the profession from automation. *The Conversation*, available at: https://theconversation.com/teaching-law-students-creative-skills-could-save-the-profession-from-automation-97615

Kuh, GD, Kinzie, J, Buckley, JA, Bridges, BK, & Hayek, JC (2006). What matters to student success: A review of the literature, Commissioned Report for the National Postsecondary Education Cooperative, http://nces.ed.gov/npec/pdf/Kuh_Team_Report.pdf

Leiter, B (2010). Legal formalism and legal realism: What is the issue?, *16* Legal Theory 111.

LETR (2013). Chapter 2: http://www.letr.org.uk/the-report/chapter-2/perceived-strengths-and-weaknesses-of-the-current-system/index.html

Letsas, G (2012). *The ECHR as a living instrument: Its meaning and its legitimacy*. SSRN: https://ssrn.com/abstract=2021836

Lin, YS (2011). Fostering creativity through education–a conceptual framework of creative pedagogy. *Creative education, 2*(03), 149.

Lord Neuberger (2012). Judges and professors – ships passing in the night? Speech Max Planck Institute, Hamburg on 9 July 2012, https://www.judiciary.uk/wp-content/uploads/JCO/Documents/Speeches/mr-speech-hamburg-lecture-09072012.pdf

LTE Bites 03 – Inclusive Assessment.

LTE Bites 06 – Strategies for Embedding Flexible Assessment.

LTE: Considerations and resources for digital platforms and tools supporting alternative assessments can be found at: https://blogs.tees.ac.uk/lteonline/digital-delivery-learning-and-support/supporting-alternative-assessments/

MacCormick, N (2007) *Institutions of law. An essay in legal theory*. Oxford University Press.

Menkel-Meadow, C (2001) Aha? Is creativity possible in legal problem solving and teachable in legal education, 6 Harv. Negot. L. Rev. 97-144 (2001) available at: https://scholarship.law.georgetown.edu/cgi/viewcontent.cgi?article=1170&context=facpub

McGinnis, J, & Pearce, R, (2014) The great disruption: How machine intelligence will transform the role of lawyers in the delivery of legal services. *Fordham Law Review, 82*, 3041–3066 https://ir.lawnet.fordham.edu/cgi/viewcontent.cgi?article=5007&context=flr

McGregor, C (February 2020) *The Show Must Go On: Creativity and thinking differently in law*, available at: https://oliver-uploads-aus.s3.amazonaws.com/2020/02/05/01/34/55/603/CKG%20Interview%20050220.pdf

McWilliam, E (2009). Teaching for creativity: From sage to guide to meddler. *Asia Pacific Journal of Education, 29*(3), 281–293.

Nedelkoska, L, & Quintini, G (2018). *Automation, skills use and training, OECD Social*, Employment and Migration Working Papers, No. 202, Paris: OECD Publishing, (https://www.oecd-ilibrary.org/docserver/2e2f4eea-en.pdf?expires=1554040951&id=id&accname=guest&checksum=06BC7F3A1E72160839AC2189A34B9B8F

Noto La Diega, G, Bessant, C, Thanaraj, A, Giles, C, Kreitem, H., & Allsopp, R (2018). *The internet: to regulate or not to regulate?" Submission to House of Lords Select Committee on Communications' inquiry*. http://data.parliament.uk/writtenevidence/committeeevidence.svc/evidencedocument/communications-committee/the-internet-to-regulate-or-not-to-regulate/written/82651.html

Orr, S & Shreeve, A (2018). *Art and design pedagogy in higher education: Knowledge, values and ambiguity in the creative curriculum*. Abingdon: Routledge.

Patterson, D (1997). *Law and Truth: Replies to Critics*, 50 SMU Law Review: https://scholar.smu.edu/smulr/vol50/iss5/2

Pearson's Higher Education Services (2016). Teaching Presence, accessible at: https://www.pearson.com/content/dam/one-dot-com/one-dot-com/us/en/pearson-ed/downloads/Teaching-Presence.pdf

Revek, M (30 March 2020). When the Tide Goes Out: Identifying and Supporting Struggling Students in Online Courses, accessible via: https://www.facultyfocus.com/articles/online-education/identifying-and-supporting-struggling-students-in-online-courses/

Rorty, R (1982). *Consequence of pragmatism*. University of Minnesota Press.

Sambell, K, & Brown, S (2020 – a collection of blog posts and resources). Covid-19 Assessment Collection https://sally-brown.net/kay-sambell-and-sally-brown-covid-19-assessment-collection/

Significance of teacher presence can be found at: https://blogs.tees.ac.uk/lteonline/2020/12/15/teacher-presence-and-learning-design/

Solomonides, I, Reid, A, & Petocz, P (2012). A Relational model of student engagement. In *Engaging with learning in higher education*, I Solomonides, A Reid, & P Petocz (Eds.). Faringdon, UK: Libri Publishing.

Spante, M, Sofkova Hashemi, S, Lundin, M, & Algers, A (2018). Digital competence and digital literacy in higher education research: Systematic review of concept use. *Cogent Education*, *5*, 1, accessible via doi: 10.1080/2331186X.2018.1519143

Stanford Encyclopaedia of Philosophy, available at: https://plato.stanford.edu/archives/fall2018/entries/technology/

Surden, H (2014). Machine learning and law. *Washington Law Review* p.89–95 https://www.law.uw.edu/wlr/print-edition/print-edition/vol-89/1/machine-learning-and-law

Tai, J, Ajjawi, R, Boud, D, Dawson, P, & Panadero, E (2017). Developing evaluative judgement: Enabling students to make decisions about the quality of work. *Higher Education*, *76*(3), 467–481.

Teesside University, Learning and Teaching Enhancement Unit.

Thanaraj, A, & Durston, P (8th March 2022). DigiFest 2022, A Trivial Pursuit: A framework for learning design. Slides accessible via: https://www.jisc.ac.uk/events/digifest-08-mar-2022/programme

Thanaraj, A, & Durston, P (10th March 2020). DigiFest 2020, In the changing future of work, how can universities prepare students for future careers? Slides accessible via: http://repository.jisc.ac.uk/7788/4/digifest-2020-in-the-changing-future-of-work-how-can-universities-prepare-students-for-future-careers.pdf

Thanaraj, A, & Durston, P (10th March 2020). DigiFest 2020, Teesside University's digital transformation journey towards educating students for the future, slides accessible via: http://repository.jisc.ac.uk/7789/4/digifest-2020-challenging-transformation-reimagining-academic-practice-in-the-digital-university.pdf

Thanaraj, A (2017) Making the case for a digital lawyering framework in legal education. *International Review of Law*, *2017*(3). 17, accessible via: https://insight.cumbria.ac.uk/id/eprint/3324/1/Thanaraj_MakingTheCase.pdf

Thanaraj, A, Chathangoth, A, Durston, P, & Sumpter, J (July 2021). Introducing the digital learning design toolkit for course teams. *Association of Learning Technologies* https://altc.alt.ac.uk/blog/2021/07/introducing-the-digital-learning-design-toolkit-for-course-teams/

Theil, S (2017). Is the 'living instrument' approach of the European court of human rights compatible with the ECHR and international law? *European Public Law*, 23(3), 587–614.

Thomson, C (20th May 2020). Is "mixed participation" in learning our future reality, accessible via: https://coronavirus.jiscinvolve.org/wp/2020/05/20/mixed-participation/

Twining, W (1997). *Law in context: Enlarging a discipline*. Oxford University Press, p.39–41.

Twining, W (2018). Rethinking legal education. *The Law Teacher*, 52(3), 241–260.

Velsberg, O (18 June 2019). The Technolawgist, Government Chief Data Officer of Estonia: Robot judges, artificial intelligence and the future of digitalisation reporting on Estonia's project to issue rulings through AI judges http://www.thetechnolawgist.com/2019/06/18/ott-velsberg-government-chief-data-officer-of-estonia-robot-judges-artificial-intelligence-and-the-future-of-digitalisation/

Verbeek, P (2005) *What things do: Philosophical reflections on technology, agency, and design*. Pennsylvania University Press.

Wegner, J (2015). The values of legal education. *24 Nottingham Law Journal*, 112 https://www4.ntu.ac.uk/nls/document_uploads/nlj_24.pdf

Weinstein, J, & Morton, L (2003). Stuck in a rut: The role of creative thinking in problem solving and legal education, 9 Clinical L. Rev. 835, available at: https://scholarlycommons.law.cwsl.edu/cgi/viewcontent.cgi?article=1138&context=fs

World Economic Forum (2016). The future of jobs (http://www3.weforum.org/docs/WEF_Future_of_Jobs.pdf)

World Economic Forum (2016). Grand challenge insight report: The future of jobs: http://www3.weforum.org/docs/WEF_Future_of_Jobs.pdf

World Economic Forum (2017). Accelerating workforce reskilling for the fourth industrial revolution, Geneva http://www3.weforum.org/docs/WEF_EGW_White_Paper_Reskilling.pdf

World Economic Forum (2018). The Future of Jobs Report, https://www.talenttalks.net/world-economic-forum-2018/

Chapter 9

Legal Tech and Sustainability

Ryan Murray and Helen Edwards

We live in interesting times. Not only do legal educators have to provide flexible study opportunities, international placements, clinical legal education, and employability skills, all in the context of the professional bodies changing the criteria for entry into the profession, but there is also the disruption of the rise of legal technology. As Hongdao et al (2019, p2) highlight: "The legal industry is experiencing a shift in delivery and business models, in turn leading to a disruptive change of the 'conventional' legal market". Law firms are embracing legal tech as core to the operations: and so those who work in this sector will need the relevant skills. Interesting times indeed.

The problem is, do students know this? Do they know why firms are using legal tech? If students do not understand the "why", teaching and assessing digital skills simply becomes one more hoop through which a student must jump to gain their qualifications. This chapter, therefore, examines how the use of practical legal tech could be adopted to enhance not only the digital skills of students but at the same time to enable them to develop an understanding as to "why" legal tech is used by lawyers and what skills need to be developed. The aim must be for a student to understand the commercial realities of legal tech; a means of achieving efficiencies or compliance, solving legal problems, and of limiting the possibility of mistakes.

The anchor for the discussion will be that of sustainability because students must be adaptable to change in order that the legal tech skills they develop are not obsolete by the time they emerge with their qualifications. Embracing and having a practical understanding of legal tech requires a holistic understanding of "how", "why", and "what next" and this chapter explores how principles of sustainability may provide a framework by which we can prepare students for a technologically advanced legal practice.

Legal Tech and Future Skills Training

The lawyer of the future will need to be equipped for a new legal landscape with technology integrated into the provision of traditional legal services. This will require new skill sets and a keen sense of business awareness. This new

DOI: 10.4324/9780429351082-9

landscape will also provide new opportunities for how businesses use their workforce. It may, however, disrupt the work of junior members of the legal profession.

Research conducted by The Law Society of England and Wales into the adoption of legal tech highlights this problem. "The often-repetitive tasks that were undertaken on behalf of clients were seen as a rite of passage and path to progression in law firms. Reducing the pool of graduates and paralegals may have significant knock-on effects on the flow of associates and partners of the future". (Lawtech Adoption Research, 2019, p43). Repetitive and time-consuming tasks, once the staple of lower-paid junior lawyers, could be completed more accurately and efficiently with software using "machine learning" (the use of algorithms and statistical models by computer systems to perform independent tasks; a subset of artificial intelligence.)

Law firms benefit from cost savings, and this may also free up junior lawyers from routine tasks meaning their time can be used for other duties. However, an alternative also needs to be considered. The reduced need for lawyers to perform repetitive tasks may simply create less need for lawyers. Rather than skills being redeployed and the role of a lawyer changing, the use of legal tech may produce a contraction in the legal job market.

That said, it is our view that some tasks that in theory could be performed by machines are tasks that are less suspectable of being imminently replaced by machines. Tasks such as managing client care and relations become not only increasingly important but also increasingly unique.

Freeing up more time and resources could play an increasingly important role in the delivery of legal services. A report by HSBC into the investment strategies of UK law firms highlights that client care is a top priority for firms, with 44% of respondents selecting this as their first choice for allocating investment within the firm (HSBC, 2019, p6).

There could be greater access to justice for some clients if technology reduces overhead costs of providing legal services and representation and firms are able to engage in pro bono activity when previously cost had been a barrier. Similarly, they might be able to offer services to some clients at lower rates. This is of course qualified by the prospect that some firms may not engage with such activity, given the reduction in income that this provides.

There may be opportunities for new types of lawyers to emerge, with specialist skills that span the gap between computer science and legal practice. Roles such as Legal Technologists are becoming more commonplace in firms and educational institutions, challenging what being a lawyer means and the skills required. At the Future of Legal Education and Training Conference 2019, Richard Susskind issued a bold warning:

> "If you are a young lawyer or you are running a law firm, you should ask yourself, should I compete with these AI/online systems or should I be one of those who is building these systems?"

It is an interesting dichotomy. Does a computer science graduate with technical skills such as programming and system design need any legal knowledge to build a piece of legal tech? Does a newly qualified lawyer conversant with legal principles and procedures need any technical skills in order to successfully practice with legal tech? Are we likely to see the convergence of these skills and the emergence of a hybrid lawyer able to converse as confidently in law as with code? Lawyer 2.0?

This latter suggestion is deliberately provocative but highlights how technology will continue to blur the boundaries of traditional legal practice and the lawyer's role and shape our understanding of what a lawyer of the future will be. A framework for developing students who are digitally empowered and future-ready needs to take account of the impact that technology may have on practice, which is likely to affect some practice areas more than others. Tasks such as conveyancing and drafting wills may require less input from lawyers as AI use develops, whereas litigation may always need specialist advocates with unique human skills to persuade tribunals of fact. Some aspects of litigation, however, may in the future involve software running sophisticated algorithms. For some time, aspects of assessment of the value of (eg personal injury) claims have been calculated with the aid of software by insurers and solicitors.

Perhaps what is most important is a synthesis of technical and legal specialists. The technical specialist needs to understand that legal concepts are interpreted and translated differently from strict rules of code and algorithms. They need an appreciation of what tasks and which areas of law are suitable for the use of technology and that systems are programmed to be doctrinally correct. Likewise, the legal specialist needs to understand the basic architecture of the technical systems they are using. The lawyer needs a sufficient understanding of the systems to know what questions to ask in order to get the answers they want from the software. They also need to know what to change when the systems are not doing what they are asked. A common but a basic understanding of these respective roles may be required to ensure they each are speaking the same language, allowing them to achieve the desired results.

The lawyer of the future will therefore need to be flexible and progressive to adapt to the challenges of a technologically advancing future. This in turn should inform the approach law schools take in training lawyers of the future. We suggest that this does not require a radical overhaul to the delivery of legal education, but that a solution may be found in the amalgamation of doctrine and practice, grounded in core principles of sustainability.

Sustainability Considerations

How does a student, graduate, or trainee develop a practice that is sustainable in light of the challenges above and how do we equip students for a digitally advancing future?

This question prompts some deeper consideration of the principles of sustainability and how they may relate to legal education and practice. The complexity of the task is summarized by Dernbach, who noted that the knowledge and skills required by future lawyers:

i began with the need "to understand the conceptual framework that sustainability embodies, particularly the integration of environment and development goals";
ii extended to "the ability to craft and apply appropriate legal rules" for restoring and protecting the environment whilst also supporting economic growth, job creation, and national security that protect and restore the environment at the same time as they help grow the economy, create jobs and protect national security;
iii also required cross-disciplinary working with natural sciences, engineering, economics, policy analysis and social sciences relating to such matters as human behaviour and institutional design;
iv finally required cross-jurisdictional working, since "sustainable development is an internationally used framework" (Dernbach, 2011, p502).

Is Teaching 'Legal Tech' Sustainable?

The Difficulties of Simply Teaching Legal Tech

One response to these challenges would be to teach legal tech as part of the curriculum in the same way that we teach legal rules, skills, and knowledge, assessing students in their proficiency in using the technology.

Is this response too simplistic and potentially flawed? Is it sustainable? Given the rate of technological development, reflecting "Moore's Law" that computer processing speed will double every two years but costs will halve and meaning that ubiquitous technology may become defunct, there is the risk that our teaching will be stale by the time it reaches the classroom.

There are further considerations as to what we teach. For example, do we teach coding, and if so, what type of code? Again, programming languages are prone to obsolescence. For instance, the need to understand MS DOS to operate every basic function of a desktop computer in the 1980s, and hence be trained in it, changed when Graphical User Interfaces were introduced from Microsoft Windows 3.0 onwards, allowed users to operate a computer by pointing and clicking on icons (which movements were translated by software).

There is a further issue of how law tutors are to develop the necessary skills to teach legal tech. Their training focuses on an understanding of legal principles, the application of legal skills, and an appreciation of appropriate pedagogy, among the many other skills required to teach. Is it realistic or reasonable to suggest that academics must also keep up to date with changing technology and how do they access such support and development?

Adopting a sustainability-based approach to teaching, using legal tech in a supportive role rather than simply teaching what happens to be the new technology, would allow students to develop core skills such as reflection and adaptability. The focus will be on producing sustainable graduates with the skills to adapt to an ever-changing professional environment.

This brings us to a consideration of sustainability and how its principles may provide an appropriate structure by which to equip students for the future of the legal practice.

The Misunderstanding of Sustainability

Unfortunately, "sustainability" may suggest merely "green" initiatives and environmental concerns. The Brundtland report (1987), published by the United Nations, articulated a definition of sustainable development as "development that meets the needs of the present without compromising the ability of future generations to meet their own needs". As Scoffham (2016) summarizes: "Sustainability is a notion that lacks clear definitions and can be interpreted in many ways. Simplistically, it is associated with specific pro-environment behaviours such as recycling waste, saving water and turning off the lights".

The temptation to focus purely on environmental factors is a trap into which institutions can also fall in promoting their sustainable credentials through eco-friendly initiatives such as the use of renewable energy and policies designed to reduce waste and through teaching modules such as Environmental Law.

Research into student attitudes towards and skills for sustainable development by Drayson et al (2014) revealed that students still defined sustainable development in ways marked by their "similarity to the definition provided by Brundtland (1987)", leading to the suggestion that "student understanding of sustainability is limited to those surrounding nature and ethics" rather than anything wider. They were concerned that those promoting education about sustainability "fall into the trap of defining sustainability interchangeably with environmentalism", raising whether "a focus on and integration with wider and 'softer' skills and competencies (ie graduate attributes) [would] be more relevant to the student population?"

This understandable association presents significant obstacles in integrating principles of sustainability into practice, particularly as the word has been overused.

However, as Bosselmann (2016, p9) observes: "While the term may have been misused, the idea remains and continues to influence our thinking about the future". The articulation of what sustainability actually is, and what it is not, is the starting point.

As Scoffham (2016) continues:

> "A more sophisticated approach sees it as the property of a whole web of relationships (Capra and Luisi 2014). Focusing on connections and associated

> notions such as balance and harmony has the advantage of shifting attention away from environmental problems towards the relationship between people, other life forms and the planet which supports us".

A more holistic approach to the idea of sustainable development is required to fully understand how it can enhance future practice. The starting point is to consider the three pillars of sustainability.

The Pillars of Sustainability

It is generally accepted that the principle of sustainable development is founded on three pillars, social development, environmental development, and economic development (commonly referred to as the pillars of People, Planet, Profit) (Kahn, 1995). The three pillars are not divorced from one another, but intersect and work harmoniously for true sustainable development to be achieved. Following the 2005 World Summit on Social Development, these three pillars were clearly defined. We shall consider each in turn.

Pillar One – People

A sustainable institution should have the support of its people, stakeholders and the community in which it operates. This involves devising mechanisms for personal and career development, creating an environment that encourages retention and a system of management that rewards achievement. These ideals may also appeal to the public more generally, enhancing public confidence and perceived integrity and, in turn, encouraging the institution to be more sustainable. The social aspect of sustainability, therefore, embraces much more than ensuring individual success. It is about ensuring human rights are promoted and adhered to; seeking opportunities to relieve poverty and, of course, the role of education and development in ensuring a fair society.

Pillar Two – Planet

As has been noted above, environmental sustainability is most familiar. Without maintaining an ecologically sound balanced environment there is little prospect of people (let alone profit) subsisting. However, focusing just on factors such as climate change and 'green' initiatives does not necessarily produce sustainable change. As Fisk has noted:

> "It is not just about 'reducing, recycling, and reusing'. Climate change is most effectively addressed by rethinking and redefining the resources we use, rather than seeking to limit the damage by belatedly planting a few more trees".
>
> Fisk (2010, p7)

The "planet" aspects of sustainability are therefore important as to how institutions plan and maintain their development. As Fisk also commented:

> "For business, they represent some of the greatest opportunities to find new markets of profitable growth, more lasting and engaging sources of competitive advantages, and more effective ways of reducing risk and cost".
>
> Fisk (2010, p2).

These are opportunities that students may not associate with sustainability. The link between the planet and suitable business practice is therefore something we must consider, including how this is highlighted through our teaching practice.

Pillar Three – Profit

What may seem controversial is the recognition of profit as a pillar of sustainability. The drive towards profit may easily be associated with the consumption of resources at the expense of the environment. Applied to educational institutions, this becomes even more unpalatable. There is no doubt that the world's wealth is already distributed inequitably, with a small percentage holding a disproportionally vast amount. As such, there would seem ample opportunities for such wealth to be redistributed and reinvested, allowing individuals to gain value in life from factors other than consumption. The pleasure and mobility that are gained from education are just one example.

However, the current prevailing ethos in society means that profit to fund improvements is a simple reality. As such, profit has a symbiotic role to play in harmonizing the three pillars of sustainability. Without profit, the organisation may not be able to carry on business. It cannot invest in its people. It cannot invest in more energy-efficient solutions. An educational institution which functioned only to generate profit might have short-term success, but sacrificing investment in its people, infrastructure, and surrounding community means it is unlikely to be sustainable. One of the roles of an educational intuition is to foster creativity and innovation and it should seek to do this through suitable business practices.

How do We Introduce Principles of Sustainability into Legal Education?

Principles of sustainability have to be introduced in ways that are practical and meaningful and promote engagement with the core ideas.

Course designers in the modern law curriculum are subject to various pressures. Key skills, knowledge and attributes need to be developed and assessed in line with the requirements of the awarding University and to the satisfaction of the relevant processional regulatory bodies. Additional pressures may be created by various enhancement projects in response to student attainment and progression and the input of the "student voice" into course developments. Within these constraints, there seems to be little room to introduce new modules dedicated to the teaching of concepts of sustainability.

In England and Wales, the introduction of the Solicitors Qualifying Exam in 2021 and the review of the requirements for a qualifying law degree by the professional bodies may offer some limited respite. Traditionally, students have been required to study the seven foundation subjects of legal knowledge as part of their degree or post graduate qualification, these being: Contract Law, Law of Torts, Public Law, Land Law, Law of Trusts, Criminal Law, and EU Law (which is still a requirement of the Bar Standards Board). Further, these had to contribute 180 credits to an undergraduate degree, making curriculum design very restrictive and potentially stifling optionality and innovation in the remaining half of the degree.

If the professional bodies are to relinquish the strict requirement for 180 credit points being allocated to the foundation subjects, this does offer some opportunities to reallocate these learning hours elsewhere. Modules that develop skills, enhance employability and allow innovative content could be developed without falling foul of any minimum requirements prescribed by the Solicitors Regulation Authority or Bar Standards Board. It is against this background that we now consider whether the use of technology can provide a solution to the problem of how we equip students with the skills for sustainable practice.

The Role of Legal Tech as Part of the Solution

Using technology to equip students for sustainable practice creates a not-so-subtle irony. Technology consumes resources. It can be disposable and prone to obsolescence. It has the potential to reduce effective interactions between people. It may have a negative impact on the user's health and wellbeing. It is expensive. Technology certainly has an accountable role in the acceleration of climate change.

If technology is part of the problem, then perhaps we can make it part of the solution? We propose that requiring students to reflect on the three pillars of sustainability, but using technology as their lens and a means by which to reflect and be critical, may be an effective way of preparing students for a digitally advancing practice.

An illustrative example is the use of a case management system, which bridges the gap between academic and professional practice. It requires students to engage with a convergence of software packages – word processing, email, spreadsheets. It requires students to think about the implications that the system has for the running of a business. It is also a relatively inexpensive way of introducing them to legal tech.

If institutions don't have access to such systems they could even create simulated, 'in-house' equivalents, drawing together different parts of a case file using standard software packages. If the technology isn't available at all, the theory could extend to more hypothetical exercises, with students being asked to think of how technology may provide a solution to an everyday problem. The key is not to focus purely on the use of technology. The aim is to encourage students to reflect on how have they engaged with the pillars of sustainability in whatever task they are set. It is their reflection on the process that is assessed, not the use of the technology itself.

Using the example of a case management system students may reflect on how they have engaged with the three pillars of sustainability.

In relation to pillar one, people, students may reflect on the training and development they have undergone in order to use the system and how this has prepared them for practice. They may reflect on how the system has impacted their working environment in light of the time-saving efficiencies. This may also prompt reflection on the future job market they will be entering: how the rise of legal tech may reduce the need for certain roles. They may reflect on the benefits for clients such as how sound data management may enhance the client experience and ensure better relationships with clients. They could reflect on the wider social benefits and how the efficiencies created by the system may enhance access to justice through more pro bono activities. The efficiencies created by technology may promote more flexible working patterns and opportunities for job shares. This may facilitate social change through more effective work/life balance and increased equality of domestic responsibilities. With countries such as Finland adopting more progressive policies ensuring equality of maternal and paternal leave (the UK only permitting two weeks of paternity leave), and the debate as to whether the UK should adopt a four-day working week, technology may be influential in supporting further social change and greater equal opportunities (see further, Kirby, 2020).

In relation to the second pillar, planet, students may reflect on how the system impacts the environment. This may include positive aspects such as the reduction of hard copy files and less waste. The reduction in the need for face-to-face meetings meaning less travel for practitioners and clients. It may include more negative aspects such as the resources used to manufacture the hardware. It may also involve reflection on how the lawyer of the future may contribute to the protection of the environment through legal rules, policy and governance.

In relation to the final pillar, profit, students may reflect on the efficiency of the system and how this is important to the business of legal practice. The system may ensure better compliance with professional body rules on the provision of legal services and codes of conduct. This may reduce issues of non-compliance and reduce the cost this may have to the business and its reputation. The system may require less human input, allowing resources to be used to enhance the services of the business that cannot be performed by software. This may produce better client care, ensuring more repeat business and more profit. Students may then reflect on how the profit could be used to invest in the business, its people and more sustainable resources. Thereby allowing students to develop a holistic appreciation of the principles of sustainability.

Another example could be developing inclusive and flexible assessment strategies that allow students to use technology in more innovative and creative ways. Students could be set an assessment task and they must then select which technology they think will allow them to best satisfy the assessment criteria. Rather than submitting word-processed documents, they may produce short videos, podcasts, presentations, or blogs. They may also reflect on why they selected that technology over other alternatives and reflect on how the pillars of sustainability have been considered as part of that decision-making process. The reasons for selecting the technology and the process of reflection undertaken can be assessed just as equally as the final assessment output that is submitted.

Follow-on Steps

Our suggestion that principles of sustainability and reflection are foundational in equipping students for the future of legal practice and should be central to the law degree is only a starting point. These principles need to be scaffolded into both the academic and subsequent professional stages of legal training to ensure they remain relevant and contextualized.

Students on an academic course of study could be introduced to different models of reflection, such as Driscoll (1994) and Gibbs (1988). These models could then be used to reflect on the United Nations Sustainability Goals. These 17 interconnecting goals focus on reducing poverty, inequality, climate, and environmental degradation, and on enhancing prosperity, peace, and justice. The aim is to achieve these goals by 2030. Students could be assessed on the quality of their reflection as to how legal tech may be relevant in limiting or achieving these goals.

For practitioners, principles of sustainability could be adopted by professional bodies as part of pre-qualification training and continuing professional development. An assessment of professional ethics and conduct, for example, could include an assessment of how principles of sustainability affect both the advice that is given and the form in which it is given. Lawyers of the future will need to make decisions as to what matters are handled by human beings and which are delegated to software. Lawyers will need to develop robust processes for making these decisions and understand any liabilities that follow. By adopting a holistic approach to sustainability that spans the academic stage of training through to continuing professional development, students and practitioners alike may be equipped for a digitally advancing and sustainable practice.

References

Bosselmann, K (2016). *Transforming law and governance*, 2nd Edition, Routledge, 8 Dec 2016.

Brundtland (1987). Report of the World Commission on Environment and Development: Our Common Future. Available at: https://sustainabledevelopment.un.org/content/documents/5987our-common-future.pdf

Capra, F, & Luisi, PL (2014). The systems view of life: A unifying vision. Cambridge University Press.

Dernbach, J (2011). The essential and growing role of legal education in achieving sustainability. *Journal of Legal Education, 60*, 489–518.

Drayson, R et al, (HE Academy, November 2014). Student attitudes towards and skills for sustainable development. https://www.heacademy.ac.uk/sites/default/files/resources/student_attitudes_towards_and_skills_for_sustainable_development.pdf

Driscoll, J (1994). Reflective practice for practise. Senior Nurse. Vol.13 Jan/Feb. 47–50.

Fisk, P (2010). People planet profit: How to embrace sustainability for innovation and business growth, Kogan Page Publishers, 3 Feb 2010.

Gibbs, G (1988). *Learning by Doing: A Guide to Teaching and Learning Methods.* Oxford: Oxford Further Education Unit.

Hongdao, Q, Bibi, S, Khan, S, Ardito, L, & Khaskheli, M (2019). Legal technologies in action: The future of the legal market in light of disruptive innovations. *Sustainability, MDPI, Open Access Journal, 11*(4), 1–19, February 2019.

Hove (2004). Critiquing sustainable development: A meaningful way of mediating the development impasse? Available at: https://pdfs.semanticscholar.org/d3c4/8aa3a38490aa20844791e901af20c6185896.pdf

HSBC (2019). Legal tech analysis, investment and growth strategies in law firms. Available at: https://www.business.hsbc.uk/-/media/library/business-uk/pdfs/hsbc-2019-legal-tech-report.pdf

Kahn, M (1995). Concepts, definitions, and key issues in sustainable development: The outlook for the future. Proceedings of the 1995 International Sustainable Development Research Conference (pp. 2–13).

Kirby, G (2020). Finland increases paternity leave to 7 months to match maternity quota. Available at: https://www.telegraph.co.uk/news/2020/02/06/finland-increases-paternity-leave-7-months-match-maternity-quota/

Lawtech Adoption Research (2019). The law society. Available at: https://www.lawsociety.org.uk/support-services/research-trends/documents/law-society-lawtech-adoption-research-2019/

Scoffham, S (2016) "Grass roots and green shoots: Building ESD capacity at a UK University." In *Challenges in Higher Education for Sustainability. Management and Industrial Engineering*, edited by J Davim, W Leal Filho Cham: Springer.

United Nations Sustainability Goals – Available at: https://www.un.org/development/desa/disabilities/envision2030.html

Chapter 10

A Polish Perspective on How Ensuring Access to Legal Information Impacts Access to Justice and Legal Education

Olga M Piaskowska and Piotr F Piesiewicz

Introduction

The right of access to justice (ATJ) – as guaranteed by Art 47 of the Charter of Fundamental Rights of the European Union and Art 6 of the European Convention on Human Rights – has core components such as the right to obtain legal advice and legal representation in court proceedings; more broadly, it also encompasses legal aid in all types of cases, including the right to legal information. It is the duty of the State to secure ATJ: the numerous obstacles to this include elevated legal fees, formalised and costly procedures, parties avoiding contact with the judiciary for economic reasons – out of fear or feeling that the goal is unattainable; the excessive number of statutes and sources of law statutes and sources of law; lack of relevant systems of legal assistance as well as lack of relevant information concerning one's legal standing; and physical barriers (Democratic Governance Group, Bureau for Development Policy, 2004, pp20–22; Organisation for Economic Co-operation and Development, 2016, pp7–9). The effective implementation of the State duty to secure ATJ is, for practical reasons, the responsibility of lawyers (McDowell and Sheikh, 2009, pp6–7), educated by law schools.

Justice may be relevant in many domains, such as procedural justice, interpersonal justice, distributional or informational justice (Klaming & Giesen, 2008, pp14–20; Colquitt, Conlon, Wesson, Porter & Ng, 2001; pp425–427; Gramatikov, Barendrecht & Verdonschot, 2008, pp9–10). Informational justice pertains to the explanations given to individuals as to why the given law or procedures are being applied (Colquitt, Conlon, Wesson, Porter & Ng, 2001, pp426–427). Provision of information at the early stages of proceedings is beneficial both in implementing ATJ and in improving the perception of justice (Klaming & Giesen, 2008, pp1–8; Shapiro, Buttner & Barry, 1994, pp346–347). The right to legal information must entail accurate information. Before they proceed, individuals should know if they have any rights and of what kind, and what they can do in the specific situation. Therefore, legal knowledge is the basis for the implementation of this right.

DOI: 10.4324/9780429351082-10

Legal information is commonly associated with legal expertise and is considered to be the exclusive domain of legal professionals (McDowell & Sheikh, 2009, p14). In Poland, however, there is no monopoly. First, there are various websites offering online legal advice, mostly in civil and family cases: as this is not monitored, it is not always known who the provider is and/or whether the information is accurate. Secondly, the legal regulations in force (such as the Act of 6 March 2018 on entrepreneur law, Journal of Laws 2019, item 1292) allow persons who have not qualified for the regulated professions, such as attorney or counsellor, to offer legal advice. This affects the implementation of the right to legal information. As this is predicated on information that is correct and this may turn on the many variables of a situation, it is more likely to be provided by those in the regulated legal professions. Any assumption that the law is a simple matter must be rejected.

In Poland, the Act of 5 August 2015 on free legal assistance and legal education (Journal of Laws of 2015, item 1255) has led to legal aid centres being established at the municipal level. Legal aid is there provided by legal professionals free of charge; the expenses are covered by the State. In addition, there are legal clinics in law schools: they date back to 1904 (Rundstein, 1904, pp229–235). Our observations are that they are perceived by law schools as a significant and valuable part of legal education. First, they allow students to practically apply their acquired knowledge, help them develop their lawyering skills, and above all, they promote the *pro publico bono* attitude. Second, by providing legal aid including legal information to people with modest resources, they implement the guarantee of ATJ. This multi-layered role of legal clinics is perceived similarly in other legal systems (Shanahan, Selbin, Mark & Carpenter, 2018, pp585–586;Kalantry, Brundige & Gupta, 2012, p9;Drew & Morriss, 2013, pp2–29). As a result of the 2015 Act, the number of cases handled by the clinics has decreased (Fundacja Uniwersyteckich Poradni Prawnych, 2019, pp18–19), though this does not affect their role in legal education or justice.

Also central to our research project was the change in the way information is stored and accessed as a result of the growth of the Internet. Since digital tools are used in education and have affected the manner in which law is practised, law schools may not remain passive in this context. What matters is not only the manner in which digital tools and the Internet are used for education, which is currently the focus of researchers all over the world (Sahin, Balta & Ercan, 2010, pp234–244; Glava & Glava, 2012, pp3556–3560; Dogruera, Eyyamb, Menevisab, 2011, pp608–611, pp608–611) but also the manner in which common access to legal information has affected the exercise of legal professions and the implementation of ATJ (Vinson & Moppett, 2018, pp551–571; Prescott, 2017, pp1993–2050), by reducing one of the barriers (geographical ones). It can also reduce other barriers (eg effective access to court, costs of justice and legal assistance), but this depends on the legal system and organisation of the judiciary in a particular country (Directorate General For Internal Policies Policy Department C: Citizens' Rights And Constitutional Affairs, 2017).

The Present Study

We noticed that students preparing legal opinions in our clinic began by using information found on the Internet: but many were unable to verify the information, which caused them to provide propositions containing outdated or incorrect information. This lack of skills undermines ATJ for clients and may significantly impair the exercise of the legal profession in the future. We wished to explore this further, and also to determine the approach of those already in the legal profession, and consider whether technological progress may improve ATJ, particularly informational justice.

Between April and June 2019, with the approval of our University ethics process, we collected data through an anonymous online questionnaire open to law students, legal trainees or law graduates and publicised, with participant information, on social media and websites dealing with legal issues. The questionnaire had 13 questions, 12 obligatory closed questions (9 of which were dichotomous ones, and three in the form of semantic differential), and one optional open-ended question; the results were only recorded if the 12 obligatory questions were answered. Out of 341 questionnaires, 340 were filled in accurately, and one inaccurately, which led to its rejection. The data generated through the questionnaire were analysed using the IBM SPSS Statistics v 25 software and Microsoft Excel.

341 people participated in the study. Among them, there were 135 law students (39.71%), 60 legal trainees (17.65%), 1 notary (0.29%), 2 prosecutors (0.59%), 11 academics (3.24%), 5 judges (1.47%), 85 attorneys and counsellors (25%), 29 persons exercising another legal profession (8.53%), and 12 lawyers not exercising the profession (3.53%).

Considering the purposes of the study, only 328 questionnaires out of 340 appropriately completed ones were taken into account. 12 persons who are qualified lawyers but do not exercise the profession were left out, given that they were not involved in giving advice. Their opinions were considered non-representative for the purposes of the study.

The 328 participants were divided into three groups according to their career status. The first group, students (135 questionnaires – 41%), was composed of people who have just begun their career as lawyers and who at the same time have the most up-to-date knowledge of law studies. The second group, legal trainees (60 questionnaires – 19%), consisted of law graduates who were following legal internships and preparing to exercise their chosen legal profession; their experience and knowledge placed them between students and practitioners of law. The third group, practitioners in various legal professions (133 people – 40% of the total number), was composed of people who had graduated from law schools and had jobs after having gathered relevant experience. Members of this group were able to observe certain loopholes in legal education, especially in terms of necessary skills.

The respondents could also be broken into four age groups as follows:

- Under 30 (ie, 18–29), of which there were 177 (54%), comprising 98 students, 48 trainees, and 31 practitioners.
- 30–39, of which there were 118 (36%), comprising 31 students, 9 trainees, and 78 practitioners.
- 40–49, of which there were 31 (9.5%), comprising 5 students, 3 trainees, and 23 practitioners.
- 50 and above, of which there were 2 (0.6%), comprising 1 student and 1 practitioner.

Only two persons aged above 50 participated in the study. Their opinion then will not be representative of the age group, but it remains significant for the research group they belong to. When designing the study, we deliberately selected the 50+ group. Statistical research in Poland clearly shows that online presence is primarily determined by age, and only secondly by education. The most infrequent users of the Internet are those aged above 50 (Fundacja Centrum Badania Opinii Społecznej, 2019)). In part, our research confirms this – which results in an unrepresentative group of two people. However, we did not combine them with the previous one on purpose, as this would modify the original assumptions.

Analysis of Data and Results

Acquisition and Verification of Legal Information via the Internet

Does Common Access to Legal Information on the Internet facilitate the Exercise of the Profession?

Overall 91.5% of respondents thought that common access to the legal information on the Internet facilitates the exercise of legal professions; 5.5% disagreed and 3% did not have an opinion. There were no major differences within the individual research groups or between them. 91.1% of student respondents agreed with Internet facilitation, as did 93.3% of law trainees and 91% of practitioners. In the 18–29 age group, 89.8% of respondents agreed; the figure for the 30–39 age group was 94.1%, and in the 40–49 group it was 90.3%. These results undermine any presumption that using digital tools is limited to young people. Irrespective of the stage of their careers and their ages, the respondents almost unanimously perceive common access to legal information on the Internet to facilitate their exercising of the profession.

Do Lawyers Use Digital Tools in the form of Internet Search Engines as a Source of Legal Knowledge?

Overall 95.4% of respondents used Internet search engines when searching for legal information needed for their work; only 4.6% did not. Again, there were no major differences within research groups or between the groups. 94.1% of students pointed out they used such sources, as did 96.7% of legal trainees and 96.2% of practitioners. In the 18–29 age group, 94.9% used Internet search engines while searching for legal information; 96.6% in the 30–39 age group and 93.5% in the 40–49 age group. Accordingly, regardless of age or professional experience, the respondents thought that Internet search engines form a source of legal knowledge, even though there are professional and trustworthy digital databases.

The finding that common accessibility of Internet search engines has facilitated the exercise of their profession for both student and practising lawyers has translated directly into the use of Internet search engines as a source of legal knowledge. This means that the development of digital technologies and accessibility of information has changed the manner in which the legal profession has been exercised in the last 20 years.

Is Legal Information Found on the Internet Useful?

Only 11% of respondents found always helpful the legal information found on the Internet; 39.3% found it often helpful, 41.5% sometimes helpful, 7% rarely helpful, and 1.2% not helpful.

Across the whole sample, Internet-based information was most frequently assessed as only "sometimes" or "often" helpful. Differences emerge between different research groups. Students assess Internet-found information in the most positive manner (14.7% always helpful and 44.9% often helpful), while both legal trainees and practitioners have a more negative opinion (trainees – 8.3% always helpful and 36.7% often helpful; practitioners – 9.7% always helpful and 34.3% often helpful). This difference shows only from one research group to another, regardless of age criteria, suggesting the importance of professional experience: the longer the experience, the more negative the respondent's opinion about the usability of Internet information.

Is Information Found on the Internet Verified?

Overall 71% of respondents always verified information found on the Internet; 17.7% did so "often"; 9.5% "sometimes", and 1.8% "rarely". No respondent declared they never verify information found on the Internet. Of the individual research groups, students were less likely to double-check information found on the Internet: only 55.6% "always" did so; 25.2% did so "often", 15.6% "sometimes", and 3.7% "rarely".

Legal trainees most often double-checked information from the Internet. 91.7% "always" verified information, 5% "often", and 1.7% "sometimes" and "rarely". In the practitioners' group, 77.4% verified information "always", while 15.8% did so "often", and 6.8% "sometimes". No legal practitioner declared they double-checked information "rarely". The discrepancy between the students and the legal trainees may reflect trainees being at a career stage which requires responsibility paralleled with continued education and so leads to greater caution.

Tools for Verifying Information Found on the Web

The respondents verify the information found on the Internet using professional tools, that is legal databases, most often digital databases such as LEX and Legalis. As many as 91.2% indicated these tools as methods for verification of information found on the Internet. Legal trainees most often used the digital databases (98.33% declared so). A high percentage was also found in the practitioners' group (91.72%), and not significantly lower amongst students (86.6%). Professional digital databases are indispensable work tools for a lawyer. They have numerous advanced functionalities that may be used to personalise the tool according to the user's needs. The ability to use all the functionalities to a large extent facilitates work. Our experience as academic teachers is that students are able to use the tools only on a basic level. Also from our experience is that they treat it as another Internet search engine. Interesting differences emerged when it came to verification of information found on the Internet by running an additional search in the same way (for example, if they originally searched for information on the Internet, they also verify the information they found by searching on the Internet): students most often verify their knowledge in this way (25.29%), then legal trainees (18.33%), and finally practitioners (17.29%), who also most often resort to their own knowledge (40.6%), compared to 36.29% of students and 38.33% of legal trainees. In turn, students more often than others reach out for paper publications (50.37%), compared to 40% of legal trainees and 36.84% of practitioners.

The Need to Teach the Skills to Search and Verify Data Using Digital Tools and the Internet

A great majority of respondents recognised the need for developing the skills to verify information found on the Internet as early as at law school (96.3%). Only 0.9% were against this, with 2.7% having no opinion. 97.8% of students and 96.7% of trainees supported the need to develop these skills during studies. Students were also clear about the need to learn how to use professional digital databases in law school: 95.6% of respondents said so, and the answers did not differ with age. The youngest practitioners were also keen (93.5%). However, older practitioners and trainees were less positive, though even in the case of practitioners from the 40–49 age group a significant majority of 73.9% of respondents gave a positive answer.

Since we were interested in the reasons for such an answer, we asked for its justification through an optional open question directed only to those who did not see a need to teach these skills. However, only three people answered and their answers do not establish any clear rationale: all indicated that the skills were needed (one referring to it being a sign of professionalism); only one suggested that the skills should be learned by people themselves.

Does Easy Access to Legal Information on the Internet Promote ATJ?

Overall 69.5% of respondents thought easy access to the legal information on the Internet promotes ATJ; 17.7% disagree and 12.8% had no opinion. Higher levels of support came from students (74.8%); persons aged 30–39 (71.2%) and 18–29 (69.5%). A positive response was most often given by students aged 30–39 (87.1%), and then trainees aged 30–39 (77.8%). These data show that young people (raised in the Internet era) treat it as a natural tool also for providing legal assistance and they have greater trust in the Internet. It is important because young people are the future of the legal profession.

Should Online Services be Used to Provide Legal Aid?

64.94% of respondents thought there should be a digital tool allowing lawyers to provide legal aid online, the support from students being 69.6%, practitioners being 62.94%, and trainees being 60%. Interestingly, the highest percentage of positive responses came from practitioners in the 40–49 age group (78.3%). At the same time, 59.8% of respondents said they would be interested in such a professional tool, with 63% of students being interested, 60.2% of practitioners, and 51.7% of trainees. 82.6% of the persons who thought there should be such a tool declared they would like to use it. It seems that the results in the group of trainees are due to the fact that it is the most careful group. Students are often unaware of the responsibilities of their chosen profession; only the professional training shows the risks and consequences of it. For this reason, lawyers seem to be the most careful at this stage of their career. But there may be different explanations as well. For legal trainees, it is also important to learn and shape skills as widely as possible. The best way to do this is by observing a practitioner. When providing online legal aid, such learning opportunities are limited.

Conclusions and Reflections

Before the Internet era, books and written materials were the main sources of legal knowledge. Teaching was also based on such sources. Sometimes information about essential cases was obtained from newspapers, but it was mainly verified with a trusted source. Moreover, there was the profession of journalist rapporteur (Barta, Markiewicz & Matlak, 2005, pp264–265;

Sobczak, 2000, p9). On the other hand, access to legal information for the public was significantly limited. The barrier was both the need to go to the library but also the language of the books (incomprehensible to the average recipient). Whilst legal guides were written for people who were not lawyers, not everyone used them and they did not cover all areas of law (Chociszewski, 1880, pp1–240). There is also a mention in Polish legal literature that before the Internet age, lawyers and legal advisers were struggling with the scourge of illegitimate legal advisers, whose activities and lack of professionalism posed a real problem in access to justice, given the damage caused by their erroneous advice (Nowodworski, 1925, pp931–943, Kowalski, 1962, p89–90).

What Our Study Shows

The study has confirmed common access to the Internet has changed the manner in which legal knowledge is acquired and has affected the manner in which the legal profession is exercised. It has also contributed to the decreasing of barriers in accessing legal information, even though the information is not verified, which may lead to new risks and a new barrier to implementing ATJ. Legal education should not remain unresponsive to these changes, which are important enough to impact not only the form but also the content of what is taught to law students, and above all, the skills that are shaped. One should then reflect upon the skills that are indispensable for a law student and the manner in which the students should be prepared for future challenges.

The conducted study has shown students are the ones who not only attach the most importance to information found on the Internet, but they are also the ones to verify it most rarely and to use professional digital tools for this purpose most rarely. Therefore, the Internet is an undoubted source of knowledge for them, but they do not always see the risks it brings. This is the first important fact for law schools.

The research has also shown that there is interest in online tools for providing legal aid. It seems that in some cases their use is imposed by the situation in the legal services market, and in other cases by external circumstances. Meanwhile, most Polish law schools still teach in a traditional way – focusing mainly on presenting legal knowledge to the student. So the academy has not responded to the fact that the student can obtain this knowledge at any time using all sorts of digital tools. This is the second important piece of information that emerges from the research for law schools.

How to Prepare Students to Become Future-Ready

It is obvious that students will continue to use the Internet as a source of knowledge, and that the changing digital reality means that teaching how to use the digital tools we actually know will not prepare students for the future. So, how can we prepare students to be ready for the future? In our opinion, the most crucial question to be addressed by law schools is then the issue of necessary skills. The ability to verify information found on the Internet is indispensable owing both to the fact that part of the information might be outdated and above all because of the risk of falsity. As the Internet may be both a source of information and misinformation, the ability to recognise the truthfulness of news, and in particular legal information, will allow students to be well prepared to exercise their profession in the future. This will help the implementation of the guarantee of ATJ, in which lawyers play a significant part. We believe lawyering skills courses should be supplemented with elements enabling the acquisition of the skill of verifying information collected via searches from Internet search engines; coupled with the parallel knowledge of professional digital tools, this will better prepare the students to be future-ready.

Professional Digital Tools & Cooperation With Companies Owning the Databases

Undoubtedly, using professional digital tools is important for lawyers. Whilst it is not part of the curriculum, at law school, students are required to be able to use the tools, meaning that universities themselves do see the need for the students to have the skills. Accordingly, Polish universities should enable students to develop such skills, especially as after graduating, law practitioners will be required to use the tools proficiently. In the Polish law system, it is particularly important, considering the recent pace of changes in the law. Acquiring the skills that enable students to use all the functionalities offered by professional digital tools will to a large degree facilitate the exercise of their profession in the future. From our experience, it follows students know how to use databases on a basic level, but they remain ignorant of more advanced functionalities of these tools. It should be remembered the databases are constantly updated. Not only are new functionalities being added, but their complexity is increasing. Gradually, they also become educational tools. Adding such elements to the curriculum or ensuring optional classes for students does not seem to be complicated. They should be developed in collaboration with the companies owning the databases, which will make it possible to quickly respond to new developments.

Essential Skills

Taking into consideration technological development including AI becoming a part of the legal world, lawyering skills - perceived more broadly than before – will allow students to find their place in the professional world. Methods by which the skills are to be taught remain to be discussed; they should be adapted to the legal system in which students will exercise their profession in the future. Undoubtedly, the methods should be based on critical reading, on basic rules of legal system operation and the rules of Internet operation. Students should develop these skills also when working in the clinics. One should note, too, that the clinics themselves should get ready to provide legal aid on-line, which will require, however, developing safe digital tools first. The first step in this direction could be setting up a digital platform where verified legal information would be published. In this manner, clinics in Poland could further grow, at the same time dismantling barriers to accessing justice or new barriers to implementing the guarantee which might emerge as a result of using unverified information. In our judgement, this topic deserves further research.

The Covid-19 pandemic has shown that the participation of clinics in providing online legal aid cannot be overestimated. Almost all clinics in Poland have switched to online help, although no common solution has yet been developed. It is therefore a field for further work.

The pandemic also demonstrated the importance of digital skills in today's world. Learning at universities had to be online. On the one hand, it required more work from the lecturers, and on the other hand, from the students. The undoubted temptation to use Internet sources during classes, with the simultaneous lack of verification or inadequate verification of the information obtained, may affect the learning outcomes.

Universities may offer their students digital tools – but only the ones that are available at a given moment. At the same time, the digital world is continuously changing, and technological development is producing new tools. What we offer to our students today might be already outdated when they graduate. Nonetheless, if we give the students indispensable skills, they will be future-ready. And it is skills that make us different from machines, giving us the edge over them. Now it is more important than ever.

References

Barta, J, Markiewicz, R, & Matlak, A (2005). Prawo mediów. Warszawa.

Berlioz Investment Fund SA v Directeur de l'administration des contributions directes, C-682/15 ECLI:EU:C:2017:373 (Court of Justice of the European Union 2017).

Chociszewski, J (1880). Mały adwokat domowy zawierający najważniejsze wiadomości o nowéj organizacyi sądownictwa [...] (pp. 1–240). Poznań.

Colquitt, J, Conlon, D, Wesson, M, Porter, C, & Ng, K (2001). Justice at the Millenium: A meta-analytic review of 25 years of organizational justice research. *Journal of Applied Psychology*, *86*(3), 425–427.

Democratic Governance Group, Bureau for Development Policy. (2004). *Access to Justice Practice Note* (pp. 1–31). United Nations Development Programme. Retrieved from https://www.undp.org/content/dam/aplaws/publication/en/publications/democratic-governance/dg-publications-for-website/access-to-justice-practice-note/Justice_PN_En.pdf

Directorate General For Internal Policies Policy Department C: Citizens' Rights And Constitutional Affairs. (2017). *Effective Access To Justice* (pp. 1–164). Brussels: Policy Department for Citizens' Rights and Constitutional Affairs. Retrieved from https://www.europarl.europa.eu/RegData/etudes/STUD/2017/596818/IPOL_STU(2017)596818_EN.pdf

Dogruer, N, Eyyam, R, & Menevis, I (2011). The use of the internet for educational purposes. *Procedia - Social And Behavioral Sciences, 28*, 606–611. doi: 10.1016/j.sbspro.2011.11.115

Drew, M & Morriss, A (2013), Clinical legal education & access to justice: Conflicts, interests, & evolution. U Of Alabama Legal Studies Research Paper, (2322825), pp. 1–30. Retrieved from https://ssrn.com/abstract=2322825

Fundacja Centrum Badania Opinii Społecznej. (2019). *Korzystanie z internetu (The use of Internet)* (pp. 1–22). Warszawa: Fundacja Centrum Badania Opinii Społecznej. Retrieved from https://www.cbos.pl/SPISKOM.POL/2019/K_095_19.PDF

Fundacja Uniwersyteckich Poradni Prawnych. (2019). *Studenckie Poradnie Prawne Podsumowanie działalności za rok akademicki 2017/2018* (pp. 1–103). Warszawa: FUPP. Retrieved from http://www.fupp.org.pl/co-nowego/9-polski/aktualnosci/289-roczne-sprawozdanie-z-dzialalnosci-poradni-w-roku-akademickim-2017-2018

Glava, C & Glava, A (2012). Teachers' views on using the internet as a learning tool. *Procedia - Social And Behavioral Sciences, 46*, 3556–3560. doi: 10.1016/j.sbspro.2012.06.104

Gramatikov, M, Barendrecht, M, & Verdonschot, J (2008). Measuring the costs and quality of paths to justice: Contours of a methodology. *Hague Journal On The Rule Of Law, 3*(2011), 1–26. doi: 10.2139/ssrn.1269328

Kalantry, S, Brundige, E, & Gupta, P (2012). Promoting clinical legal education in India: A case study of the citizen participation clinic. *NYLS Clinical Research Institute Paper, 21*, 1–56. doi: 10.2139/ssrn.2112429

Klaming, L & Giesen, I (2008). Access to justice: The quality of the procedure. *TISCO Working Paper Series On Civil Law And Conflict Resolution Systems*, 1–40. doi: 10.2139/ssrn.1091105

Kowalski, R (1962). Korespondencja. Palestra, (8), 89–90. Retrieved from http://bazhum.muzhp.pl/media//files/Palestra/Palestra-r1962-t6-n8(56)/Palestra-r1962-t6-n8(56)-s89-90/Palestra-r1962-t6-n8(56)-s89-90.pdf

McDowell, W & M. Sheikh, U (2009). A lawyer's duty to ensure access to justice. The Advocates' Society, 1–15. Retrieved from https://www.advocates.ca/Upload/Files/PDF/Advocacy/InstituteforCivilityandProfessionalisDuty_to_Access_to_Justice.pdf

Nowodworski, L, Pokątne doradztwo. (1925). Palestra, (8-9), 931–943. Retrieved from http://dlibra.umcs.lublin.pl/Content/26801/Palestra_1925_8_9.pdf

Organisation for Economic Co-operation and Development. (2016). Leveraging the SDGs for Inclusive Growth: Delivering Access to Justice for All (pp. 1–22). Open Society Foundation. Retrieved from https://www.oecd.org/gov/delivering-access-to-justice-for-all.pdf

Prescott, J (2017). Improving access to justice in state courts with platform technology. *Vanderbilt Law Review, 70*(6), 1993–2050. Retrieved from https://ssrn.com/abstract=3080615

Rundstein, S (1904). *Studya i szkice prawne* (pp. 229–235). Lwów: Polskie Towarz. Nakladowe.

Sahin, Y, Balta, S, & Ercan, T (2010). The use of internet resources by university students during their course projects elicitation: A case study. *The Turkish Online Journal Of*

Educational Technology, *9*(2), 234–244. Retrieved from https://www.researchgate.net/publication/259439481

Shanahan, C, Selbin, J, Mark, A, & Carpenter, A (2018). Measuring law school clinics. *Tulane Law Review*, *93*(3), 547–586.

Shapiro, D, Buttner, E, & Barry, B (1994). Explanations: What factors enhance their perceived adequacy?. *Organizational Behavior And Human Decision Processes*, *58*(3), 346–368. doi: 10.1006/obhd.1994.1041

Sobczak, J (2000). *Dziennikarz sprawozdawca sądowy*. Warszawa.

Vinson, K & Moppett, S (2018). Digital Pro Bono: Leveraging technology to provide access to justice. *St. John's Law Review*, *92*(551), 551–571. Retrieved from https://ssrn.com/abstract=3347381

Chapter 11

Legal Education Meets Computer Science: An Interdisciplinary Approach to Teaching LawTech

Lucia Otoyo, Alan Russell, Kim Silver, and Andy Unger

Introduction

The Solicitors Regulation Authority have introduced an Innovation Space, or "regulatory sandpit" to encourage the innovative application of technology to the delivery of legal services in England and Wales (SRA, 2019). This is a reflection of an increasing recognition throughout the legal profession of the importance of innovation and technology. The Law Society Report, The Future of Legal Services (Law Society, 2016), reviewed the likely impact of technology and other factors on the legal services market from 2020 onwards. Its predictions include greater flexibility of work and employment contracts; an increased number of diverse business models; and the development of an hourglass-shaped employment market, with technology hollowing out the middle of the workforce, resulting in an increased use of paralegals, fewer trainee, and newly qualified positions and increased competition for senior roles. See also their more recent report, Horizon Scanning: Digital Futures (Law Society, 2020). There is therefore an urgent need for Law Schools to recognise and respond to the likely impact of these developments on the legal career choices of their current and future undergraduates.

The initial spark for the development of our law and technology option was a presentation at the Legal Education, Legal Practice & Technology Conference, organised by the Centre for Legal Education, Nottingham Law School in June 2017. One of the presentations showcased a predictive analytics tool, Case Crunch, developed by Ludwig Bull and fellow Cambridge University students. It aimed to correctly predict the outcome of European Court of Human Rights cases based on the fact summaries contained in the judgments. Case Crunch was then put to the test in a challenge with working lawyers to see who could most accurately predict the outcome of payment protection insurance claims based on the relevant law and short fact summaries. At the end of the challenge, Case Crunch had a better success rate than the lawyers by 86.6%–62.3% (see https://www.legalfutures.co.uk/latest-news/ai-crunches-lawyers-case-prediction-challenge). There is a debate as to whether this demonstrated that artificial intelligence ("AI") could outperform

DOI: 10.4324/9780429351082-11

lawyers in their own field of expertise or whether the trial was inconclusive, involving untested methodology. Critics asked how expert and diligent were the lawyer volunteers and whether post facto case summaries give subtle clues to the decision and reasoning in the case. Whatever the answer, we were alerted to the rapid pace of developments in the application of technology to law and legal services.

Digital Empowerment Through LawTech

Student Employability

Three decades of predictions by experts such as Richard Susskind (see Susskind, 1987, Susskind, 2017 and Susskind and Susskind, 2017) seemed to be turning into facts. We could see that automation was already changing lawyers' roles and that AI was likely to have an even greater impact. For example, technologies such as Kira Systems (https://kirasystems.com/), Luminance (https://www.luminance.com/), and LawGeex (https://www.lawgeex.com/) can conduct due diligence, discovery, and contract review faster, cheaper, and more accurately than lawyers can and are receiving investment (Artificial Lawyer, 2019, 2020). Loss of work to automation will mean fewer training contracts and junior lawyer positions, particularly in the large commercial city law firms. The rapid growth of lawtech start-ups is best captured by the Legal Geek Start Up Map (Legal Geek, 2019), showing over 250 start ups and 15 larger, more established "scale ups" across Europe. One global law firm reacted by setting up a tech incubator in 2017, giving start-up firms space within its London office to work on projects "to explore, develop and test legal, regulatory and deal-related solutions" (Allen & Overy, 2020). Large city firms have also started to recruit trainees to work in the lawtech area (Legal Cheek, 2018). Barclays also support a lawtech start up incubator in London's Notting Hill Gate (Barclays, 2021).

We are not anticipating the replacement of lawyers by technology, but we have joined those predicting that technology will play an increasingly important part in the delivery of legal services with significant changes to lawyers' work as a result. The implication is that students studying law today are preparing for different roles and careers than those of their predecessors. Susskind predicts the emergence of a range of new legal roles including legal knowledge engineer, legal technologist, legal hybrid, legal process analyst, legal project manager, legal data scientist, R&D worker, ODR practitioner, legal management consultant, and legal risk manager (Susskind, 2017, Table 13.1). These roles will require additional knowledge and skills compared to what is generally offered on traditional law degrees. Susskind (2017) argues that this is something that Law Schools need to address urgently.

We considered what additional skills and knowledge might be needed to empower our students to survive and thrive in a rapidly changing environment.

Given the potential for integrating technology into the delivery of legal services, it seemed obvious that students need greater experience of project management and working in cross-disciplinary teams. Familiarity with technology and how technologists work is essential to avoid misunderstandings in cross-disciplinary work. Budding legal technologists also need to understand the importance of legal design. The challenge is to bring together the existing technology and legal expertise in ways that are helpful and easy to use for clients, especially vulnerable clients. This is the domain of good legal design. Like many others, we have been inspired by the work of Margaret Hagan: see her blog (https://medium.com/@margarethagan) and the Stanford Legal Design Lab (http://www.legaltechdesign.com/).

Access to Justice

We are a community law school with a strong commitment to social justice, including our Legal Advice Clinic (LAC) (see https://www.lsbu.ac.uk/about-us/facilities/lsbu-facilities/legal-advice-clinic), opened in 2011, which offers a drop-in service where students give immediate, face to face supervised advice on social welfare law problems: principally housing, employment, welfare benefits, family, and debt. Undergraduate students volunteer at the clinic as an extra-curricular activity but may use the experience as a placement for their core "Working in the Law" module, which is partly assessed by a reflection on a period of legal work experience. We have assisted nearly 3000 local people, trained nearly 300 student legal advisors and collaborated with a large number of solicitors and advice agencies in our local legal advice network. Our students also volunteer at other advice providers across London and we have developed helpdesks for local courts, offering support to litigants in person (LiP).

We chose to concentrate on access to justice projects because of our expertise and interests but also because social welfare law has been largely ignored by the initial wave of lawtech start-ups, who have concentrated on the potentially richer pickings of commercial law applications. In addition, as a result of the Legal Aid, Sentencing and Punishment of Offenders Act 2012, it is now virtually impossible for people to obtain early social welfare law advice from a lawyer paid for out of central public funds (see eg, Legal Action Group, 2020). This is despite a wealth of research evidence demonstrating that early intervention in social welfare law problems can avoid social and economic costs down the line, whereas unresolved social welfare problems impact adversely on health and well-being (see eg, Drummond & McKeever, 2015). Early social welfare law advice is precisely what we offer LAC clients, though the enormous demand outstrips our capacity. LAC records show that the most common problems people approach us with are housing and employment, so we started there. Could we use technology to assist and empower our clients whilst at the same time improve our students' future career opportunities?

Designing and Delivering the Module

Interdisciplinary and Collaborative Approach

Although we now know that lawyers do not necessarily need to code (for the debate on this topic see, eg, Lawtomated, 2019), we did not know that when we started and so, as none of us could code, we approached a colleague in computing. She was enthusiastic about collaborating, particularly because we could provide real clients for her students' project work. We held a hackathon (a time limited design and programming challenge) to explore how to work together, putting law and computing students into teams and asking them to solve problems set by law staff, mainly practising lawyers, as well as academics, including some working in our Legal Advice Clinic.

At the conclusion of the hackathon we felt that we knew what we wanted to do: to adopt a collaborative and practical approach to teaching law and technology. We also had adapted a tool used on our Family Court Help Desk and created an automated form to help LiP prepare for a First Hearing and Dispute Resolution Appointment (Practice Direction 12B – Child Arrangements Programme, para 14.1, 2014). This tool indicates what information the judge will require at the hearing and allows the LiP to find and record the information in advance and then print it or send it to the court. It assists both the client and the court by ensuring that the LiP is prepared for the hearing.

The Law and Technology Module

Our computing students are taught and assessed over several modules based around projects and group work. This fitted in well with the law division's engagement with experiential learning and clinical legal education. We created a law and technology credit bearing module as an option for final year LLB students. It runs in parallel with a mandatory final year project management module for the computer science undergraduates. We have adopted a collaborative, cross disciplinary approach, putting law and computing students into working groups of five or six members and teaching and assessing them together. The groups are encouraged to adopt an agile project development methodology called "Scrum" (Cadle & Yeates, 2008), which enabled students to work closely with their clients, holding regular face to face meetings to review development progress and get feedback. This methodology aims to ensure flexibility in the design process to accommodate changes requested by the client throughout the project. This is particularly important as the projects are innovative and the clients themselves do not know exactly what they want until they start to see the ideas being generated by the teams and can respond.

Given the variety of projects (as noted below), the teams have to research and evaluate technologies available before choosing the most suitable tools for implementation. The choice is influenced by the project requirements and its required features, as well as the tool's ease of use and students' existing expertise with the tools.

As time and resource did not permit us to teach law students to code within this module, we initially thought to use one of the available no/low code development platforms which allow expert systems to be developed without coding. (We used Neota Logic (https://www.neotalogic.com/) and Outsystems (https://www.outsystems.com/) and have also looked at Josef (https://joseflegal.com/) and Bryter (https://bryter.io/).) However, contrary to our initial expectations, they were not popular with our students, mainly because no/low code systems have fairly steep learning curves (20 hours plus). The computing students preferred to use tools and systems they were familiar with and the law students were mostly happy to take on legal design and project management roles. Institutionally, intellectual property issues and the cost of hosting finished tools and resources are other factors mitigating against the commercial no/low code systems. Nonetheless, there are also potential advantages to no/low code solutions, primarily that law students can use them to explore the design and development of lawtech without having to learn to code or rely on others to build their designs, so we will continue to explore them.

The traditional "full code" development technology stacks (data structures) preferred by the computing students included the following key technology layers:

- **HMTL** and **CSS** required when creating websites, where HTML is used to create the basic structure of the web application and CSS to add formatting and layout.
- A **programming language,** such as **JavaScript**, **PHP,** and **Python**, which is used to program the functionality and add interactivity to the website/application.
- A **database**, such as **MongoDB**, **MariaDB**, **QSLite**, **Microsoft QSL server**, and **PostreQSL** which is required to store data for the created applications.
- A **server/web hosting**, such as **Nginx** or **AWS**, which is needed for the user to access the application services over the internet, normally through their internet browser.

In addition to these core layers of "full code" technology stacks, developers often choose additional tools to make the development faster through reusable code and other helpful tools and services:

- A **framework/Content Management System**, such as **Django**, **Drupal**, **Wordpress, Framework7,** or **React.js** which makes development faster through reusable code and enable non-technical users to add content to the site.
- **Development environments,** such as **Android studio** and **Visual studio**, which offer tools and services for developing applications.

We weave classes on law and technology, legal design, access to justice, group work, and project management, including talks by practitioners, around the lab-based group work, on a weekly basis. We want our students to encounter the uses of technology and to develop practical professional skills, rather than reading about them. There is an initial formative task, student teams are given a small legal design project, presenting user-friendly terms and conditions for a new social media app, which gives them experience in working together, as well as an understanding of legal design. Students then move on to the main project, which is the basis of their final assessment: each group is assigned a client and a brief to develop a piece of lawtech software.

Students are assessed by two pieces of coursework, an individual reflective essay on careers and skills and a presentation and a written report. The latter is group work, with which the computer scientists are familiar but which is a novelty for the law students. With student involvement, we have devised a method to address the problem of the free-rider without undermining the collective responsibility for the outcome of the project work, which we feel is an important employability lesson. Students evaluate themselves and their fellow group members on a scale of 1–5 under five headings (attendance, contribution, completion of tasks, co-operation, and listening and participation). The group work mark is then adjusted for each student depending on their personal score in relation to the average score.

The Projects

There are usually around 15 teams, each of which requires a client. Law staff (outside the core teaching team) are an invaluable resource as clients, particularly those involved in our clinical legal education activities. In addition, we invite local lawyers to volunteer as clients, giving them an opportunity to develop their own thinking on if and how to adopt lawtech into their practice. We have also worked with members of the anti-racism organisation The Monitoring Group (http://www.tmg-uk.org/). The clients do not take part in the assessment of students, although they observe the final presentations by their groups.

The clients bring their own project tasks. One team of students was asked to develop a prototype for a website/smart phone application which would explain the duties owed to homeless and poorly housed people in our local authority area (Southwark), how to apply to Southwark for social housing, and sources of face to free face independent housing advice in Southwark (in addition to our LAC). Another team worked on a website/app for tenants facing eviction on the basis of rent arrears. The brief was to help tenants self-assess for eligibility for legal aid: if they were eligible, to connect them with local specialist housing solicitors in advance of their court hearing; if they were not eligible, to help them collate all the information they would need to present to the court duty solicitor at their hearing, if there was a duty solicitor, or to represent themselves effectively, if there was no duty solicitor. A third team worked on a website/app that described basic employment rights, including wages, holidays, notice and unfair dismissal, and signposted clients to local face to face sources of employment advice. A fourth team were tasked with finding a solution to help local people to find a lawyer. A local solicitor provided the brief to create a chatbot which might be integrated with the local law society website, though in the end the students persuaded their client that a web-based system would be more effective and a working prototype was produced, intended for use by accredited lawyers specialising in domestic abuse cases. The team working for The Monitoring Group were asked to design and build a prototype app for reporting incidents of racism that could also provide out of hours advice and referrals to local lawyers and community groups for further help.

The student teams quickly grasp they have to distil large amounts of complex information into simple, accessible (but accurate) bite-sized pieces of information and, despite the difficulty, their final designs are generally useable, intuitive, and accessible. Projects can be repeated both in the same year and in the following year. Different teams may come up with different approaches and strategies, which is a valuable contribution to the access to justice aspect of the project. The limitation of the exercise is that there is only time to design a prototype, as developing a full application generally requires more time and effort than the module allows.

Future Readiness – New Skills and New Roles

Introducing any new module carries potential risks and rewards for academics and students alike. When the content, the context, the teaching methods, and the skills required are all new and the module is being delivered by two completely different disciplinary teams to final year students from both disciplines working together in teams, the stakes are even higher. The modules (separate for law and computer science) had to be approved by not one, but two, internal committees and aligning learning outcomes and assessment criteria was a delicate task. The law students were stepping away from traditional legal topics into an unfamiliar world, which, for final year students, carries some risk. That said, the initial results have encouraged us to continue and expand our collaboration and our engagement with lawtech.

Aoun (2017) argues that a new discipline of "humanics" will be required for the digital age. In addition to the "old literacies" of reading, writing, and mathematics, graduates in the future will need data literacy, technological literacy, and human literacy (humanities, communication, and design). These skills will be coupled with "a set of cognitive capacities": systems thinking; entrepreneurship; cultural agility; and critical thinking.

Our new module begins to introduce law students to new ways of working with data, perhaps selecting appropriate data to use on an information and signposting website, planning how to capture and present data for a racism monitoring app or ensuring that sensitive data are appropriately managed. For the first time in some cases, law students see under the technological bonnet. The emphasis on access to justice and legal design inculcates new ways of thinking in both law students and computer science students. Designing a user-centred product and communicating clearly, whilst understanding the political, social, economic, and legal context is human literacy of a high order. We think that legal design is an important future skill, and a useful tool for legal education. It requires students to imagine the needs of diverse legal clients and to break down legal solutions into algorithms (sets of simple rules) that can be automated by lawtech. Our module may also be the first opportunity for law students to encounter systems thinking or entrepreneurship. External and internal clients have noted how students thought creatively about the problems they presented. Although Aoun situates cultural agility within "varied global environments", it is arguable that working across disciplines can also enable students to develop the necessary flexibility. Although critical thinking skills are essential throughout legal education, particularly in the final year, a module such as this offers plenty of opportunities to use them in a real life and practical context. Finally, the computing students now know a great deal about housing and employment and other rights. They also understand how the law might be used to resolve the problems that they, as well as local citizens, may face. One unforeseen benefit of the module's inter-disciplinarity is its potential for engendering awareness and, it is hoped, social activism in the student body: not just in our law students but our computing students too.

The module is unusual, at least in legal education, in its use of expert clients, both internal and external. In the clinic or on the court helpdesk, clients are lay people who are reliant on the clinic or helpdesk team for their legal knowledge. Simulated lay clients have also been used for assessment purposes in professional skills competences in various disciplines (see eg, Barton et al, 2006). Simulated clients have no long-term contact with the students and no genuine relationship is developed. The situation is purely artificial and designed purely for the purpose of testing one or more professional skills, and clients may be assessors (see however, Paul Maharg's simulated client initiative (Maharg, 2019)). In our module, the clients put forward a genuine problem and hope for a prototype which might eventually contribute to their legal practice. In this respect, students and the clients are partners and co-producers in the process (see Healey et al, 2014). The clients could not produce the software without the students, but the client input is essential to the project as well. Just as the law students in the team have to learn fast how the tech world operates, so do the clients. For example, for lawyers it is enlightening to be present at the start of a "stand up"– a way of starting a sprint meeting where everyone stands up to report on progress (Techtarget, 2019) – for the speed and focus that is provides. Lawyers and legal academics gain an insight into this and from other project management techniques taught on the module. This exposure is a further benefit of an interdisciplinary module.

The first presentation of the module was in semester 2 of 2018–19. The 2019–20 presentation was well underway in March 2020 when UK university teaching went online because of the COVID-19 pandemic. The rest of the module was taught online. At the time of writing, the 20–21 presentations are also likely to be online.

Despite the well-documented problems of the move online, the module proved resilient under pressure. Students were interested in and involved in technology anyway so there were fewer issues of access and aptitude. Groups and relationships were already established by the time of the lockdown and the team projects were just starting in earnest. For the experts, online meetings were easier in some ways as there was no travel time and slightly more flexibility. It was also easier to view the work in progress on a shared screen in Microsoft Teams rather than huddled over a student laptop.

The more important lesson to be drawn from 2020 was that the changes to the legal system and legal practice identified earlier in this chapter are coming and their arrival has been significantly accelerated, making it all the more important to ensure that our students are ready to meet the challenges of the digital age.

Conclusion

We believe we have begun to develop an exciting, innovative, and relevant new course, one that addresses employability and justice, as well as legal learning and the development of professional skills. The collaborations between disciplines and between the law school and local lawyers have been vital in pursuing these aims. We have also begun to engage with the emerging lawtech community across the United Kingdom, with practitioners coming to the University to share their experience. We hope that individual projects will be developed further, perhaps using students as paid interns or as part of postgraduate study, and contribute to the development of a national suite of lawtech access to justice resources. We see a clear potential for technology to expand the reach of the currently very limited resources available to address unmet legal need in the community, not by replacing lawyers, but by assisting clients so that they need to spend less time with experienced practitioners to get the help they need. There is currently an attempt to provide more co-ordination and collaboration between all those interested in and experimenting with lawtech and access to justice. One such network is the Justice and Innovation Group, led by the the Access to Justice Foundation (https://atjf.org.uk/network-for-justice) and Rightsnet (https://www.rightsnet.org.uk/). Resources for Law Schools include the newly-formed International Future of Law Association (https://futureoflawassociation.org); that offers an international network to support teaching and research into the future of law. Our next steps are to seek modest funding to try and develop the best of our student projects into prototypes and minimum viable products. We are also beginning to receive enquiries to use our students as alpha (early) testers of lawtech prototypes, such as the Access Social

Care Chatbot (see www.accesscharity.org.uk) which is win–win for the developers and our students.

In conclusion, we have found rich potential for future collaborations involving law, computing science, the Legal Advice Clinic, local lawyers, lawtech start-ups, and the emerging access to justice law tech community. It is by no means the only way to teach the many varied aspects of law and technology but is it is fruitful, accessible, and easily adaptable to an experiential/clinical legal education teaching philosophy.

References

Allen & Overy (2020). Fuse. Retrieved August 24, 2020 from https://www.allenovery.com/en-gb/global/expertise/advanced_delivery/fuse

Aoun, J (2017). *Robot-proof higher education in the age of artificial intelligence*. Cambridge, Mass: MIT Press Kindle Retrieved from http://www.amazon.co.uk

Artificial Lawyer (2019) Product Review - Luminance Retrieved from https://www.artificiallawyer.com/2019/12/09/al-product-review-luminance-part-one/

Artificial Layer (2020). Law Geez Bags $20m Retrieved from https://www.artificiallawyer.com/2020/05/12/lawgeex-bags-20m-shows-vc-funding-still-flowing/

Barclay's Eagle Lab in collaboration with The Law Society (2021). Retrieved March 11th, 2021 from https://labs.uk.barclays/our-industries/lawtech/

Barton, K, Cunningham, CD, Jones, GT, & Maharg, P (2006). Valuing what clients think: Standardized clients and the assessment of communicative competence. *Clinical Law Review, 13*(1), 1–65. Retrieved July 4, 2022 from https://strathprints.strath.ac.uk/3212

Cadle, J & Yeates, D (2008), Chapter 6.3.3, *Project management for IT systems*, 5th Edition, Pearson.

Drummond, O & McKeever, G (2015). Access to justice through University Law Clinics. Ulster University Law School and the Legal Education Foundation. Retrieved August 30, 2020 from https://www.ulster.ac.uk/__data/assets/pdf_file/0003/132654/Access-to-Justice-through-Uni-Law-Clinics-November-2015.pdf

Healey, M, Flint, A, & Harrington, K (2014). *Engagement through partnership: Students as partners in learning and teaching in higher education*. York: The Higher Education Academy. Retrieved July 4, 2022 from http://www.heacademy.ac.uk/sites/default/files/resources/engagement_through_partnership.pdf

Law Society (2016). The Future of Legal Services, The Law Society of England & Wales, p. 11, Retrieved July 4, 2022 from: https://www.academia.edu/36753171/THE_FUTURE_OF_LEGAL_SERVICES_THE_LAW_SOCIETY_OF_ENGLAND_AND_WALES_EXECUTIVE_SUMMARY

Law Society of England and Wales (2020). Horizon scanning: Digital futures, Retrieved March 8th, 2021 from https://www.lawsociety.org.uk/en/topics/research/digital-futures

Lawtomated (2019). To code or not to code: should lawyers learn to code? Retrieved August 25, 2020 from https://lawtomated.com/to-code-or-not-to-code-should-lawyers-learn-to-code-3-2/

Legal Action Group (2020). Research into London advice provision finds large gaps in services, Retrieved August 28. 2020 from https://www.lag.org.uk/article/208764/research-into-london-advice-provision-finds-large-gaps-in-services

Legal Cheek (2018). Clifford chance launches lawtech training contract that leads to qualification as a solicitor, Retrieved August 28, 2020 from https://www.legalcheek.com/2018/08/clifford-chance-launches-lawtech-training-contract-that-leads-to-qualification-as-a-solicitor/

Legal Geek (2019), Legal geek StartUp map, Retrieved August 30, 2020 from https://www.legalgeek.co/startup-map/

London South Bank University (2019). Legal Advice Clinic Retrieved August 30, 2020 from https://www.lsbu.ac.uk/about-us/facilities/lsbu-facilities/legal-advice-clinic

Maharg, P (2019). Simulated Client Initiative, Retrieved August 30, 2020 from http://paulmaharg.com/tag/simulated-client-initiative/

Practice Direction 12B – Child Arrangements Programme (2014). Retrieved August 30, 2020 from https://www.justice.gov.uk/courts/procedure-rules/family/practice_directions/pd_part_12b

SRA (2019). SRA Innovate, Solicitors Regulation Authority, Retrieved August 30, 2020 from https://www.sra.org.uk/solicitors/resources/innovate/sra-innovate/

Susskind, R (1987). *Expert systems in law: A jurisprudential inquiry*. Clarendon Press.

Susskind, R (2017). *Tomorrow's lawyers: An introduction to your future*, 2nd Edition, OUP.

Susskind, R & Susskind, D (2016) *The future of the professions*, 1st Edition, OUP.

Techtarget (2019). Sprint – software development Retrieved August 30, 2020 from https://searchsoftwarequality.techtarget.com/definition/Scrum-sprint

Chapter 12

Integrating Innovation into a Law School Curriculum: The Galway Experience

Rónán Kennedy

Introduction – Why this Project?

Recognising that rapid developments in "artificial intelligence" are changing the workplace for which our students require preparation, the School of Law at NUI Galway undertook a transversal project to examine how to incorporate innovation into its teaching, particularly at undergraduate level. The background to the decision was that many of the predictions regarding the future of law and of the legal profession – the end of law (Hildebrandt, 2009), the end of lawyers (Susskind, 2009), or even the end of law schools (Campbell, 2014) – involve information and communication technology. In this context, how does a university education remain relevant, and how does (or should) it interface with preparation for the legal professions? The chapter documents a particular project which seeks to explore this question in Ireland, and highlights some reproducible learnings that can be applied in other jurisdictions and disciplines.

The legal profession in Ireland remains split into solicitors (who deal directly with the public and tend to do more transactional and advisory work) and barristers (who rarely deal directly with the public and specialise in drafting pleadings and advocacy). Legal education and training is also split: most intending lawyers take an undergraduate law degree, then study in either the Law Society of Ireland (known as Blackhall Place, its location) to become a solicitor or the Honorable Society of King's Inns (which awards the degree of Barrister-at-Law, a pre-requisite for being called to the Bar of Ireland and practicing as a barrister). Although it is possible to become a practitioner without a law degree, most people who intend to become lawyers do obtain one (and often also a master's degree before professional training, to acquire a specialisation or become a more attractive candidate for more competitive traineeships as a solicitor.)

Ireland, a common law jurisdiction, is likely to be subject to similar winds of change (Denvir, 2020) as have impacted other common law jurisdictions. Hook Tangaza's review on the education and training of legal practitioners, as required by Section 34 of the Legal Services Regulation Act 2015 (Hook Tangaza, 2018), is an early step towards extensive reform of the legal

DOI: 10.4324/9780429351082-12

profession in Ireland (Hall, Hodgson, Strevens, & Guth, 2019; Brennan, 2020). This was one of the requirements of the so-called "troika" EU/IMG/World Bank bail out of Ireland (Hosier, 2014, pp84–85). Although the report focuses on the professional component of legal training, it also notes some issues relevant to third-level education, including aspects of technology. Some consultees suggested that the topic of artificial intelligence and technology be added to the Law Society's Professional Practice Course (Hook Tangaza, 2018, pp115–116). Is this call also relevant to third-level institutions, and how should they respond to it?

This project attempts to provide a partial answer. It begins with the fundamental question: What is the purpose of a university education? This chapter suggests an answer through collaboration across disciplines (cf Denvir, 2020), a contentious issue, particularly in a quasi-vocational field such as law. It may be possible to distinguish education from training, with the former focusing more on high-level skills and understanding, and the latter dealing more with efficiently and effectively engaging in repeated behaviours or actions in order to achieve specific outcomes. As the legal academy becomes more socio-legal and less "doctrinal" (which is seen by some as too connected to practice, and not worthy of scholarly consideration (Kennedy, 2016, pp26–28)), legal education, particularly at the graduate level but also increasingly in undergraduate degrees, has begun to move away from a black letter practice- and doctrine-focused approach and more towards critique, theory, and socially informed perspectives that interrogate the suitability of legal regimes to solve particular problems (Mohr & Schweppe, 2011, pp6–7; Byrne, 2011, p62).

However, this does not necessarily match the expectations of degree entrants or their long-term needs. This may indicate a need to draw a balance between providing students with critical perspectives on the law that will serve them for years to come; and hands-on skills that will help them to get started on a career from which they will have the vantage point to look back and realise what it was that they really learnt at third level. Adding to the challenge of getting this balance right is the divergence between what students want, what they need on graduation, and what they may need in the future. An individual may begin a law degree as a first step towards a career in practice, decide that they would prefer a career in policy, and then, after some years' experience, find themselves in a workplace context which is not the one imagined either by their lecturers or by their younger selves. This complexity means that third-level education must be more than knowledge transfer or skills training, although these are also valuable and difficult elements in the process; there must also be the development of critical thinking, creativity, and resilience. This project illustrates one way in which this can be done, involving collaboration with industry but also a focus on access to justice (Brescia, McCarthy, McDonald, Potts, & Rivais, 2014; Lupica, Franklin, & Friedman, 2017), and a design which encourages the development of deeper skills, self-reflection, and critical perspectives, similar to Brescia's (2016).

There are multiple practical problems in implementing such a balance (Denvir, 2020, p4). As one of the "selling points" for an undergraduate law degree is preparation for professional training, much of the "space" in a student's programme of study is already taken up with mandatory subjects (the traditional "core" subjects, such as contract and tort) and optional subjects required for entry into one or both professions (eg, jurisprudence is required by the King's Inns). Adding new modules means that something else must go. Within individual modules also, the explosion of law and regulation plus the increasing international and comparative perspective means that there is little opportunity to add yet another topic. Individual lecturers in a chronically underfunded tertiary system (Brennan, 2019, p375) have little capacity to take on new areas of expertise or to rethink their teaching, and large changes to programme structure can take years to plan and implement, and need general support to be successful. Nonetheless, small pilot initiatives are possible.

Mapping the Journey

Curriculum reform with a focus on skills should be grounded in an understanding of the needs of the professions. The first step was therefore to learn about what was happening in practice. This involved semi-structured interviews with a dozen practitioners (six solicitors, four barristers, and two technologists), in a "snowball fashion", to better understand what changes are underway, and to get suggestions on what skills graduates should have. In addition to this focused information-gathering, the topic was also broached in other discussions with colleagues, practitioners, and judges. However, this was not a comprehensive study, did not seek to be representative, and sought to inform teaching rather than provide a deep understanding of views and perceptions in the professions.

Perhaps the most interesting finding was that suggestions focused on practical and basic skills, such as document redaction. One mentioned an awareness of technology; one mentioned a capacity for problem-solving. None mentioned skills in innovation or entrepreneurship, although interviewees included individuals who were starting their own boutique firms or had transitioned from being a solicitor to bootstrapping a software start-up.

Lawyers generally did not seem to think that innovation belonged in the curriculum. (As a counterpoint, colleagues from the School of Business and Economics were enthusiastic about the idea and quick to help.)

Practitioners using technology sometimes downplayed its importance. They felt that it was not always relevant to everything; for example, one criminal barrister was clear that document management and display technology would only be relevant to hearings that involve large numbers of documents, such as fraud cases. A civil solicitor mentioned that some individuals and firms were making their adoption of technology a key selling point but not doing a great deal of implementation in practice.

Looking to the future application of legal technology in Ireland, some pointed to technologies that have been "just around the corner" for quite some time, such as artificial intelligence or alternative/online dispute resolution. However, the main innovation was in new business models, such as subscription-based "all-you-can-eat" retainers for solicitors. One barrister interviewee put forward the view that "people won't use [technology] until they are told to. Judges need to lead"; another made similar claims. Although another solicitor interviewee hoped that Ireland could be a centre for radical change within his international firm, in general, practitioners seemed to be expecting others, such as the courts or the judiciary, to provide leadership.

It was clear from discussions with judges that their capacity to lead is not significant due to years of underfunding, although important steps have been taken, such as the Courts Service Online website, which allows users to create, review, and advance civil claims, and the COVID-19 pandemic has accelerated progress towards online filing and hearings. Nonetheless, several senior judges were enthusiastic about the potential for technology to make their working lives easier and better (and to save time and costs).

During the life of this project, some of the practitioner interviewees were elevated to the bench, perhaps enhancing the prospect for change. However, the sample is small and clearly selected for an interest in technology; these views are not universally held across the Irish bench. Nonetheless, although this project did not investigate the barriers to wider use of technology by the courts in detail, there is some evidence that this may be due to lack of public investment and the general inertia of any large institution rather than a lack of interest or leadership. In addition, as some interviewees indicated, the technology may not be uniformly transformative, and could be irrelevant to some areas of practice and very important to others. The future, as we are often reminded, is not evenly distributed; neither are its benefits.

Setting Sail

After this groundwork, the project proceeded along the following three strands.

Introducing Innovation

Beginning from the NUI Galway graduate attributes, and the Law School's perspective on these, the School examined how innovation can be made a more central feature of teaching. As there was considerable other reform underway, including the re-structuring or introduction of new undergraduate programmes, a comprehensive review was not possible in the time available. However, independent of this project and led by other colleagues (Larry Donnelly and Nicola Murphy), first year undergraduate teaching was significantly reformed. The Law School moved from teaching foundational modules, such as Irish Legal System and Legal Research and Method, in parallel to substantive courses.

Instead, the first four weeks of first year were devoted entirely to the block teaching of "Understanding the Law", an intensive combination of basic knowledge and skills, involving considerable group work, presentations, and new tools, such as LEGO Serious Play (LSP) which can be used to guide a group discussion towards a clearer shared understanding. There was mandatory training on LSP by the LaunchPad, an on-campus innovation resource. Once students had been given the foundational knowledge which they required, they had to work in a group using LSP to prepare a presentation on one aspect of the Irish legal system which they thought should be reformed. Once this introductory four weeks were completed, the remainder of the year proceeded along more usual lines, with other modules (Constitutional Law, Contract Law, and Tort Law) taught in parallel.

Back to Basics

Many students now graduate without formal training in the use of commonly used computer applications, such as word processors or spreadsheets, which often leaves a gap in the skills needed for university study and for the workplace. This was a common feature of university degrees in the 1990s, when digital technology was unfamiliar to undergraduates. (I taught and assessed such sessions for first years while I was a postgraduate student.) As the fallacy of the "digital native" has spread, and budgets have become tighter, these have been phased out. The School explored the idea of requiring that students have a relevant "digital badge" or Microsoft Imagine Academy certificate before they can submit essays or apply for clinical placements, but ultimately adopted the Procertas "Legal Technology Assessment" (LTA) tool as an essential element of the assessment of foundational modules.

This provides online video tutorials and automated tests covering basics in Microsoft Word, Excel, and PDF editing. It was attractive because integrating an online tool which can be entirely completed by the student without needing classroom instruction or lecturer effort to mark was relatively painless and kept workloads manageable. The introduction of the LTA was part of the reform of first year teaching, and also applied to Arts students in a joint honours programme. There were inevitable hiccups, from which learnings will be taken, and it is difficult to assess it after only one year, but the usual basic errors in formatting of essays were eliminated and the quality of visual presentations produced was very high. Overall, therefore, it seems to have been a useful addition to the curriculum.

Flagship Collaborations

The cornerstone of the project was a new module, *Law and Innovation*, for final year undergraduate students. It was designed to be practical, but with a pedagogical and theoretical underpinning to develop deeper learning rather than just straightforward skills training. Because students worked on "real-world" app projects, enrolment had to be limited to a dozen in the first year, and students had to apply (with a short personal statement) for admission. The learning outcomes required the student to demonstrate a capacity to:

1 Critically assess the suitability of ICT to solve particular practical issues.
2 Conduct preliminary information gathering and analysis for a particular application of ICT.
3 Work in a team in order to develop a coherent design and presentation for the users for the system.
4 Integrate legal and ICT knowledge to develop an appropriate solution.
5 Develop, plan, and complete a high-quality research essay.

Amongst the pedagogical practices employed for this purpose were small group, hands-on workshops in which students were facilitated in developing bespoke applications. After an introductory session from the module leader, colleagues from the disciplines of Management and Business Information Systems gave sessions. Most of the remaining workshops were led by staff from the LaunchPad who are highly experienced in leading groups through the application of design thinking to the development of practical solutions. (For more on these approaches to law teaching, see Hagan, 2020).

The apps had real-world application, and came from NGOs with an access to justice focus. The aims included enabling better access to environmental information or freedom of information requests; reporting illegal hedge-cutting during the nesting season; assisting in applying for Irish citizenship; and helping adoptees to obtain information on their birth parents. Assessment was through a combination of internal blog posts, learning journals (following the recommendations of Leering, 2019), an academic essay on an aspect of innovation in the legal services market, the app itself, and a written report and oral presentation on the development process. The intention was to get students to go further than learning a skill and to develop a capacity for self-reflection on change, career development, and the relationship between individuals and technology.

Taking Stock

Delivery

Delivery of the module involved stepping outside of comfort zones for everyone involved. As module co-ordinator, even with a background and considerable practical experience in systems analysis, design, and development, the broad range of skills required were outside of my expertise, particularly as I have not written very much software since the 1990s. The module therefore proceeded on somewhat of a "stone-soup" basis, bringing in individuals from a variety of disciplines to provide a curated learning experience for students.

The delivery was considerably facilitated by the kind assistance of the LaunchPad staff. Working with law students was a new experience for them, to which they took with aplomb. Colleagues from the School of Business and Economics were also happy to contribute, delivering two separate sessions on "innovation" as a concept and on converting business rules into a decision table. They rose to the challenge of condensing a longer and large presentation of four to six hours into a one or two hour session, respectively with an audience about whose knowledge they could make no assumptions.

The session on business rules was disconcerting to the law students – although some of the class were in their final year of a Commerce degree with a specialisation in law or a Corporate Law degree, and had therefore some exposure to Management Information Systems, most had little or no experience with the details of software development. The challenge which this presented to them, and the discomfort which they felt, was a common theme in their first set of monthly learning journals.

Development

The students had a relatively brief period, the 12-week semester, within which to develop a functional app. They did not know the end-user, or the context in which the app would be used. Everyone involved had many other demands on their time. Therefore, so that the process could begin as soon as possible, little time was taken up with theory at the beginning of the module. Once the groundwork had been laid, the students were able to select their groups for the four projects on offer. They also moved directly into a sequence of design thinking workshops and a session on the use of one of the two recommended tools, Josef Legal, delivered by video-conference from Australia.

This again moved them out of their comfort zone, asking them to think about individual interactions with the law from a perspective of empathy and to consider the role of emotion in the lives of the users of legal services. This is not part of the standard law school curriculum in Ireland; although they were not so alien to those who had taken business subjects (who also saw themselves as more creative and less focused on rote learning), there was still a process of re-orientation required for everyone.

Students were also keen to get to the end – to develop a solution and an app, not realising that they were not ready for this. This impatience caused them further discomfort. Information from end-users was sometimes incomplete or contradictory, and developing a clear conception of a "user persona" was challenging. Wide-ranging ambition on the part of both students and NGOs had to be tempered by the reality of the limitations of technology and time available, and the scope of the projects had to be constrained. Nonetheless, after some bumps in the road (which of course were in the projects that seemed most straightforward at the outset), each group managed to move forward. This successful outcome was not guaranteed – at least one project could easily have failed entirely – and although this could have been a valuable learning experience in a safe context, it would not have been positive for students who were putting real effort into progressing towards their goal.

Once the projects had moved through the sequence of design thinking workshops, moving from developing a user persona, mapping that user's journey, and developing a solution, the groups were given a session on business pitches. (Although this module is not an incubator, this is nonetheless a valuable skill for those who hope to develop a career in legal innovation, and a presentation is part of the final assessment.) There was also a session on the theory and practice of innovation in legal technology, which would logically have come at the beginning but had been deferred to ensure that the practical component could be wrapped up in good time.

Wrapping Up (Suddenly Online)

At this point, the context for the module changed dramatically. The university shut its doors due to the COVID-19 pandemic. Students were told to return home. Teaching moved online. Presentations were pre-recorded for upload. Fortunately, all of the substantive material had been delivered, and there were relatively few user requirements remaining to be elicited before everyone's work arrangements were disrupted by the closure of schools and child care facilities. Unfortunately, the final sessions, including presentations from practitioners with hands-on experience of developing legal technology, had to be deferred. It also created an external context in which the calls for the Irish legal services industry (and particularly the courts) to move more quickly to a digital method of operation grew much stronger. It brought into the frame a new set of digital skills.

There were ironies in this transition: although learning journals and essays were enthusiastic about working in a technologically intermediated way, students also expressed frustration at the difficulties it created for coordination. They also reflected on what they had learned over the semester: human-centred skills of collaboration, empathy, and creativity. Some groups had delved deep into the legal background to their projects, whereas others had taken a lighter approach. All learned to be patient when developing a project, iterate through alternative approaches in a resilient and reflective way to overcome roadblocks, and how legal tech might alter the dynamics of the marketplace. Crucially, they had learned how to take an innovative project from a short description through information-gathering to a finished product. A key insight was that not everyone involved will be keen on disruption – students were surprised at how unreceptive state agencies were to new tools that would make it easier for them to do their work. However, the NGOs were very pleased with the results, which met the needs that had been agreed earlier in the process. Again, the individual dimension and the unpredictability of the world outside the controlled classroom intervened: one key contact changed employer and resource constraints prevented the live deployment of the apps. This will require further attention in the future, and continued engagement should enable them to be used on a day-to-day basis.

Students also enjoyed the module: anonymous feedback highlighted how they liked the control they had over their projects, the complete contrast to their other modules, and the new problem solving techniques which they learned. Practicality was repeatedly highlighted as a benefit. However, they found the workload was quite heavy.

Looking to the Next Iteration

This project aims to prepare students for a changing environment. However, the nature and extent of that change is not clear, even at the end of the project. In addition, the project seeks to provide education, not training – the aim is not to teach students how to use particular applications or environments, but to have a good grasp of the basics of the use of technology, an awareness of innovation and change that they can turn to their benefit and to the benefit of society, and a capacity for self-reflection. The aspects of the module that were most striking within the context of a relatively traditional legal curriculum – the use of online app platforms, the design thinking workshops – were the least important from a pedagogical perspective. The intention was not to teach students how to build apps but how to adopt a perspective of "how can we do this differently in the future?", and to consider the perspective of the user of legal services, rather than prioritising the lawyer (as the nature of the market has tended to reproduce).

The focus of this project was not directly on digital empowerment. The goal was simultaneously to familiarise students with technologies which could be applied in legal practice, and to enable them to take a critical distance from it. Students were encouraged to "get their hands dirty" by specifying and building apps themselves, but also exposed to critical literature on information technology, and "law-tech", so that they develop a higher level capacity to stand back from the "shiny toys" and make informed decisions about the appropriateness and usefulness of particular technologies.

The approach taken, therefore, was to prepare students to build their own future, one in which they can make informed and (one hopes) values-driven choices about which technologies should be developed and favoured. If the target is moving, graduates should be empowered not only to hit it better but to make it easier to hit because they can move it into their own immediate vicinity. The NUI Galway experience suggests that it is possible to assemble a cross-disciplinary module which engages and stimulates students, and that design thinking can be an effective means of teaching innovation (echoing Lee & Benza, 2015). This lesson transfers across disciplines; the module design considered the student journey rather than thinking of the course content as an interchangeable collection of topics, which can be re-arranged at will.

A real-world experiential component will create challenges (often unanticipated ones), but motivated individuals can find solutions. Technology can enhance law teaching – for example, using bots helped students to think about law in a different way. However, it is best combined with a focus on the human (Jackson, 2016); design thinking requires students to think about emotions and makes them defer thinking about the solution until later in the process, when more information has been collected. Others have documented the lack of focus on the emotions of law students (eg, Jones, 2018); this project indicates that a focus on the emotions of those whom our graduates will serve would also be valuable.

What has been achieved so far is relatively limited. Without significant staffing (which is very unlikely), the pedagogical approach will always limit the number of students who can be taught in this fashion. Aspects of the module require further development in future iterations, including better engagement with the literature (which is still relatively sparse when it comes to legal technology, and very limited when it comes to the Irish legal services market), fine-tuning the integration of guest speakers from other disciplines, and collaborating with external organisations to provide more real-world projects on which undergraduate students can make meaningful progress in a relatively short time. There will be a need to engage in further fieldwork and to re-engage with practitioners to see what has changed, and what new needs or problems are emerging.

For this project to have a wider impact, the ideas it embodies will need to be fully integrated into the curriculum. One way to achieve this, and an aspect of the project which did not come to fruition in the time available, was deeper cross-campus collaborations, in which the Law School would work with the School of Business and Economics and the Launchpad to develop ideas, such as a graduate module, an industry-focused final year project, or links to campus-based start-ups. Work on this continues and will be developed in the future, particularly as more government funding for skills-based initiatives becomes available.

Acknowledgement

This project was part-funded by the National Forum for the Enhancement of Teaching and Learning in Higher Education and the Higher Education Authority of Ireland, through the Learning Enhancement Projects scheme.

References

Brennan, G (2019). Irish undergraduate legal education. *The Law Teacher*, *53*(3), 370–377.

Brennan, G (2020). Pending reform of Irish legal education. *The Law Teacher*, *54*(2), 308–319.

Brescia, RH (2016). Law and social innovation: Lawyering in the conceptual age. *Albany Law Review*, *80*, 235.

Brescia, RH, McCarthy, W, McDonald, A, Potts, K, & Rivais, C (2014). Embracing disruption: How technological change in the delivery of legal services can improve access to justice. *Albany Law Review, 78*, 553.

Byrne, R (2011). "Four thoughts on legal writing and law reform." In *Thirty years of legal scholarship: The Irish Association of Law Teachers*, edited by T Mohr & J Schweppe. Thomson Round Hall.

Campbell, RW (2014). The end of law schools: Legal education in the era of legal service businesses. *Mississippi Law Journal, 83*, 15–17.

Denvir, C (2020). Introduction. In *Modernizing legal education*. Cambridge: Cambridge University Press.

Hagan, M (2020). "Design comes to the law school." In *Modernizing legal education* edited by C. Denvir. Cambridge: Cambridge University Press.

Hall, E, Hodgson, J, Strevens, C, & Guth, J (2019). "What we did over the summer": Updates on proposed reforms to legal education and training in England and Wales and in the Republic of Ireland. *The Law Teacher, 53*(4), 536–546.

Hildebrandt, M (2009). "Technology and the end of law." In *Facing the limits of the law*, edited by E Claes, W Devroe, & B Keirsbilck, p. 443. Berlin: Springer.

Hook Tangaza. (2018). Review of Legal Practitioner Education and Training.

Hosier, M (2014). *The regulation of the legal profession in Ireland*. Quid Pro Books.

Jackson, D (2016). Human-centered legal tech: Integrating design in legal education. *The Law Teacher, 50*(1), 82–97.

Jones, E (2018). Transforming legal education through emotions. *Legal Studies, 38*(3), 450–479.

Kennedy, R (2016). "Doctrinal analysis: The real 'Law in Action'." In *Legal research methods: Principles and practicalities* edited by J. Schweppe & L. Cahillane pp. 21–38. Dublin: Clarus Press.

Lee, C & Benza, R (2015). Teaching innovation skills: Application of design thinking in a graduate marketing course. *Business Education Innovation Journal*, 7(1), 43–50.

Leering, MM (2019). Perils, pitfalls and possibilities: Introducing reflective practice effectively in legal education. *The Law Teacher, 53*(4), 431–445.

Lupica, LR, Franklin, TA, & Friedman, SM (2017). The apps for justice project: Employing design thinking to narrow the access to justice gap. *Fordham Urban Law Journal, 44*, 1363.

Mohr, T, & Schweppe, J (2011). "Irish scholarship, Irish law and the Irish Association of Law Teachers." In *Thirty years of legal scholarship: The Irish Association of Law Teachers*, edited by T. Mohr & J. Schweppe. Dublin: Thomson Round Hall.

Susskind, R (2009). *The end of lawyers?: Rethinking the nature of legal services*. Oxford: Oxford University Press.

Chapter 13

LawTech Education: A View from Oxford

Rebecca Williams and Václav Janeček

Introduction: The Transformation of Law and Legal Practice

We are on the cusp of the transformation of law and legal services through the application of Artificial Intelligence (AI). The near future will see changes to the way in which legal services are delivered and the business models underlying them (Armour and Sako, 2020), and the motivations for adopting technology to automate or augment legal practice are obvious (Armour, Parnham, and Sako, 2020). From the perspective of a private enterprise, gains in efficiency can translate into reduced prices and thus greater competitiveness. From a broader public perspective, these reduced prices can also translate into increased access to justice, particularly for small- and medium-sized businesses and individuals.

In addition, technology seems likely also to have an impact on the substance of legal practice as lawyers increasingly have to grapple with the application of their particular area of expertise to new problems arising from the use of technology. Thus, employment lawyers will have to consider the use of algorithms in hiring and monitoring staff; property lawyers will deal increasingly with digital assets; public lawyers will challenge decisions made by or with automated systems, and so on. What skills, then, will lawyers need in order to be "future ready" and how can educators empower them with the necessary skills to optimise these digital aspects of the future and their role in it?

As part of a large-scale interdisciplinary research project "Unlocking the Potential of Artificial Intelligence for English Law",[1] bringing together experts in law, business, education, computer science, and economics, we sought to answer both questions through two main forms of research. First, in order to identify the skills gaps, we conducted a series of semi-structured interviews with a range of legal professional organisations and analysed this data both in combination with data collected by our Oxford colleagues in a survey about lawtech adoption in England and Wales (Sako, Armour, and Parnham, 2020), and also in the context of wider debates and scholarship regarding 21st-century skills more widely, ie, beyond the legal profession (Janeček, Williams, and Keep, 2021). Second, in

DOI: 10.4324/9780429351082-13

order to understand the role of university law schools in the 21st century and the opportunities and challenges presented by the adoption of advanced digital technology, we combined our findings with the literature regarding legal education and with empirical data regarding trends in university law student numbers and their career destinations (Williams, Janeček, and Keep, 2021).

In this chapter, we summarise our findings from these two strands of research and show how we translate our research into practice via our Law and Computer Science masters-level course[2] and our practice-oriented Oxford LawTech Education Programme.[3]

Our Research: Skills Gaps, "Future Readiness" and the Transformation of Lawyers

Analysis of our interviews identified five interlocking areas in which respondees felt that further education and training would be necessary (Janeček, Williams, and Keep, 2021). The five skills gaps that have to be filled and that might therefore be thought of as necessary in order to achieve the "future readiness" were:

- The ability to understand the differences in mindset between lawyers and computer scientists.
- The ability to recognise data as such when it flows through one's fingers, and in particular to recognise its value and the uses to which it might be put.
- The ability to adopt a more agile and design-oriented approach when helping clients and the ability to see the relevant issues from a systems perspective.
- Greater commercial awareness.
- An understanding of the law and ethics that might apply to digital technology in the future.

The fifth of these skills is likely to be equally applicable to all lawyers in relation both to the changes to legal practice and to the challenges facing the substantive law such as employment law with regard to algorithmic management (Adams-Prassl, 2019), administrative law with regard to automated decision making (Williams, 2022; Williams and Melham, 2020), commercial law with regard to data trading (Janeček and Malgieri, 2020), and so on. But all five skills, especially if accumulated in one organisation or one individual, are particularly important in relation to the first of the impacts identified in the introduction, namely the ability to augment and automate legal practice. Whilst the importance may differ according to one's role in a firm, it would be helpful for all lawyers to have an awareness of the data to which they have access and the likely uses to which it might be put, even if they merely flag it to someone else in the firm.

Similarly, in terms of agility of thinking, a lawyer who cannot themselves think about how a particular issue might be assisted by technology but who can develop an instinct that "there must be a more efficient way of doing this" and then flag that to someone else in the firm is making an important contribution. Several of our interviewees mentioned that we might therefore see the development of "Legal Technologists" who could act as a key point of contact within a firm, helping to make greater use of data and developing technical solutions to assist, augment or automate parts of legal practice. Such people will need at the very least to be "bilingual" enough to work with computer scientists in developing a technical solution and may need to act as a translator between the technicians and those in more mainstream practice.

In relation to both the data and the agility, an understanding of the mindset of computer scientists could be particularly helpful. If an interdisciplinary team comes to work on the particular data source or problem identified, it will be necessary for the lawyers involved to understand how they need to frame their instincts in order to be well understood, and developed by those on the technical side. If a piece of technology is then produced as a result, it will be important for all those involved in the strategy of the firm to understand the benefits but also the potential costs involved in adopting it, so as to reach a balanced decision.

In terms of the fifth knowledge and skills gap—law, and ethics—Legal Technologists would not need a detailed grasp of all the substantive areas of law and their application to technology, but they would need an understanding of the particular IP rules, professional regulations and other rules likely to be applied to the particular piece of legal tech they were developing. They would need at least a basic understanding of the areas of legal practice in which such a piece of tech might be deployed and for which it might need to be developed. They might also be able to play a role in supporting an understanding of the technology giving rise to substantive issues of law in particular departments. And finally, they would be best placed to outline the advantages and disadvantages of a particular piece of tech for those in the firm making a policy decision about whether or where it should be deployed.

In summary, our research here suggests a growing need for these five areas of knowledge and skills: (1) law and computer science mindset understanding; (2) data-oriented thinking; (3) agile systems and design thinking; (4) commercial awareness; (5) digital ethics and knowledge of the law relating to AI and digital technology. Relatedly, law firms seem to be increasingly interested in hiring talent from science, technology, engineering, and mathematics (STEM) (Qian, Saunders and Ahrens, 2020) and there is thus more room for either multi-disciplinary teams or multi-disciplinary individuals, typically referred to as Legal Technologists, who would be able to bring better legal services to their clients.

Our Research: The Transformation of Legal Education?

If digital technology brings about new learning needs amongst established and aspiring lawyers, it also brings about new teaching opportunities. After all, the five skills identified above do not feature in a traditional University law school curriculum. At the same time, however, it is not clear from the outset whether it should be Universities rather than practice-led professional training programmes that will satisfy these learning needs. Thus, we have also examined what all this might mean for University law schools, both in terms of the need to empower lawyers with these skills for the digital age, and also in relation to the sense more generally that lawyers should become more T-shaped (Smathers 2014), D-shaped (Runyon and Carrel, 2019), or O-shaped (O-Shaped Lawyer Research Report 2020), possessing a variety of interpersonal and commercial skills in addition to their core of legal knowledge (Williams, Janeček, and Keep, 2021). On this front, we have reached various conclusions relevant to this chapter.

First, benefiting from the inherent multi-disciplinarity of Universities, law schools are optimally placed for the development of more interdisciplinary "law and [another subject]" courses, particularly "law and computer science", because as established places of learning in multiple disciplines, they have both the subject-domain and educational expertise relating to a range of areas. This clearly sets Universities apart from virtually all other educational providers.

Second, University law schools are also optimally placed to provide the lifelong learning that is necessary as people are now far more likely to have "lattice" shaped career structures with lateral moves as well as vertical ones and so need additional education for pivotal moves. Individual corporations or law firms cannot provide such education, not least because they are not in the business of education. More importantly, University law schools are a stable presence.

Third, in providing this lifelong education Universities are able to draw not just on market demand but on a strong, objective and independent peer-reviewed research base of both substantive contents and also in the design and shaping of the syllabus. This research-led nature of our learning provision was highly praised even by the participants in our practice-oriented Oxford LawTech Education Programme (see below).

To summarise, Universities are very well placed to serve as interdisciplinary, life-long and research-led places of learning that could meet the current demand for training and education of lawyers in the field of digital technology. The significance of these three aspects cannot be emphasised enough. In legal practice, there is often very little time to do any interdisciplinary work, let alone to do interdisciplinary research and develop digitally powered prototypes of legal services or products. Indeed, there is no such thing as a "beta-contract" in law and law firms or legal institutions rarely have their own Research & Development units. It can thus be argued that if lawyers want to stay on top of their game and be "future ready", rather than become uncritical consumers of digital legal tools, they need to educate themselves, and independent and trustworthy educational institutions which can combine educational and subject-domain expertise in both Law and Computer Science should try to satisfy this need.

From Research to Practice: Two Case Studies

Academic research is one thing, but it is another to translate such research into practice. Our goal from the beginning was to do both. We aimed to be more ambitious than simply to identify the knowledge and skills needs that will shape lawyers' "future readiness" and the role that Universities can play in this shift towards digital empowerment of legal services providers. We also felt the responsibility to lead the way in this regard by our own example.

Having identified the skills gaps to be filled for "future readiness" as the first component of our research, the second was to identify how to fill them and how to empower lawyers (and computer scientists) with the necessary skills to navigate law and legal practice in the digital age. This involved two things: designing and teaching an experimental course in Law and Computer Science in 2019, jointly with the Department of Computer Science, and setting up an online learning platform for those already in practice in 2020.

Law and Computer Science

Our experimental course for masters-level students in the Departments of Law and Computer Science[4] is interdisciplinary: it is co-convened by Prof Tom Melham from the Department of Computer Science, student numbers are capped to ensure equal numbers from each discipline, and every session is co-taught by at least one representative of each Department. The course takes place over 22 weeks from early October to March (with a six-week winter break in the middle). Each week there is a two-hour "theoretical" session which involves introductory lectures on the relevant material followed by group problem-solving exercises which require students from each discipline to engage with one another to solve the problems from both perspectives. The course proves to be heavily oversubscribed by students from both Departments and we, therefore, allow a few additional auditors to observe the expository part of these theoretical sessions.

The first block of theoretical sessions (sessions 1–3) is designed to introduce the two disciplines to each other and to encourage thinking about the similarities and differences between the two fields, between the professionals working in those fields, and how these might present both opportunities and challenges. The second block (sessions 4–7) is devoted to examining how technology can automate and augment legal practice, dispute resolution and so on and what the ethical and other challenges of doing so might be. In the third block (sessions 8–15), students are introduced to a different substantive area of law each week and asked to examine how the use of technology will raise new challenges for that area and how law and computer science might be expected to work together to solve those challenges. Session 16 brings together some of the key concepts and strands encountered throughout the course.

Alongside these theoretical sessions, students are introduced to a specific type of digital technology and asked to create a lawtech tool using this technology, working in groups of three students from law and three students from computer science. In 2019/2020, the technology was blockchain-based smart contracts; from 2020/2021 onwards, students have been able to choose between blockchain-based smart contracts and natural language processing (NLP) using one of a series of available datasets kindly provided by our industry partners.

The most important goal of these practical projects is meaningful interdisciplinary collaboration, which tests their understanding of each other's assumptions, working patterns, and so on. For law students, the challenge is to think about the legal applications for the technology and the regulatory and other legal challenges of implementing such a tool, while for computer science students the challenge is to design the tool itself. We emphasise to them that this should be seen as a process of co-creation in which both disciplines play an equal part. It regularly happens that computer scientists point out some salient legal issues and lawyers suggest better software design or systems design.

As well as their own work in groups, which spreads over 21 weeks from late October till March, the students have six formal project sessions as part of the course. The first session takes place in the second week of the whole course and introduces them to the technology (or technologies)[5] and collaboration and project management tools such as GitHub (a software development and version control platform ubiquitous in the computer science community and thus part of the interdisciplinary experience). In the second session, the students pitch their initial ideas and receive feedback. Projects have spanned a range of topics from proxy shareholder voting to an online tool identifying risky clauses in contracts.[6] In the third session, the students submit a timeline for completion and can bring any questions to a "clinic". In the fourth session, they are introduced to the concept of an investor pitch and report on their progress. In the fifth session, they do a dress rehearsal of their pitches, and in the sixth session, they do a formal presentation to academics from both Departments and external guests, who all are experts in the field of LawTech, innovation, and start-up funding.

For the first cohort (2019/2020) guests from legal practice, industry and so on were only involved during the final project presentations, while for the second iteration of the course (2020/2021) we formed a panel of industry mentors to be involved throughout the whole course.[7] These industry mentors attended the first, second, fourth, and final project sessions and were available for informal consultation by individual teams. In the second iteration of the course, we also introduced an additional workshop on design thinking in law,[8] and students also had access to a special seminar series related to the wider research project "Unlocking the Potential of Artificial Intelligence for English Law".

The course is assessed by means of two 3,000-word essays completed during the Easter vacation, one dealing with the common themes and automation of law section of the course, the second asking more detailed questions such as algorithmic discrimination, transparency of machine learning, etc, with reference to two or three legal contexts in which it arises.

The course has succeeded in addressing the skills gaps identified in our interviews. From the point of view of the first gap, addressing the differences in mindsets between lawyers and computer scientists, teaching the two disciplines together proved vital both to understand and then to try to bridge those differences, making both cohorts more "bilingual". We surveyed the students at the end of the first iteration of the course and this came out very strongly in some of their comments. As one law student said: "I was … grateful to be able to speak to, and ask computer scientists about the technicalities of certain codes, amongst other technical discussions". Another law student told us: "The worst aspect of the interdisciplinary coursework … lies in the differences in methodology, language and culture of law and computer science and this accounted for why it was, at some points, difficult for us to agree on some salient issues. Happily this is part of the training and I developed new skills in dealing with interdisciplinary issues".

The practical project was at least as important as the theoretical sections in this respect, probably more so. Thus, one law student told us that "[t]he best aspect of the interdisciplinary course work … is the practical project. This project exposed me to why and how law … and computer science should collaborate in developing emerging technologies. For instance, in the course of the project, the lawyers on the team consistently assess some of the technical solutions proposed by the computer science students and how [they] will fit into the legal framework with less friction". In addition to giving students the opportunity to work together on the practical projects and the problem questions in the theoretical sessions, it was also helpful that the first three theoretical sessions were entirely devoted to exploring these interdisciplinary challenges and thinking about how they might be resolved.

The course also responded to the need to provide lawyers with more data-oriented thinking in various ways, from considering data privacy law in one of the theoretical sessions to looking at how important it is to ensure that that data does not contain inherent discrimination or imbalances. For all our practical projects, the understanding of input and output data proved to be critical. Naturally, students undertaking the NLP-based practical project developed this skill further as they needed to organise their data meticulously before the processing began.

In order to enable students to be more agile and design-oriented in their thinking, the second block of our theoretical sessions (sessions 4–7) examines how various aspects of law and legal practice might be automated and encourages the students to think about what problems they are trying to solve and which discipline might best be able to provide the solution. Similarly, the discussion exercises in our theoretical sessions (especially sessions 8–15) require the students to think systematically about the challenges and solutions that advanced digital technologies present to the law and that law presents to these technologies. The practical projects also give them an experience of this kind of approach, as does the specific design thinking workshop.

Having to present their practical projects in a pitch-like session at the end of the course as if they were a start-up company also, we hope, develops students' commercial awareness, as does their interaction with the industry mentors. Moreover, the need to manage their own project and to use wisely their allocated time and further resource budget for the project (such as our licensed software and access to computational facilities) is a way to learn these skills too.

With regard to the fifth skills gap, the third block of theoretical sessions (sessions 8–15) examines the challenges presented by technology to various different areas of law such as employment law, property and intellectual property law, competition law, public law, criminal law, and so on. These all enable our students to develop an understanding of the law and ethics as they should be applied to digital technology. Here again, we are able to add to that core of legal knowledge which is essential to legal education regardless of the need for additional skills. In addition, the students enhance their existing knowledge so that it is applicable to the future legal challenges as well as those that have already arisen.

While our research into the skills gaps has so far focused on the perspective of lawyers, there is no doubt that the course has had a positive impact in both Departments. We hope to research the equivalent skills gaps on the part of computer scientists, but it seems at least likely that the course may go some way towards filling these too. In particular, our surveys revealed that seeing their own area of expertise through the eyes of another actually allowed each discipline to reflect on itself. Thus, as one Computer Science student put it: "it allows one to really take a step back on the code, the maths and ask ourselves higher-level questions … Interacting with lawyers permitted [us, that is computer scientists,] to confront and compare our point of view and reflect on our own knowledge and mindset, but also understand how our discipline is perceived by another. I really believe these kind of reflections are crucial for computer scientists, and traditional computer science courses could not have provided them". Similarly, one of our Law students commented that "this course allowed for a conversation about the law with students from another discipline and I honestly feel this increased my personal understanding of the law by leaps and bounds".

The Oxford LawTech Education Programme

If interdisciplinary education of the kind just described is increasingly more relevant to students as they go through their degrees, it is even more important for lawyers in practice who did not have access to this kind of opportunity during their formal legal education. To seize the opportunities of digital technology in their work and become digitally empowered and future ready, these lawyers need relatively quickly to catch up on the learning gaps created by the rise of such technology. It, therefore, seemed imperative to use the ideal position of Universities, as identified above, to reach this audience too.

Accordingly, we established the Oxford LawTech Education Programme (OLTEP). OLTEP is a joint initiative by the Oxford Law Faculty and the Oxford Department of Computer Science and its mission is simple—to train future leaders in the legal market, confident providers of tech-enhanced legal services and successful innovators who can spot, analyse, and utilise trends in digital technology.

Based on our research into the skills gaps, we took a systemic approach to satisfy these needs and finding the methods best suited to fill these gaps through a practice-oriented educational programme. We partnered with several organisations, including Slaughter and May and the Government Legal Department, to understand how these learning needs can be satisfied in very concrete terms, ie, alongside the daily duties of both public and private lawyers and their support staff and alongside all the other training they undertake. To this end, we organised a series of deep-dive interviews to tailor a pilot programme that was run at the end of 2020.[9]

Almost 700 participants from our partner organisations attended our two fully online modules during the initial phase and more are currently enrolled in our follow-on educational activities. During the pilot phase, one of our modules was focused on digital literacy and the mindset gaps between lawyers and IT specialists in a commercial law firm setting. The other module was focused on issues concerning the use of algorithms in the public sector.

After running the pilots, we evaluated this experience. As the follow-on feedback survey and interviews revealed, the participants "liked the pace and the balance between using academic sources, theoretical puzzles (well [they] found them puzzling and interestingly challenging) and practical examples". They also noted that the biggest takeaway was "thinking about how to combine the power of CSs [computer scientists] and lawyers effectively to deal with new challenges". Others praised "[t]he myth-busting and no-nonsense approach".

Overall, we have learned that the development of the Oxford LawTech Education Programme is not without its challenges, many of which will be familiar to anyone who has designed an entirely new educational programme. These challenges are also magnified by the fact that University organisational structures often do not have any existing templates for such practice-oriented activities and because law professionals who participate in this learning opportunity typically have very high demands. Despite these challenges, there seems to be a very positive attitude towards a carefully tailored educational programme in LawTech that builds on Universities' unique ability to provide interdisciplinary, lifelong, and research-led education. This is positive news for Universities.

Conclusion

Lawyers' clients and consumers of legal services increasingly rely on digital technology. Relatedly, law professionals are increasingly expected to be able to unlock the potential of such technology in the provision of their legal services. This applies both to the tech-enhanced process of lawyering and to the law as it applies to issues raised by digital technology. Our research has identified a concrete set of knowledge and skills that lawyers need to acquire if they want to fulfil this expectation: (1) mindset understanding between lawyers and computer scientists; (2) data-oriented thinking; (3) agile systems and design thinking; (4) commercial awareness; (5) digital ethics and knowledge of the law relating to AI and digital technology. Currently, these learning needs also represent a learning gap because most professional lawyers and University law students do not (yet) possess such knowledge and skills. To this end, our research has also identified concrete opportunities for Universities in closing this knowledge and skills gap. The aim of this chapter was to demonstrate that through the provision of interdisciplinary, life-long and research-led education—such as our academically-oriented "Law and Computer Science" course or the practice-oriented "Oxford LawTech Education Programme"—University law schools are very well placed to satisfy those learning needs and thus contribute to the future-readiness of the legal profession.

Acknowledgement

This work was supported by the UK Research and Innovation (UKRI) Industrial Strategy Challenge Fund: 'Next Generation Services' (ES/S010424/1) and by the 'ERDF Postdoc2MUNI' project (CZ.02.2.69/0.0/0.0/18_053/0016952).

Notes

1 For more details, see https://www.law.ox.ac.uk/unlocking-potential-artificial-intelligence-english-law [last accessed 25 Feb 2021].
2 For more details, see https://www.cs.ox.ac.uk/tom.melham/LawAndCS/# [last accessed 22 Jul 2022].
3 For more details, see https://oltep.ox.ac.uk/ [last accessed 25 Feb 2021].
4 For more details, see http://www.cs.ox.ac.uk/teaching/courses/2020-2021/LawandCS/ [last accessed 26 Feb 2021]; http://www.cs.ox.ac.uk/teaching/courses/2019-2020/LawandCS/ [last accessed 26 Feb 2021]; https://www.cs.ox.ac.uk/teaching/courses/2020-2021/LawandCS/ [last accessed 22 Jul 2022]; https://www.cs.ox.ac.uk/tom.melham/LawAndCS/# [last accessed 22 Jul 2022].
5 Oxford researchers with expertise in smart contracts (Alastair Janse van Rensburg) and NLP (Matthias Qian) gave these introductions and were ready to support the projects teams from the technical side.
6 For more details, see https://www.law.ox.ac.uk/news/2020-12-07-law-and-computer-science-students-working-together-again [last visited 26 Feb 2021]; https://www.law.

ox.ac.uk/news/2020-03-13-law-and-computer-science-final-project-presentations [last accessed 26 Feb 2021].

7 Our thanks are due to Stuart Hopper for his help with setting up the industry mentor group.

8 For more details, see https://www.law.ox.ac.uk/events/design-thinking-law [last accessed 26 Feb 2021].

9 For more details, see https://www.law.ox.ac.uk/news/2020-12-18-oxford-lawtech-education-programme-pilots-first-modules [last accessed 26 Feb 2021].

References

Adams-Prassl, J (2019). What if your boss was an algorithm? The rise of artificial intelligence at work. *Comparative Labor Law & Policy Journal, 41*(1), 123.

Armour, J & Sako, M (2020). AI-enabled business models in legal services: from traditional law forms to next-generation law companies? *Journal of Professional Organization*, 7(1), 27–46.

Armour, J, Parnham, R, & Sako, M (2020). Augmented lawyering. *European Corporate Governance Institute - Law Working Paper 558/2020.*

Janeček, V & Malgieri, G (2020). Commerce in data and the dynamically limited alienability rule. *German Law Journal, 21*(5), 924–943.

Janeček, V, Williams, R, & Keep, E (2021). Education for the provision of technologically enhanced legal services. *Computer Law & Security Review, 40*(1), 105519.

O Shaped Lawyer Working Group. (2020). Transforming the training and development of lawyers. *O Shaped Lawyer Research Report.*

Qian, M, Saunders, A, & Ahrens, M (2020). "Mapping LegalTech adoption and skill demand." In *The LegalTech Book*, edited by Chishti, S and others. Chichester: Wiley, 211–214.

Runyon, N & Carrel, A (2019) *Adapting for 21st century success: The delta lawyer competency model*, Legal Executive Institute/Thompson Reuters.

Sako, M, Armour, J, & Parnham, R (2020). LawTech adoption and training: Findings from a survey of solicitors in England and Wales. *Oxford University (online)* https://www.law.ox.ac.uk/sites/files/oxlaw/oxford_lawtech_adoption_and_training_survey_report_18_march_2.pdf

Smathers, RA (2014). The 21st century T-shaped lawyer. *ABA Law Practice Magazine, 'Big Ideas Issue'*, July/August 2014, 34–39.

Smith, A & Spencer, N (2020). "Do lawyers need to learn to code? A practitioner perspective on the 'polytechnic' future of legal education." In *Modernising legal education*, edited by Denvir, C. Cambridge: Cambridge University Press.

Susskind, R (2013). *Tomorrow's lawyers: An introduction to your future.* Oxford: Oxford University Press.

Williams, R (2022). Rethinking administrative law for algorithmic decision making. *42*(2) OJLS 468-494.

Williams, R & Melham, T (2020). Automated decision-making in the public sector. *Practical Law Public Sector* (online).

Williams, R, Janeček, V, & Keep, E (2021). What Is the role of law schools in the 21st century?. (forthcoming).

Chapter 14

A Master's Degree: Empowering Digital-Age Lawyers in Legal Technology

Cemile Cakir

The call for Legal Technology and Innovation has been heard and the demand for lawyers to be innovative and technologically accomplished recognised (Tech Nation, n.d.). The legal sector in England and Wales, confronted with allegations of being left behind (Cohen, 2018) has accelerated its adoption and integration of legal technologies in the Courts (Susskind, 2019), the Justice System (The Law Society Commission, 2019), and Legal Practice (The Law Society, 2019). Lawyers now, in addition to digital skills, require an aptitude for change to find new ways to better meet their clients' needs and an understanding of legal technology to critically evaluate, contest and seek accountability for its outcomes in the digital age.

This enterprising perspective has led to much discourse on the role of legal education and how best to prepare future lawyers for legal practice in the fourth industrial revolution, the digital age. Although the new regime for the Solicitors Qualifying Examination (SQE) presented an opportunity for the Solicitors Regulation Authority to incorporate digital and technological competence within the assessment framework, this was not realised (SRA, 2019).

Whilst the development of digital literacy is generally accepted as a core skill that needs to be developed amongst lawyers and various frameworks have been widely integrated into law schools (JISC, n.d.) (LTC4, n.d.), there is growing consensus that a more progressive curriculum is needed if the legal sector is to lead in this space. This has inspired forums and collaborations to map out what such a curriculum might present (Chaplin, n.d.).

Law Schools across the globe, such as the University of Law in the UK (ULaw), Harvard Law School in the United States, and Swinburne Law School in Australia, have pioneered new programmes dedicated to legal technology and innovation to grow and empower a new breed of lawyer, increasingly referred to as the "legal technologist". These are professionals who are "experienced and skilled individuals who can bridge the gap between law and technology" (Susskind, 2017, p136).

These courses are designed to provide students with an in-depth study of legal technology and how 'innovative technologies are changing the way the legal sector operates' (University of Law, 2020), acknowledging that "With law often

DOI: 10.4324/9780429351082-14

playing catch up …, the study of how the law interacts with science and technology is more critical now than ever before (Harvard Law School, 2020)" and thus creating STEAM (Science, Technology, Engineering, Arts and Mathematics) programmes by the integration of Arts and STEM disciplines in the study of law with "engineering, computer science, or innovation and design" (Swinburne University of Technology, n.d.).

Professionals with a multidisciplinary understanding can make valuable contributions at all stages and thus can improve the successful deployment of legal technologies from inception at the ideating and design phase to completion and integration in the delivery of legal services.

A Masters

By 2016, the developments in technology and the changes this had driven across industries had become apparent. From communication systems, entertainment, and media to business systems, operations, and finance, there were overt and significant shifts in the methods and quality of services. This led some to hypothesise the prospects for future employment (Rogerson, 2019).

The legal sector was lagging behind. Custom, precedent and established practices continued to prescribe the delivery of legal services and training. Yet firms, lawyers and technologists who were alive to the opportunities that technological innovation could bring began to explore new initiatives. As with many innovations, there were failures and lessons learnt, which inspired new and improved projects. The motion and appetite for legal technology had gained momentum, attracting large investments, the allocation of designated resources, and an increase in start-up technology companies. Stakeholders began to assemble at conferences and innovation hubs (Eagle Lab in Partnership with the Law Society: A LawTech Centre of Excellence, 2020) to share knowledge, experience, and networks.

Faculty members at ULaw were among the enthusiasts who embraced this vibrancy and promoted the significance of technology in legal practice. Further, they recognised the fundamental role that legal education providers have in developing the necessary skillset in future lawyers. The University of Law Tech Research Academy (ULTRA) was established to bring together the body of knowledge, research, and experience in law, technology and education.

ULTRA is actively engaged with legal tech panels, conferences, and thought leadership such as the Law Tech Delivery Panel, tech events with Legal Cheek and the co-authored publication The Legaltech Book (Chishti, Bhatti, Datoo, & Indjic, 2020). There is an annual Student Law Tech Fair and a Law for Good Conference held in partnership with Legal Geek, which showcases the start-ups and established providers in the Legal Tech industry. Connections have been built with law firms' legal and tech innovation teams and legal tech companies, enabling members to be actively involved in projects designing and building legal technology for education. Further, bespoke events, such as the Online Courts Hackathon, supplement a Legal Tech Speaker series and a not-for-profit coding club that was run throughout the year to inspire innovation and networks across the legal and tech industries.

To encourage students' understanding and awareness of the prevalence of legal technology, resources were created and built to be shared across all Programmes of study. However, the demand for more focused in-depth study opportunities for legal practitioners and non-lawyers ensued. A masters was identified as an opportune way to bridge the industry skills gap in England and Wales by providing a course for lawyers, technologists and new graduates to advance their foundation in law or computer science by concentrating on the specialism of legal technology.

ULaw launched its MSc in Legal Technology as part of its thought leadership undertaking with ULTRA in September 2019. The programme was designed by building on faculty research and collaborations with the legal tech industry and research institutions specialising in technology. These interactions fed into both the design and delivery of the masters to enable students to benefit from insights across the disciplines to see how tech manifests in legal practice. As a postgraduate, higher-level 7 programme of study in England, Wales and Northern Ireland (Gov.uk, n.d.), or level 9 on the Australasia rating scale (Australian Qualification Framework Council, n.d), it allowed for the depth and breadth warranted by the intersect of the complex disciplines, whilst offering flexibility in study through its fulltime, part-time, face to face, and online learning modes using ULaw's virtual learning environment.

The MSc was structured to include both compulsory and elective modules that provide students with comprehensive knowledge, understanding, and critical insight into legal technology from an evolutionary perspective geared towards responsible, innovative thinking. This ensures the students achieve core knowledge and understanding whilst having the ability to tailor their qualifications and concentrate on the areas that leverage their expertise and areas of interest either as graduate law students, qualified lawyers, or developers who wish to migrate into law within the tech industry. As future roles in legal practice and services continue to be shaped and emerge in response to market demands and innovations, a versatile MSc places students in a prime position to be both responsive to and/or instigate these transformations.

All students must complete the award-linked module AI and Blockchain, plus three further electives and a dissertation. The combination of elective subjects includes those within the MSc and the other Masters in Law that are offered (eg the LLM Corporate Governance, LLM Business Law and LLM Arbitration and Alternative Dispute Resolution). To ensure non-law students have an understanding of fundamental legal principles and concepts, a foundation module in law is provided as part of the induction and is a prerequisite to the study of the modules on the MSc Legal Technology.

The modules on the MSc employ constructivist learning and teaching methods (Ackermann, 2001) which provide students with the advantage of experiential, collaborative, and exploratory learning opportunities. The ability to share lived, practical insights and research from the legal and tech industries allows fundamental knowledge exchange and distribution, bringing current and emerging matters to the fore: this should promote thought leadership. These methods nurture confidence, skill, and resilience to prepare students for: the iterations of design involved in legal-tech innovation; the barriers and hurdles experienced in the implementation of legal tech; and the critical evaluation of its effects against legal, commercial, and ethical frameworks. This cultivates an inquisitive and reflective perspective essential to future lawyers aspiring to achieve the growth mindset required for the digital age.

Artificial Intelligence

The study of Artificial Intelligence (AI) is a central component of the compulsory module AI and Blockchain. One of the key learning outcomes is understanding the concept of disruptive technologies. Grasping the characteristics, capabilities and practical parameters of these technologies used in law is required. The array of technologies, often sweepingly referred to as AI include:

- automation and intelligent machines which are based on the codification of human processes step by step into programmes using rule-based algorithms to reach precise and unambiguous outcomes (Fry, 2019);
- machine learning, often referred to as strong AI, incorporates pattern recognition technologies that are able to learn and produce classification outputs or decisions from the machine's analysis of data to unknown instances (Hartung, Bues, & Halbleig, 2018);
- natural language processing which is the use of computer technology for the analysis, interpretation and understanding of natural language (Hartung, Bues, & Halbleig, 2018);
- optical character recognition, which involves the extraction of data from various documents and images, is often used for data processing, analysing, and electronic editing (Memon, Sami, Khan, & Uddin, 2020).

The module is taught through a range of knowledge acquisition methods involving video, comprehension, and literature review of legal practice-related and technical resources, as well as applied problem-based learning tasks involving case study analysis and exploratory learning methods as part of preparatory, workshop, and consolidation activities. For example, students will use interactive web-based resources to trial and test the different functionalities of various technologies to realise the technological progression in the use of Natural Language Processing technology in law. The ability to appreciate the functionality; prospects and limitations of the different types of technology together with an understanding of how people adjust to disruptive technologies is fundamental. Comprehension of the changes to cognitive processes by drawing on sociology, psychology, neurophysiology, and digital anthropology better prepares students for the possible ways people might adapt to new technology and the skillsets that are liable to automation.

Another learning outcome is to demonstrate the ability to use disruptive technologies to address practical issues and problems. AI technologies are increasingly integrated within legal practice as projects and collaborations strive to identify the pain points in legal transactions, processes, and the delivery of client services to find efficiency gains in costs, time, and improvements in quality. The interdisciplinary approach equips students to complete varying activities: this requires them to diagnose the legal "problem" and pair it with the appropriate technology by dissecting the lawyer's tasks into its micro components which can then be translated to an outcomes model, thus allowing various aspects of legal services to be matched with the relevant AI. For example, one such activity requires students to research the different types of technologies by contacting different providers in order to decipher the appropriate choice of technology for a specific legal practice-based problem. Students are thus being taught to strategize around legal technology and to recognise which tools could be mapped to specific legal issues, enabling them to see how technology manifests in law. Further, the requirement to independently engage and conduct self-directed research with tech providers in real-time establishes key networks within the tech industry.

Tasks designed to encourage students to research past, current, and new legal technologies, presenting opportunities for interaction with developers, provide a real and practical dimension to the student's learning and give insight into the technologies that have been successfully introduced within legal workstreams. Students learn about the practical use of AI tools which are now becoming ubiquitous in commercial practices. For example, market leaders in document analysis that focus on due diligence draw on a number of disciplines within the field of machine learning, including natural language processing and pattern recognition. Students also look at other advanced data analytics platforms used by leading firms for investigations, e-discovery, intelligence mining, and compliance. They consider applications that combine machine learning and interactive data visualisations that augment intelligence by improving speed and working through high volume and complex data to provide greater insight for informed decision making. Other case studies look at the use of machine learning and natural language processing to provide automated risk review and remediation of contracts. Students realise how the reduction of low-value manual work and risk demonstrates the user case for automating aspects of a legal transaction.

By examining the range of technologies, different approaches to creating innovative solutions become apparent. For example, technologies are not only created for individual tasks but to provide end to end solutions. Students look at online transaction management platforms that simplify and automate traditional legal processes, which allows for detailed analysis of their functionality, design challenges, and practical user benefits.

The above examples are but a few of the technological achievements that have increased the appetite to explore further technology-based solutions in legal practice. Good tech design processes revolve around its defined "users" and factor their goals, needs, and problems, reflecting on trials and testing at each iteration. Currently, the end-users in legal technologies are the lawyer and/or the clients. These may be existing or future clients. In the public sector, the technology may be available and intended for everyone. Careful consideration of the functionality, user interface, and intuitiveness are at the core of "design thinking" to generate a future age of user-centric tech solutions. It is the lawyer's insight into the legal processes and requirements that gives them the advantage to lead in the development of future innovations.

Blockchain

The study of blockchain and how it works is the second compulsory component of the award-linked module. Understanding how technologies could be utilised to build an effective, coherent, and secure legal ecosystem is another outcome of the module. Students are introduced to the blockchain by looking at its origins, the motivations behind it, and its structures. They then examine the most popular applications of blockchain, smart contracts, and cryptocurrencies.

Simply put, a blockchain is an online ledger where digital information is grouped into blocks. The first block is called the genesis block. Thereafter, each block is linked to the preceding block to form a chain which is fused by code (or a hash) in a way that means the information cannot be altered. Each blockchain is collectively powered by its users, known as "nodes", who join the chain, replicate, and update it on their devices. This enables transparency, auditability, and security by limiting the possible loss or destruction of the information. The decentralised or distributed network of nodes operates in accordance with the rules coded into the system, thus enabling anonymous or "trustless" networks using public-private key cryptography.

Blockchain was popularised by Satoshi Nakamoto who in 2008 proposed a cryptocurrency called Bitcoin (Wright, 2019) which launched in 2009, conceived to address the "double-spend problem" where the same digital token can be spent more than once due to duplicity or falsification. The controversy surrounding its lack of control, regulation, and undermining of fiat currencies, however, branded it as "crypto anarchy" (May, 1992). Blockchain as a disruptor is thought by many to have since earned its respect and place within the world of finance, with governments and banks now looking to capitalise from cryptocurrencies (Inman, 2020), (HM Revenue and Customs, 2019).

Although blockchain technology is mainly known as a form of cryptocurrency, it has a much wider use and is heralded to be the next "foundational" and "underlying" technology, like the Internet in its day (De Filippi & Wright, 2018). Many industries and governmental authorities all over the world are actively experimenting and deploying blockchain solutions (PWC, n.d.) (Lauren Tombs, 2019) (HM Land Registry, 2018) (BBC, 2014) (Australian Government Digital Transformation Agency, n.d.). Blockchain was considered to be one of the solutions for the tracking and tracing of Covid-19 (Ledger Insights, 2020b), immunity passports (Ledger Insights, 2020a) and "paperless travel" such as the Known Traveller Digital Identity (KTDI) project (KTDI, 2020) and the global supply chains during the pandemic (Mariam Obaid AlMuhairi, 2020).

Students look at which governments have introduced legal frameworks for blockchain technology and gain an overview of the types of projects appropriate for the implementation of blockchain technology. Tasks require the students to project the industries that would benefit from the adoption of blockchain as a fundamental technology and illustrate their understanding by researching global user cases in, for example, the medical, energy, intellectual property, and real estate sectors.

As part of this study, students look at tokenisation, which involves the representation of a physical or digital asset by a token (Williams, 2019) and offers an alternative way to organise and manage data and transactions. At its extreme, the theory of a potential overthrow of existing governance and systems has been explored (Atzori, 2017). Its more immediate and viable potential is integration into existing structures to secure and encode the current order. Several states have explored blockchain's merits through tokenisation including the UK Land Registry, which completed their first transaction in March 2019 (Lauren Tombs, 2019). Other states, such as Estonia, have fully adopted the blockchain technology (E-estonia, n.d.) in order to reinforce trust and security in their central records and benefit from blockchain's transparency, immutability, and auditability among other attributes (Niranjanamurthy, Nithya, & Jagannatha, 2019). Most notably, Estonia has used blockchain to run its democratic elections. Students analyse and evaluate the case studies to propose future implementation of blockchain technology.

In law, with AI having taken centre stage, blockchain has until recently been disregarded as a viable technology with a promise of reform that never arrives (De Filippi & Wright, 2018) (McKinlay, Pithouse, McGonagle, & Sanders, 2018) (The Law Society, 2020). Yet the prospects of decentralised, distributive, secure systems with the capacity to set aside existing establishments present the vision of a new order. Though conceptually challenging for a legal institution grounded in tradition and precedent, to dismiss its potential is an oversight of its distinguished features and the yield in democratising access to data. The prospects are much greater than the commonly associated cryptocurrency Bitcoin. Post the Covid19 pandemic, there has been a significant increase in use, cases and more applications across the industry. Consequently, "ledger lawyers" are bringing on board more clients where blockchain is employed as a fundamental technology and this is driving a specialism in legal practice (Lawtech Insight, 2020).

Blockchain technology also presents opportunities for firms and advances in legal practice through the partnering of blockchain and smart contracts (Consensys, n.d.) (Broadridge, 2018), particularly in finance and legal transactions (Williams, 2019). This has been propelled by the Legal Statement on Cryptoassets and Smart Contracts which provides that smart contracts are capable of having legal force as a symbiosis of natural language and code (UK Jurisdiction Taskforce, 2019). The students thus examine how lawyers are adapting their practice to integrate blockchain and smart contracts.

Whilst these prospects are exciting, as with all technologies, there are drawbacks. A comprehensive understanding of how blockchain technology works enables the student to evaluate the suitability of the technology for different tasks. For example, the lack of human control over processes run entirely by code can make the correction of errors near impossible. The elements of blockchain technology and its functionality, such as its global access and transparency, also raise concerns regarding its compliance with existing and newly emerging privacy legislation discussed below. Further, the high levels of security, though commendable, are not unhackable (Bambrough, 2020) (Chavez-Dreyfuss, 2020). As lawyers' clients increasingly use and explore blockchain technology, lawyers have to understand this technology to be able to advise properly. For example, using blockchain with personal data creates a host of different implications with respect to compliance with the EU's General Data Protection Regulation (GDPR). It is these intricate considerations weighed up against the legal risk and process that can differentiate between viable innovations that incorporate blockchain technology.

The Internet of Things

The marvel of the fourth industrial revolution is not only the capability of the individual AI and blockchain technologies or even the sum of them but their collective accomplishment via the Internet of Things (IOT). IOT is the ability of these technologies, objects, and devices to communicate with one another on networks using wireless sensors, the internet, the cloud and data stores, algorithms, and personalised computers. Moving from "man to machine" to "machine to machine" interactions, enables devices to be controlled by other machines, thus enhancing their performance. Students, therefore, build on their technical knowledge and understanding of the IOT ecosystem with social sciences to evaluate studies on the economic and social impact of IOT, with a particular focus on the legal sector. For example, students analyse research and reports such as that by the McKinsey Global Institute which estimates that IOT has a potential economic impact of up to £11.1 trillion a year by 2025 (Nakamura et al, 1997), presenting significant prospects for the digital-age lawyer.

The IOT has improved connectivity, speed, accessibility, and archiving across devices that can operate seamlessly, and more responsively to current data, which can be tracked and managed using predictive analytical tools. The process and information can be visible to all stakeholders via portals and user-friendly interfaces. These "machine to machine" interactions, or IOT eco-systems, have created many prospects across industries and governments. For example:

- Smart Cities are thought to be a significant part of the solution to the challenge of growing populations living in cities across the UK (Fairhead, 2018), by helping to manage matters such as pollution, energy, water, and waste.
- Intelligent transport systems look to improve safety, mobility and efficiency by using technology, data and communications to ease congestion, reduce crashes, minimise environmental damage, and deploy help in emergencies.
- Businesses are able to leverage the instant, real-time gathering of data to respond to consumer needs by mobilising supply chains on a just in time basis by analysing customer loyalties and predicting behaviours to identify their needs (Seppo Leminen et al, 2012).
- Smart systems automating healthcare look to track the use of space and equipment to ensure service needs are prioritised where there is most need (David Paul, 2020), to aid diagnosis and patient monitoring in real-time.

Given the involvement of the IOT within our daily lives, lawyers need to appreciate the implications of the merging of the physical, biological, and digital in order to truly be able to engage and identify with their clients' needs. Digital-age lawyers ought to be at the forefront, advising clients on their obligations when using these systems, assessing the fitness of the law surrounding IOT and monitoring its application to legal practice in this new age (DLA Piper, n.d.) (Lovells, n.d.).

Lawyers also need to look ahead. New technologies often bring new challenges that lead to further technological innovations. For example, the security of data with IOT networks is a real concern, exposing businesses, firms, and clients to various repercussions. The next generation of tech innovation is the prospect of integrating IOT with blockchain to improve network security (Atlam, Alenezi, Alassafi, & Wills, 2018). Legal technologists who can meaningfully participate in these developments would be invaluable.

Data and Technoethics

Technologies are powered by data, be it in the form of storing, sharing, organising, managing, or processing. In particular, the rise of AI goes hand-in-hand with, and only derives meaning from, the exponential rise in the amount of digital data ("big data"). Although the main driver for these technologies often lies in economic values, social and cultural considerations must also be given weight. The logistics and sensitivities around the use, capture and processing of personal data are so fundamental that these are enshrined in the European Charter of Fundamental Rights: Article 8 of the Charter gives citizens of the EU a fundamental right to protection of their personal data, a right allied but additional to the right of privacy. The protection of personal data has now been given real force and become centre stage with the coming into force of the General Data Protection Regulation (GDPR) in May 2018. This detailed and complex Regulation imposes serious obligations on businesses and organisations in the processing of data. Failure to adhere can result in criminal sanctions and significant fines. As such, a digital-age lawyer must be fully informed and able to advise on the parameters and duties relating to data protection laws.

There are, however, many arguments calling for more prominent regulation of the design, build, and use of technologies. The Cambridge Analytica scandal – where personal data was harvested from social media and processed to manipulate behaviours to interfere with the US elections and the UK Brexit referendum (Parkinson & Osborne, 2018) – demonstrated the risks. The Information Commissioner's Report on Big Data, Artificial Intelligence, Machine Learning, and Data Protection (Information Commissioner's Office, 2017) also called attention to public concerns of breaches of privacy rights, consent, surveillance, trust, and security. The Law Society Report on Algorithms in the Criminal Justice System (The Law Society Commission, 2019) raised further awareness of issues surrounding predictive analytics, racial and gender bias, and inequality through the use of AI in policing and enforcement.

It is not only the technologies' processing of personal data that presents ethical issues but the way people and society at large use and interact with the technology. The Online Harms White Paper (Home Office and Department for Digital Culture Media and Sport, Great Britain, 2019) stressed the need for responsibility and accountability for online harms caused via online platforms, which can facilitate the dissemination of disinformation and misinformation, anti-social and criminal behaviours, such as online trolling, bullying, racial and sexual harassment, and the glorification of self-harm. Indeed, some harms are the consequences of well-intentioned technological innovations designed to aid good causes (Samaritans, n.d.). This magnifies the complexity of designing ethical technologies that adequately factor the implications on communities, culture, and vulnerable groups among other considerations. The discussion also emphasises the importance of balancing freedom of expression and agency with the need for online safety and privacy.

Students, therefore, not only draw on their technical and legal knowledge but call on the ethics, humanities, and social science disciplines to frame their analysis of the AI and blockchain technology. Through their examination of science led reports and studies, evaluated against philosophies such as deontology, consequentialism, and virtue ethics, as well as the professional codes of practice and the law, they engage in a comprehensive and multifaceted analysis of AI technology. The students' findings and the nature of the ethical concerns thus impress upon them the urgency of measures to ensure technologies are designed, tested, and integrated responsibly and with accountability.

The Centre for Data Ethics and Innovation (Gov.uk, 2020) has been tasked with the exploration of these ethical concerns through collaborative exchange with the public, to offer guidance and recommendations to the government on prospective regulations for data-driven technology. There is much, however, to be settled upon, particularly as both the law and guidance continue to play catch-up to new technology. Data and technoethics are pervasive across all tech-related disciplines and ought to be a priority consideration when shaping the legal and regulatory frameworks that protect the public interest and security whilst facilitating innovation. A legal technologist would be invaluable to these advisory committees in stipulating proactive as opposed to responsive measures.

It is with this perspective that the interdisciplinary masters provide an opportunity for informed analysis, debate, and evaluation of the current issues. Working with case studies and simulations students are confronted with the fundamental questions of ethics and the balancing of conflicting interests which have been overlooked. The tension between the various ethical perspectives and human rights, meshed with the wider legal, commercial, professional conduct, and social obligations, weighs upon all stakeholders. In this way, the digital-age lawyer can be prepared to recognise and avoid the pitfalls on behalf of their firms and when advising their clients on the implementation of legal technologies and also in the design of new tech innovations whereby "ethics by design" processes are embedded within the creative process.

Empowering the Digital-Age Lawyer

Since the launch of the MSc Legal Technology, the student numbers on the course have increased considerably. Their commitment to the MSc has rewarded many not only with knowledge and understanding but the confidence to engage in their field with legal technology in the age of the digital-age lawyer. Since completing the masters many students have progressed:

- to more tech-focused roles within law firms;
- by embracing the incorporation of legal tech into their own legal practice;
- to roles in legal tech companies;
- to further specialist computer science/technology education.

A solid foundation in legal tech can empower a digital-age lawyer not only in the implementation of technology but also when embarking on the trending but elusive phenomenon that is "technological innovation". Though easily recognised, innovation is challenging to succeed in and can be equally challenging to accommodate. For every accomplished legal technology, countless start-ups and prototypes have failed and been abandoned.

Among the many factors determining the success of legal-tech innovations is the ideating and design process; and the strength and diversity of the collaboration team. It is now readily acknowledged that legal technologies are best built collaboratively among technologists and lawyers to avoid failings in integration, incompatibility, process, and professional breaches fundamental to ethical legal practice (Cohen, 2019) (Pooley, 2019) (Langenhoven, 2018). Clients, employers, investors, and the public in this era need the reassurances that a steadfast "legal technologist" could bring.

Engaging lawyers qualified in legal technology on the innovation journey of "design thinking", technology advisory boards and consultations earns them positions of leadership and influence. Training directed to focused outcomes, geared towards end solutions involves the rewiring of lawyers' thinking to accommodate the logic of technology and creative solutions alongside the rationale traditionally employed in legal reasoning. This demands a cultural shift that is more collaborative and emotion led, thus departing from the lawyers' accustomed working routines (Destefano, 2018). A Masters in Legal Technology rounds the lawyers' skillset empowering them for the digital age.

Acknowledgements

The ULaw Masters in Legal Technology was possible through the support of colleagues at ULaw, ULTRA, and ULaw's wider legal and tech partners. A special thanks to Mike Butler, Anna Elmirzayeva, Simon George, Patrick Grant, Jill Howell-Williams, and Leyanda Purchase for their hard work and dedication in its realisation.

References

Ackermann, E (2001). Piaget's constructivism, Papert's constructionism: What's the difference? *Constructivism: Uses and perspectives in education*, 1–11. 10.1.1.132.4253

AlMuhairi, MO (2020). Why COVID-19 makes a compelling case for the wider integration of blockchain. Retrieved June 14, 2020, from https://www.weforum.org/agenda/2020/05/why-covid-19-makes-a-compelling-case-for-wider-integration-of-blockchain/

Atlam, HF, Alenezi, A, Alassafi, MO, & Wills, GB (2018). Blockchain with internet of things: Benefits, challenges, and future directions. *International Journal of Intelligent Systems and Applications*, *10*(6), 40–48. 10.5815/ijisa.2018.06.05

Atzori, M (2017). Blockchain technology and decentralized governance: Is the state still necessary? *Journal of Governance and Regulation*, *6*(1), 45–62. 10.22495/jgr_v6_i1_p5

Australian Government Digital Transformation Agency. (n.d.). Simple, clear and fast public services Blockchain. Retrieved August 1, 2021, from https://www.dta.gov.au/help-and-advice/technology/blockchain

Australian Qualifications Framework. (n.d.). Retrieved July 18, 2021, from https://www.aqf.edu.au/aqf-levels

Bambrough, B (2020). Massive hack exposes Bitcoin's greatest weakness. Retrieved August 1, 2021, from https://www.forbes.com/sites/billybambrough/2020/12/23/massive-hack-exposes-bitcoins-greatest-weakness/?sh=7bcc1bbeda7d

BBC. (2014). *Ecuador gives details of new digital currency*. Retrieved from https://www.bbc.co.uk/news/world-latin-america-28992589

Broadridge. (2018). Santander and Broadridge complete a first practical use of blockchain for investor voting at an annual general meeting. Retrieved June 7, 2020, from https://www.broadridge.com/press-release/2018/santander-and-broadridge-completed-practical-use-of-blockchain

Chaplin, D (n.d.). Voices from the World Cafe. Retrieved March 5, 2020, from https://www.scl.org/articles/10740-voices-from-the-world-cafe

Chavez-Dreyfuss, G (2020). Crypto crime slows in 2020, but "DeFi" hacks rise – CipherTrace report. Retrieved August 1, 2021, from https://www.reuters.com/article/crypto-currencies-crime-int-idUSKBN27Q29W

Chishti, S, Bhatti, SA, Datoo, A, & Indjic, D (2020). *The Legaltech Book*.

Cohen, MA (2018). Law is lagging digital transformation – why it matters. Retrieved March 5, 2020, from https://www.forbes.com/sites/markcohen1/2018/12/20/law-is-lagging-digital-transformation-why-it-matters/#552179a0515c

Cohen, MA (2019). The legal industry is starting to collaborate – why now and why it matters. Retrieved August 7, 2021, from https://www.forbes.com/sites/markcohen1/2019/07/22/the-legal-industry-is-starting-to-collaborate-why-now-and-why-it-matters/?sh=1b1bdbb343d1

Consensys. (n.d.). Real-world blockchain case studies. Retrieved June 7, 2020, from https://consensys.net/blockchain-use-cases/case-studies/

De Filippi, P & Wright, A (2018). *Blockchain and the law*. Harvard University Press.

Destefano, M (2018). *Legal upheaval*. ABA Publishing.

DLA Piper. (n.d.). Internet of things. Retrieved June 7, 2020, from https://www.dlapiper.com/en/us/focus/internet-of-things/

E-estonia. (n.d.). Healthcare. Retrieved June 7, 2020, from https://e-estonia.com/solutions/healthcare/

Eagle Lab in Partnership with the Law Society A LawTech Centre of Excellence. (2020). Eagle Lab in Partnership with the Law Society will bridge the gap between emerging LawTech innovation and major law firms to help to transform the legal industry. Retrieved March 5, 2020, from https://labs.uk.barclays/lawtech

Fairhead, R (2018). Speech The UK's leadership in smart cities. Retrieved from https://www.gov.uk/government/speeches/the-uks-leadership-in-smart-cities

Fry, H (2019). *Hello world* (Black Swan). Penguin Books Ltd.

Gov.uk. (2020). Centre for data ethics and innovation. Retrieved June 8, 2020, from https://www.gov.uk/government/organisations/centre-for-data-ethics-and-innovation

Gov.uk. (2021). What qualification levels mean. Retrieved July 18, 2021, from https://www.gov.uk/what-different-qualification-levels-mean/list-of-qualification-levels

Hartung, M, Bues, M-M, & Halbleig, G (2018). *Legal Tech A Practitioner's Guide*. Verlag C.H. Beck of oHG.

Harvard Law School. (2020). Law, science and technology. Retrieved March 5, 2020, from https://hls.harvard.edu/dept/academics/programs-of-study/law-science-and-technology/

HM Revenue and Customs. (2019). Policy paper Cryptoassets: Tax for individuals. Retrieved June 10, 2020, from https://www.gov.uk/government/publications/tax-on-cryptoassets/cryptoassets-for-individuals

HM Land Registry. (2018). HM Land Registry to explore the benefits of blockchain. Retrieved August 1, 2021, from https://www.gov.uk/government/news/hm-land-registry-to-explore-the-benefits-of-blockchain

Home Office and Department for Digital Culture Media and Sport, Great Britain. (2019). *Online Harms White Paper.* Retrieved from https://assets.publishing.service.gov.uk/government/uploads/system/uploads/attachment_data/file/793360/Online_Harms_White_Paper.pdf

Information Commissioner's Office. (2017). Big Data, artificial intelligence, machine learning and data protection. *Data Protection Act and General Data Protection Regulation*, 144. Retrieved from https://ico.org.uk/media/for-organisations/documents/2013559/big-data-ai-ml-and-data-protection.pdf

Inman, P (2020, January 21). Bank of England to consider adopting cryptocurrency. *The Guardian.* Retrieved from https://www.theguardian.com/technology/2020/jan/21/bank-of-england-to-consider-adopting-cryptocurrency

JISC. (n.d.). Building digital capabilities: The six elements defined. Retrieved March 5, 2020, from http://repository.jisc.ac.uk/6611/1/JFL0066F_DIGIGAP_MOD_IND_FRAME.PDF

KTDI. (2020). Unlocking the potential of digital identity for secure and seamless travel. Retrieved July 11, 2020, from https://ktdi.org/

Langenhoven, L (2018). The symbiotic relationship between lawyer and legal tech. Retrieved August 8, 2021, from https://www.herbertsmithfreehills.com/latest-thinking/the-symbiotic-relationship-between-lawyer-and-legal-tech

Lawtech Insight. (2020). Blockchain: legal and regulatory guidance report. Retrieved August 7, 2021, from https://www.lawsociety.org.uk/en/topics/research/blockchain-legal-and-regulatory-guidance-report

Lawtech UK, L. T. P. (n.d.). Transforming the UK legal sector through technology Our vision. Retrieved June 8, 2020, from https://technation.io/lawtechuk-vision/#our-vision

Ledger Insights. (2020a). European consortium develops blockchain COVID-19 immunity passport. Retrieved July 11, 2020, from https://www.ledgerinsights.com/european-consortium-develops-blockchain-covid-19-immunity-passport/

Ledger Insights. (2020b). IoT blockchain platform Nodle launches Coalition COVID-19 contact tracing app. Retrieved June 14, 2020, from https://www.ledgerinsights.com/covid-19-contact-tracing-iot-blockchain-nodle/

Leminen, S, Rajahonka, M Westerlund, M, & Siuruainen, R (2012). "Towards IOT ecosystems and business models." In *Internet of things, smart spaces, and next generation networking*, edited by S. A. S. Balandin & Y. Koucheryavy, p. 15. Berlin, Heidelberg: Springer. 10.1007/978-3-642-32686-8_2

Lovells, H (n.d.). Internet of things. Retrieved June 7, 2020, from https://www.hoganlovells.com/en/knowledge/topic-centers/internet-of-things

LTC4. (n.d.). Legal technology core competencies certification coalition. Retrieved March 5, 2020, from https://www.ltc4.org/about-us/

May, T (1992). The crypto anarchist manifesto. Retrieved June 10, 2020, from https://www.activism.net/cypherpunk/crypto-anarchy.html

McKinlay, J, Pithouse, D, McGonagle, J, & Sanders, J (2018). Blockchain: Background, challenges and legal issues. Retrieved August 8, 2021, from https://www.dlapiper.com/en/uk/insights/publications/2017/06/blockchain-background-challenges-legal-issues/

Memon, J, Sami, M, Khan, RA, & Uddin, M (2020). Handwritten optical character recognition (OCR): A comprehensive systematic literature review (SLR). *IEEE, 8*, 142642–142668. 10.1109/ACCESS.2020.3012542

Nakamura, H, Hishinuma, T, Tomioka, Y, Ishiwata, S, Ido, T, Iwata, R, … Mizugaki, M (1997). Effects of haloperidol and cocaine pretreatments on brain distribution and kinetics of [11C]methamphetamine in methamphetamine sensitized dog: Application of PET to drug pharmacokinetic study. *Nuclear Medicine and Biology, 24*(2), 165–169. 10.1016/S0969-8051(96)00204-1

Niranjanamurthy, M, Nithya, BN, & Jagannatha, S (2019). Analysis of blockchain technology: Pros, cons and SWOT. *Cluster Computing, 22*(s6), 14743–14757. 10.1007/s10586-018-2387-5

Parkinson, HJ & Osborne, H (2018). Cambridge Analytica scandal: The biggest revelations so far. Retrieved August 19, 2019, from https://www.theguardian.com/uk-news/2018/mar/22/cambridge-analytica-scandal-the-biggest-revelations-so-far

Paul, D (2020). NHS highland to use iot to aid efficiency and enhance hospital experience. *Digit*. Retrieved from https://digit.fyi/nhs-highland-to-use-iot-to-aid-efficiency-and-enhance-hospital-experience/

Pooley, CR (2019). Lawyers' next challenge: Too much technology. *Financial Times*. Retrieved from https://www.ft.com/content/d9d475c2-d544-11e9-8d46-8def889b4137

PWC. (n.d.). PwC's global blockchain survey. Retrieved August 8, 2021, from https://www.pwc.com/gx/en/industries/technology/blockchain/blockchain-in-business.html

Rogerson, P (2019). AI revolution could cost 35,000 UK legal jobs - Law Society research. Retrieved June 8, 2020, from https://www.lawgazette.co.uk/news/ai-revolution-could-cost-35000-uk-legal-jobs-law-society-research/5102442.article

Samaritans (n.d.). Samaritan's radar. Retrieved June 24, 2020, from https://www.samaritans.org/about-samaritans/research-policy/internet-suicide/samaritans-radar/

Solicitors Regulation Authority (2019). Assessment Specification for SQE Stage 1 pilot. Retrieved from https://www.sra.org.uk/sra/policy/solicitors-qualifying-examination/pilot/sqe-assessment-specification/#:~:text=Assessment format,a period of two days

Susskind, R (2017). *Tomorrow's lawyers: An introduction to your future* (2nd ed.). Oxford University Press.

Susskind, R (2019). *Online courts*. Oxford University Press.

Swinburne University of Technology. (n.d.). Laws. Retrieved March 5, 2020, from https://www.swinburne.edu.au/study/find-a-course/law/laws/

The Law Society. (2019). *Lawtech adoption research*. Retrieved from https://www.lawsociety.org.uk/support-services/research-trends/lawtech-adoption-report/

The Law Society. (2020). *Blockchain legal and regulatory guidance*. Retrieved from https://www.lawsociety.org.uk/topics/research/blockchain-legal-and-regulatory-guidance-report

The Law Society Commission. (2019). Algorithms in the criminal justice system. *The Law Society*, 1–80. Retrieved from https://epic.org/algorithmic-transparency/crim-justice/

TS United Kingdom. (2016). Intelligent Transport Systems (ITS) and Their Benefits, 16. Retrieved from https://its-uk.org.uk/wp-content/uploads/2017/02/ITS-UK-Benefits-of-ITS.pdf

Tombs, L (2019). Could blockchain be the future of the property market? Retrieved from https://hmlandregistry.blog.gov.uk/2019/05/24/could-blockchain-be-the-future-of-the-property-market/

UK Jurisdiction Taskforce. (2019). *Legal statement on cryptoassets and smart contracts*. Retrieved from https://technation.io/about-us/lawtech-panel/

University of Law. (2020). MSC legal technology. Retrieved March 5, 2020, from https://www.law.ac.uk/study/postgraduate/law/msc-legal-technology/?utm_source=Adwords&utm_medium=ppc&utm_campaign=Nottingham&utm_ID=12198&mh_matchtype=b&mh_keyword=%2Bmsc %2Blaw %2Btechnology&mh_adgroupid=67318838870&mh_network=g&gclid=CjwKCAiA44LzBRB-Eiw

Williams, S (2019). *Blockchain: The next everything*. Scribner UK.

Wright, CS (2019). Bitcoin: A peer-to-peer electronic cash system. *SSRN Electronic Journal*, 1–9. 10.2139/ssrn.3440802

Chapter 15

Legal Education As An Anchor Towards Shaping and Regulating the Digital World: Models of Law-Tech Curriculum

Ann Thanaraj

The Fraught Identity of a Law Degree

As has been discussed in more detail in chapter 8, law schools operate in an evolving landscape. Technology that is more comprehensive and all-encompassing than anything we have ever seen is changing the world around us: every sector, profession, and industry is affected, the future of education is disrupted, disciplines, identities, professional skills, and knowledge are blurred and re-formed. In addition, there are complex drivers of change for the Higher Education sector as a whole. Further, the operation of legal education is set within a multiplicity of conflicting but coexisting narratives about the past, present, and future telos and axiology of law degrees. Regulatory changes to legal education are requiring law schools to question their role and identity in addressing the demand for different and to some extent unknown knowledge and skills (World Economic Forum, 2016, 2017, 2018, 2019), whilst legal educators are unable to confidently answer how the legal profession is changing or how the law degree can be designed to be relevant in the changing professional landscape.

In 2010, the eminent Professor Richard Susskind predicted the emergence of new hybrid roles within the legal profession, such as legal knowledge engineer, legal technologist, legal process analyst, legal project manager, legal management consultant, and legal risk manager (Susskind, 2010). He argued that the focus of preparing for a career in law or for using a law degree for a variety of careers not only lies in legal competencies, but in upskilling and becoming able to learn entirely new skills and competencies that reflect the new reality of how law is used in the legal profession and more broadly in a multidisciplinary setting. The latter covers a broad range of work within sectors providing legal services and in areas of work where legal skills and knowledge are important, such as in advising on contracts and on legal risks, which will benefit from the knowledge and skillset of a law graduate. I argue that with digital technologies transforming the role of legal professionals and the use of law degrees for a variety of different careers, there is a need to reimagine how substantive areas of legal issues are taught in law degrees,

DOI: 10.4324/9780429351082-15

alongside the wide variety of skills needed in the digitally transforming professional world where it is likely that we will have multiple careers during our lifetime.

Legal practise, if that is the career path chosen, is now more dynamic than ever, requiring different skills and capabilities, such as project management, interdisciplinary working, and a need to speak and understand the language of tech, in order to offer competent legal advice to clients. The role of a legal professional is evolving: on one hand, there is a continued need to be able to negotiate, advocate, interpret legal rules and documents, draft and write, manage risks, liabilities and duties of care; on the other hand, the role technologies, such as blockchains and smart contracts have in the daily work of a legal professional has to be understood. Chapters 9–14 discuss these topics in more detail. As such, the need to gain a critical awareness and understanding of knowledge around how emerging technologies are influencing and impacting the world around us, and the role of law in shaping and enabling this in an ethical and safe manner, is a core outcome of a law degree.

This leads to the question: What knowledge is necessary to secure this sort of thinking and solving and deciding? Within the realm of law and technology, the ability to use technology is only one component of a multi-dimensional approach to formulating what a law-tech degree would look like (Thanaraj, 2017). Digital transformation, change, and advancement brought on by the Fourth Industrial Revolution (4IR) has offered an opportunity to reimagine legal education, particularly how a law degree can provide stewardship towards the challenges imposed by the 4IR that can be both new and greater and unknown in the evolving environments in the digital age, which necessitates a new narrative. Together with the challenges and new dimensions brought by the 4IR, outlined in the introduction chapter of this book, this chapter is also influenced by and responds to the UK Government's EdTech strategy (Department for Education, 2019), accepting that the world of future work looks very different for our students. This leads to the question of how can we better equip them with the skills and knowledge to succeed in the digital age, including identifying key considerations for academics in re-designing curricula and delivering excellence within the 4IR. Similarly, the House of Lords' report on Regulating the Digital World (House of Lords Select Committee on Communications, 2018) is one example of a multitude of parliamentary enquiries challenging policymakers around how the digital world is being used and can be used to communicate and transact business with one another on a scale previously unimaginable (Her Majesty's Government, 2017).

Creating a curriculum set against these backdrops requires a significant shift in the thinking, debates and narratives around the purpose of law and of a law degree, the objectives of studying law, and how all of this can be relevant to the already changing legal profession and wider future of work. It will require different knowledge and skills from those currently being developed through the academic and vocational stages of legal study. Although a law degree is a versatile academic course affording a variety of career opportunities, it is central to admission to the legal profession (and in many jurisdictions is a pre-requisite): and it is increasingly accepted that a law degree must provide opportunities for students to acquire the tools necessary to meet the demands of new clientele, preparing them to stand out as they define new legal frontiers. A law degree can be designed to provide the necessary stewardship towards the challenges imposed by the 4IR, which are both new and greater and unknown in the evolving environments in the digital age, and require a new narrative.

A distinctive vision for legal education should address the future-readiness needed in a time of digital change and transformation in the future of work, where legal careers are likely to be pluralistic, diverse, global, and multi-dimensional, and people are likely to have multiple careers within the legal sector and beyond in their professional lifetime. It should involve preparing students for the changing and digitally transforming future of work equipped with a sense of a limitless repertoire of actions and interpretations, particularly with deep interdisciplinary digital and critical thinking of technology and its influence, capable of producing new literacies that reach beyond tech skills, demonstrating their own practical wisdom drawn from new ways of problem identification and solving to make connections and find new solutions. This requires not just work-readiness but the ability to contribute to finding solutions to challenges in our changing landscape. The scale and pace of change requires something different from law schools.

With this intended outcome in mind, legal education should:

- Be an anchor discipline within Higher Education, capable of contributing towards the societal and ethical challenges of digital transformation and the 4IR.
- Contribute to the shaping and adaptation of the legal system and its relationship with technology, with a focus on using law for good. The law's critical role in regulating technology mediates the risks, benefits, and ethics of technology, and establishes accountability and liability in the impact of technology on society. There is both a need for flexible solutions to protect the values and interests of society, including the need for certainty in the provision of legal advice and broader needs, such as the protection of human dignity. The law degree creates space for contributing in theory and debate towards tomorrow's scientific breakthroughs and how they will affect politics, business, culture, and society.
- Create a distinctive vision for legal education by redrawing of boundaries, re-negotiating knowledge structures and broadening the telos and axiology from its multidimensional characteristics, bringing insights together in new and relevant ways to creatively identify problems and solve problems using the law as an anchor, augmented with sciences, arts and design, technology, the social sciences, and the humanities. Within

> this structure, this model has the capability of disrupting the nature of legal knowledge whilst celebrating in the constructivist episteme of law. This also affords a change to the narrative that preparing for the digital change is more than operational and transferable tech skills, and that it is about creating digitally critical and creative law graduates through models of law degrees which map a journey from digital awareness to digital understanding to digital criticality and creativity towards using the episteme of the rule of law to critically analyse and shape the (digital) transformation and consequences of digital technologies.

This chapter will make a case for interdisciplinary learning within law degrees and the flexibility that a law degree offers to benefit from this approach. In a quest to digitally transform legal education, the chapter brings law and technology into an academic context, using two proposed models for law degrees.

The Need for Interdisciplinary Learning Within Law Degrees

The world faces significant challenges that cannot be addressed by any one discipline in isolation. This is a powerful starting point for reimagining an interdisciplinary law-tech discipline. The grand challenges of today invite us to adapt novel solutions (Department for Business, Energy & Industrial Strategy, 2018).

The Value of Interdisciplinary Approaches Towards Future Readiness of Students

In this chapter, I suggest that the potential of the undergraduate law programme can best be secured through an interdisciplinary programme of tech literacies in law. This will anchor and augment the skills and knowledge for the digital age with cross-boundary and interdisciplinary learning grounded within the episteme of law. It will afford students studying a law degree the cognitive flexibility and learning opportunities necessary to become equipped for the digitally transforming landscape in which a wide variety of industries and professions operate, so "future-proofing" them for the changing world. To be future ready is to be equipped with a wider philosophical and epistemic set of disciplinary values, drawn from different threads of learning, especially given the disruptive and changing landscape and the new jobs being created with hybrid skillsets. Learning through the coming together of a variety of disciplines into the parent discipline to create integrative learning augments the parent discipline and can disrupt the nature of legal knowledge whilst celebrating in the episteme of law. To harness this opportunity effectively requires a shift beyond linear thinking and discipline structures. As such, the introduction of law and technology as an academic construct will benefit from models of tech literacies relevant to subject disciplines and professional identity.

Interdisciplinary learning is essential to teach students that people from other disciplines approach problems in a different way (Coonan and Pratt-Adams, 2019). This will allow students to understand the cognitive flexibility and learning opportunities necessary to become equipped for a tech-mediated evolving future, as a method of "future-proofing" for the changing world. In this way, digital transformation of the curriculum is not only enraptured in technology but also in its wider aspects of impact. Reimagining the law degree at a time of digital transformation requires renegotiating and redrawing boundaries of legal knowledge through an interdisciplinary programme of tech literacies in law.

An interdisciplinary curriculum, grounded in the multidimensional episteme of law, not only prepares students with the digital skillset needed for a variety of new and different emerging hybrid careers (Deloitte, 2016, 2017), but also equips them with interdisciplinary knowledge which can offer them the leadership needed to shape the conversation around regulating in the digital age. This will involve using new and existing laws and the episteme of the rule of law to shape the (digital) transformation of social, economic, democratic, political, and ethical structures which are being reimagined in the 4IR landscape.

An interdisciplinary perspective grounded in the episteme of law allows for knowledge creating to bring novel thinking to grand challenges and wicked problems. This also seeks to address the limitations of a single and linear and specialist disciplinary approach that, on its own episteme and theory, is not capable of addressing these grand challenges, nor creating structures to address the plurality of educational aims. It affords a learner the cognitive flexibility along with the capability and criticality to challenge knowledge, knowing what to challenge, the reasons for doing so, and grounds actions and interpretations in a credible and reliable way. The richness of an interdisciplinary approach is capable of disrupting the nature of knowledge and its linkage with our own reflexive awareness and assumptions about what there is to know (ontology) and how they can come to know about it (epistemology). A cross-boundary approach to learning challenges and questions, reconstructs, and reimagines the frames within which components of a discipline are encountered. It will draw on the epistemic frame of a law degree and include the core competencies of the profession, such as deep legal expertise drawn from critical understanding of the law, critical thinking to evaluate how the law and legal analysis of a claim and its corresponding evidence could impact upon their client, and creatively considering the appropriate advice and best possible solution to offer. This will be complemented by an appreciation and understanding of interdisciplinary concepts to enable students to collaborate and find solutions that are broader than just the law itself: this is the crux of the value of a law degree in addressing some of the grand challenges around technology and innovation at this time. This is in addition to the necessary broader skillset, such as creativity, working in multidisciplinary teams, managing change and flexibility, visualisation techniques from design thinking methods, to name a few.

Through interdisciplinary learning embedded into the ethos of learning law, knowledge has the " … power to transform reality", offering "a sense of a limitless repertoire of actions and interpretations that professionals can bring to the presenting situations" (Freire, 1970, p52; Pinker, 2018), allowing creative solutions and knowledge transfers. This prepares students to navigate their futures, and leverage their ability to deal with uncertainty: this is a necessary skill (Universities UK, 2018), for the future of multiple careers and change, where agility, creativity, and adaptability complement the augmentation of technology in our legal expertise.

The Need for Law to have a Pivotal Role and Its Flexibility that Allows it to Take on this Mantel

As we equip learners for the opportunities of the 4IR, educators need to challenge the traditional ways of defining disciplines and deciphering future-readiness in a time of change.

Legal education is something that I have termed a "borderless and boundless field", which allows the law degree to be positioned at the forefront of curriculum innovation, modelling the change necessary in our education system and providing the necessary stewardship within higher education. Law's borderless and boundless characteristics allow legal academics to disrupt, re-create, and reimagine legal education and support our capacity and "readiness to let go—say, release ourselves from our most comfortable thoughts, unloosen our fixed assurances, be ready to live in a new way" (Standish, 2012, p163), so that we can challenge existing ways of perceiving legal knowledge. Consequently, the study of law is an art of cultivating this multidimensionality through an intellectual endeavour of finding practical and creative solutions for complex problems. Grounded in its multidimensional episteme, legal education is an ideal anchorage for innovation and interdisciplinarity because of its relatively unbounded nature, complemented by a widely interpreted telos and inquiry of study, allowing movement beyond the legal sphere to provide solutions to complex world challenges and meeting the needs of society 5.0 (World Economic Forum, 2019).

Extending this thinking towards technology within law degrees, tech literacies are multiple, and impact many disciplines, going beyond practical activities and the operational skillsets of using technology. Higher education generally has tended to rest on such operational skillsets and practical activities rather than examining the deeper criticality of technologies, probably because there is not yet a disciplinary framework or global benchmarking of technology as a recognised academic discipline of study, unlike subjects such as Science, Mathematics, or Engineering. As such, technology is viewed as a technical skill, in the form of methods, tools, and instruments used to create or produce something. Pedagogically, Barnett (2004) focused on skills but de-contextualised it from the professional context or knowledge context. Along the same vein of deciphering the challenges with tech literacies, the Dearing report (1997) set the agenda for the use of technology in education as an operational and transferable skillset, and the recent EdTech strategy (2019) focused on transferable skills through technology. Although these are paramount for the changing practices brought about by the digital transformation of industries, sectors, and professions, developing a critical and deep understanding of technologies within the realm of the operation of law and legal rules is missing from many law degrees.

Furthermore, given that tech competencies are not stipulated as a key area in a law degree or the vocational elements of study, tech competencies remain open to interpretation. They appear to be understood to include technology to the degree to which an individual understands technology to be (Prensky, 2001), with a fundamental misunderstanding of tech competency as either mechanical mastery, bounded to practical activities and using technology, or working towards an IT profession.

Given the role of law in regulating technology, knowledge is made meaningful and relevant when it reflects the needs and realities of our practice in the world (Bhaskar, 1989; Klein, 2015) as opposed to focusing on the needs of a profession or towards meeting a competency standard. There is value in legal education as a tool to inform public policy through research-informed decision-making for real-world problems. As such, learning that is re-orienting along thematic rather than disciplinary lines encourages a move beyond fixed ways of knowing and working. Moving beyond linear disciplines affords more agility and creates empowered and responsive learners in a time of uncertainty and transformation. This broader perspective is also necessary to address concepts of justice and the rule of law in the digital age, providing the knowledge of the law and legal skills to use the law degree across a wide variety of existing and new hybrid careers. It can contribute academically, professionally, practically and personally to making students future-ready and contribute towards broader regulatory, ethical and design policies around the complexities and uncertainties affecting the digital landscape.

The capability to address this unknown, uncertain and disruptive concept of "futuring", contributes to the meaning of future-readiness, a fuzzy multi-field study of possible realities, as a framework for understanding the axiology of education. The breadth of legal knowledge augmented by theories and practice from other disciplines affords continual learning, adapting and applying relevant, creative and meaningful theories, practice, research, and methodologies drawn from a wider epistemic framework.

Digital Transforming Law Degrees

In a quest to digitally transform legal education, particularly in today's rapidly changing legal landscape, becoming a digital lawyer is vital to success within the legal profession.

This "Digital lawyering" (Thanaraj, 2017, 2018) requires a body of theory that begins to formulate the sorts of learning required for law students and future professionals to thrive in a digital age. It is a relatively new body of literature containing theoretical frameworks created through one's own professional and personal development and reflection to thrive in the radical transformation of the legal profession and the justice system.

The implications of this for the law degree leads us to the opportunity to reimagine our curriculum to afford learning fit for a 4IR landscape: as such, it is an opportunity to celebrate. Through the law's character of proof, accountability, and liability, it is instrumental in addressing a variety of grand challenges around digital transformation, making a wider contribution towards controlling risks, promoting benefits, and addressing ethical implications in this new landscape. These create a synergy between the impact of tech and its regulatory environment, using the episteme of the rule of law to critically analyse and shape the (digital) transformation and consequences of digital technologies on professional, social, cultural, economic, democratic, political, and ethical structures which are being reimagined for the 4IR. Within this context, interdisciplinarity around law-tech will allow technology to have meaning within academia, as a subject of academic study, creating inquiries that define new knowledge, helping students to see things differently when they look at the same phenomena, going beyond the boundaries of technology as a functional tool or skillset. A key factor in the success of being a digital professional is the need to continually learn and evolve our mindset, skills, and knowledge as digital solutions develop in fast-paced environments (Digital Lawyering, 2021).

To bring law and technology into an academic context, to realise the vision of the proposed purpose of a law degree as an anchor discipline contributing towards digital transformation and the 4IR, in this chapter, I propose six grand challenges.

Grand Challenge 1:	Designs and operations of autonomous and predictive technologies and the critical understanding of how AI systems explain how they reach their decisions, and identifying algorithmic bias
Grand Challenge 2:	How technology can be harvested for the administration of the rule of law, justice, ethics and democracy
Grand Challenge 3:	Interrogating the practical challenges in data analysis, understanding and using the data revolution through a deep understanding of methods in science, humanities, and ethics
Grand Challenge 4:	Philosophical, anthropological and human-technology relations in cybercrimes, professionalism and legal identity and values
Grand Challenge 5:	Leading digital transformation through sustainability and entrepreneurship in a digital economy
Grand Challenge 6:	Governance and public policy on connections and interoperability through technologies in the digital ecosystem

These six grand challenges will require the legal system to address its relationship with technology; but they cannot be addressed by one discipline alone. A reimagined law degree can contribute to responding to the challenges and prepare students for the digital transformation of society by giving them the means to understand and face the challenges that the digital world presents, drawing on the law's interpretive flexibility and the epistemically constructive nature of law. These six grand challenges are depicted through two models of designing a law degree to prepare students for the challenges of the digital transformation of society, drawing on the law's interpretive flexibility and the epistemically constructive nature of law.

Both models position Law as an anchor discipline in Higher Education in preparing solutions for future challenges; and show how a law degree can provide stewardship towards the challenges imposed by the 4IR, which are both greater and unknown in the evolving digital age environments. They move away from focusing on work-readiness and legal practice alone to a wider contribution towards the much needed regulatory, legal and ethical debates and challenges arising from the blurring identities, disciplines, professions, and structures of what we know, and the operations and impact of exponential digital transformation.

- Model 1: Using the episteme of law through thematic lines of enquiry as an integrative interdisciplinary methodology for law
- Model 2: Interdisciplinary modules alongside law modules

Model 1 – Thematic Lines of Enquiry

Model 1 is an interdisciplinary model of legal education, involving a more critically grounded law-tech education which moves the focus away from educating for legal practice alone to emphasising law's role in driving forward the regulatory and ethical landscape through the synergies among science, technology, and law. The curriculum, grounded in the episteme of the law, involves an integrated learning of the interdisciplinary knowledge, research methods, and skills required to enable critically digital and creative future-ready law graduates. The grand challenges of the 4IR are prevalently addressed throughout the degree.

The six thematic threads of the grand challenges are interwoven across the law curriculum, with the coming together of law (L), science (S), technical understanding (T), ethics (E), philosophy (P), humanities (H), design (D), and entrepreneurship (Ex) into the parent programme, the law degree. This affords revolutionary insights and positions a law degree to contribute towards tomorrow's technological breakthroughs (Table 15.1).

Model 2 – Interdisciplinary Modules Alongside Law Modules

Model 2 is created alongside the Foundations of Legal Knowledge modules, using seven core tech-law interdisciplinary modules and two core law-tech

Table 15.1 Using Model 1 to meet the proposed purpose of a law degree as an anchor discipline contributing towards digital transformation and the 4IR

Law degree purpose 1: Contributing to the shaping and adaptation of the legal system and its relationship with technology

Selected module example: Constitutional Law and Democracy through Technologies

This module addresses grand challenge 2.
It consists of interdisciplinary threads from: T, E, P, H, L

Building upon the core focus of a constitutional law curriculum, such as the role, responsibility, and powers of government, parliament, and the judiciary, the module will examine technologies' role and effects in evolving democracy and the democratic process. With more people being able to access the internet globally than ever before and with powerful communication tools including social media available and being used more at an exponential rate, the way we live, how and with whom we communicate, interact and pursue everyday activities are evolving, changing and transforming notions of identity, interaction, interpersonal skills, and boundaries of responsibilities with global impact. Other technologies, such as smart cameras and phones produce on-the-scene reporting of events that can be put up for international analysis, leaving the need to reconcile the notion of trial by media against the rule of law and the burden of proof.

Students will determine how democracy can be supported rather than undermined in a digital world. Through a theoretical underpinning of the "wisdom of the crowd" towards the doctrine of the rule of law, transparency in political campaigns, privacy and anonymity, misinformation, and the effects of digital technologies on public discourse, students will undertake a critical evaluation of how technology can facilitate democracy and the development of effective digital literacy for the public.

In light of public discourse, one of the foci in this module will involve examining social media use and the need for regulations. Students will draw on a breadth of technical, philosophical, legal, and humanities perspectives to explore arguments for and against regulation, control over content on networks and the possibilities of reducing online harms, users' mental health, online bullying, privacy and data protection issues, so that scrutiny, accountability, and responsibility can be created whilst balancing freedom of speech and freedom of expression. Philosophical theories around knowledge, truth and reality will be used as a framework for students to determine how best fact-checking and reality-checking should be implemented.

By delving deep into the technical mechanisms of different forms of technologies – such as the increasing use of encrypted messaging and private groups – and their impact on the democratic process, students will be able to contribute towards addressing the extent to which different types of media platforms can shape public debate, including how trust is developed in the democratic process and institutions. Using examples from the media, students will seek to address how digital technology has impacted the way that democracy works across the globe and the effect this has had and how the design of algorithms used by social media platforms have shaped democratic debate.

Selected module example: Property Law and Digital Estates

This module addresses grand challenge 3.
It consists of interdisciplinary threads from: T, D, L

Threaded through the conventional topics covered in Land law and Equity and Trusts, Property law in a Digital Age will cover the potential of Blockchain technology in radically

(Continued)

Table 15.1 (Continued)

changing the property landscape, particularly in the conveyancing process, and in the nature and acquisition of asset ownership. Drawing upon the affordances and limitations of a step-by-step system map approach (using flow charts) to problem finding and solving, law students will create a design roadmap of how the technology could operate in a conveyancing transaction, ascertaining the roles and responsibility of the different stakeholders in the transaction.

Students will need to assess the current state of laws on the operationalisation of property law, ownership and execution in a digital age, including estates, equitable interests, and the three certainties of object, subject matter, and intention. Alongside this, students will need to critically assess the legal status of crypto-assets, the factors relevant in determining whether the law governs the proprietary aspects of dealings in crypto-assets and in what circumstances is a distributed ledger capable of amounting to a register for the purposes of evidencing, constituting and transferring title to assets. In a similar vein, the doctrine of "ownership" of assets will be analysed, particularly what constitutes assets in the digital sphere and how cryptocurrencies can be used to create factional ownership of assets online. Whilst property law and land registration rules are yet to address these matters, amid blockchain technology being piloted by HM Land Registry in England and Wales (Her Majesty's Land Registry, 2018) and in law firms, students' research into these questions can be useful resources for the wider profession and legislature in understanding how blockchain technology can be harnesses safely and efficiently in property matters. Similarly, a review of fiduciary duties, the doctrine of the three certainties, creation of wills and establishment of trusts in digital estates will be critically analysed to ascertain the extent to which current precedents and laws are effective.

Law degree purpose 2: Creating a distinctive vision for legal education by redrawing of boundaries, re-negotiating knowledge structures

Selected module example: Legal Skills and Computational Design Thinking

This module addresses grand challenge 1.
It consists of interdisciplinary threads from: T, P, D, L

Laws have the appearance of complexity, shrouded in mystic and intellectual language and may come across as inaccessible to those without knowledge in law. As students begin learning about the sources of law, finding the law, legal research, interpretation, analysis, creating arguments, and legal writing, the module also offers an excellent space for students to be introduced to creating more accessible opportunities to make the law relatable and understandable. As a key component of modern legal skills, using the format of how flow diagrams typically operate, students will grasp the basics of computational design thinking as a problem-solving paradigm aimed at constructing and evaluating solutions to problems which a computer can carry out effectively, in an interdisciplinary setting. Students will gain experience of developing flow diagrams for a variety of legal rules, legislation, precedents, and case studies which range from simple to complex problem-finding and -solving scenarios.

Given that the episteme of law is its interpretive flexibility and constructive application to individual matters that allow the law to come to life, as opposed to the law being a fixed set of non-negotiable rules, students will critically begin to reconcile how logical reasoning, algorithmic thinking, and the episteme of law can work together. Students will create roadmaps and decision-making trees through problem-finding and

(Continued)

Table 15.1 (Continued)

-solving methods, using a variety of graphic designs and data visualisation software. Building onto the initial work on flow diagrams and conceptual charts for problem-finding and -solving, using an open-source coding platform to examine how machines undertake thinking processes, students will gain insight into a typical design, development, and execution of a technical solution to a legal problem, developing a deep and critical understanding of core concepts of computational thinking around logic, rule-based instructions vs constructivist approaches to learning, and the rich tapestry of facts, circumstances and evidence, mediated by social ontology that makes law come alive.

Alongside this, students will be able to evaluate how machine thinking and human thinking can be reconciled and the gaps which remain from our intellectual, cognitive, and epistemic processes which influence solutions to complex social issues using concepts of justification and rationality from a philosophical perspective. Using their coding experience in this module, students will identify the sorts of data and instructions fed into their designs, the relevance and validity of such data and instructions, the effectiveness of the creation to capture the episteme of laws.

Selected module example: Corporate Social Responsibility and Professional responsibility in Digital Transformation

This module addresses grand challenge 5.
It consists of interdisciplinary threads from: E, L, Ex

As the global business environment becomes ever more complex and volatile, there is a need for more entrepreneurial, innovative, and creative thinking in order to be able to change and adapt and shape and deliver digital transformational change. Students begin to develop deep understanding of how digital transformation is impacting and is capable of impacting further on legal services, understanding how the digital era is transforming the way legal services are delivered, analysing the disruption of the legal services market and studying new delivery channels/models, analysing the digitalisation of the delivery of legal services. With a focus on the environment, an understanding of the global business landscape equips students with a deep understanding to respond to complex, cross-industry, regulatory challenges in the global marketplace. The digital transformation setting will introduce students to critical thinking around the doctrine of professional responsibility when algorithms are enabled to make predictions and decisions. Students will critically assess what it means for professionals to work responsibly with big data sets and algorithms. This leads to a critical examination of rule of law standards, such as transparency, predictability, accountability, and oversight of a professional in relation to algorithmic decision-making systems. Through the concept of sustainability in a digital era, students will develop a distinctive set of knowledge and tools to help the systems and processes in organisations to evolve in the context of digital transformation, helping organisations to shift and renew cultural mindsets and capabilities to reach sustained strategic and mission-led values. This will include developing future-ready leadership skills of research and development, agility, process-driven, unbundling, and methods of undertaking due diligence on alternative legal services that can deliver new types of ancillary services. The module also examines a range of strategies and tactics for alternative dispute resolutions, and does so in the context of developing students' professional ethics and conduct skills.

experiential modules. The Future of Law research hub space aims to empower interdisciplinary connectivity and creativity to undertake a substantial piece of written or practical research project around technology and the law. As an integrated degree it meets the requirements of a Qualifying Law Degree in England and Wales (and can be adapted for other jurisdictions). The core law-tech interdisciplinary modules complement the core legal knowledge modules and enable digital and creative future-ready law graduates, and law-tech experiential modules offer an integrated learning of interdisciplinary knowledge, research methods, and skills required to complement the Foundations of Legal Knowledge modules and enable a critically digital and creative future-ready law graduates.

The six thematic threads of the grand challenges are interwoven across the law curriculum, with the coming together of law (L), science (S), technical understanding (T), ethics (E), philosophy (P), humanities (H), design (D), and entrepreneurship (Ex) into the parent programme, the law degree. This affords revolutionary insights and positions a law degree to contribute towards tomorrow's technological breakthroughs. (Table 15.2)

The Outcomes of a Reimagined Law Degree are Ambitious

A future-ready law graduate is one who is equipped with the capability to become the pathfinder, navigator, and trailblazer of the inquiry process. Interdisciplinary learning within the parent programme affords this opportunity. It positions the law degree as a contributor towards solutions for the challenges and emphasises the opportunities and innovations. As such, it reimagines the law degree with a distinctive vision, highlighting the relationship of knowledge across academic disciplines and everyday life.

An overarching question in the redesign of a law degree is to determine what digital literacies means to you and your law school. Related to this is that the 4IR will impact upon intellectually intensive jobs and the many facets of what lawyers are being trained to do at present. Therefore, how can legal education future-proof its students? What challenges will we face in order to create a law curriculum which addresses the needs of the 4IR? For law schools seeking to reimagine and remodel their law degrees, perhaps adapting the models above, here are some broader questions to help shape the conversation around future readiness and the purpose of a law degree:

- When introducing an interdisciplinary dimension into the parent degree, you may wish to consider the extent to which an interdisciplinary dimension to the study of law prepares student to thrive in a highly technologically-mediated legal practice? What sorts of knowledge and skillsets do law students require for the professions that benefit from the study of law? What are other interdisciplinary dimensions that have not

Table 15.2 Using Model 2 to meet the proposed purpose of a law degree as an anchor discipline contributing towards digital transformation and the 4IR

Law degree purpose 1: Contributing to the shaping and adaptation of the legal system and its relationship with technology

Selected module example: Digital ethics and cybersecurity in the Internet of Things

This module addresses grand challenge 3 and elements of grand challenge 4.
It consists of interdisciplinary threads from: H, P, D, L
Chapters 1, 3, 5, 9, 11, 13 also provide examples of innovation in this area

The rapid advancement of technologies is changing the types of crimes to be investigated and the ways in which evidence is collected and disclosed and also the ways of working in the criminal justice service. Given that online crimes lack physical and geographical borders, this is a challenge to the rule of law, jurisdictional limitations on the application of the law and the complex ethical and legal considerations arising as law enforcement is becoming a more digital-network profession, in a complex regulatory environment: this is at present quite poorly understood. The prevention of cybercrimes is also a key focus of this module: therefore students will begin to formulate strategies for the prevention of cybercrime, through making our current legislation more accessible in guidance for the public. Working with students from cybersecurity, digital forensics and policing/investigations, law students will develop detailed knowledge around the challenges which Internet of Things devices pose to existing digital forensic tools and methods. Students will begin to understand how data can present evaluation challenges for forensic scientists, and can contain vulnerabilities that pose privacy risks including how hacking to undermine a device.

Students will undertake simulated investigations using forensic techniques to gain awareness of the practice of extracting data and other forms of evidence designed to provide students with a rich understanding of the various sources of evidence and/or intelligence in a digital forensic investigation, whilst developing a deep and critical examination of existing criminal laws to tackle the challenges of the IoT, assessing whether it is possible to police activity online whist striking the fine and fair balance between protecting society and respecting legitimate privacy rights. Drawing on scientific research, and technology-based studies, public debate, computer ethics, and engineering science, students from across the disciplines will develop guidance for the creation of admissible evidence from IoT investigations along with a set of considerations that investigators must take into account when investigating the IoT, including the challenges posed by devices crossing the boundaries of jurisdictions.

Selected module example: Digital Transformation of industries and professions (Patents and Healthcare technologies)

This module addresses elements of grand challenge 4.
It consists of interdisciplinary threads from: T, H, E, P, L

As digital health technologies develop at an increasing pace, this module raises understanding around the governance of digital health. An example is, drawing on philosophical theories of what constitutes valid and accurate knowledge, students will undertake detailed research in the form of case studies to debate the extent to which AI image analysis produces accurate knowledge as opposed to mere true belief in making a reliable diagnosis. Alongside, students will evaluate the guidelines available on how AI is

(Continued)

Table 15.2 (Continued)

being designed to make such prognosis and diagnosis and the extent to which the design engineering can be improved. With an evolving ecosystem of connected health technologies, such as wearables, health care apps, digital health solutions, telehealth, AI, virtual reality, and others that support targeted, personalised health and well-being services, students will gain an understanding of how this valuable data is being leveraged. Issues around consent, privacy and data use will be critically assessed resulting in recommendations of how big data can be utilised ethically for the wider good whilst protecting the needs and security of individuals. Students will evaluate, through technical understanding of AI computational and design thinking, when is an invention patentable; what types of invention are excluded from patentability and whether through machine learning technologies machines themselves can invent new solutions to health care.

Law degree purpose 2: Creating a distinctive vision for legal education by redrawing of boundaries, re-negotiating knowledge structures

Selected module example: Legal Values in technological innovations

This module addresses grand challenge 2.
It consists of interdisciplinary threads from: S, T, E, P, H, L

Using philosophy and ethics to shape the rule of law, students will explore and critically evaluate through a variety of case study examples the extent to which important legal values are maintained and supported through the use of technology. From the perspective of digital truths and algorithmic decisions, this module will explore, question, and critically debate the role of big data in establishing certainty, absolute objectivity and impartiality; methods of verification in the role of technologies to achieve the rule of law: democracy, transparency, predictability, proportionality; fairness; equality; equitability; justification and explanation for legal outcomes; transparency in legal substance and process; adequate access to justice for all; integrity and honesty in creation and application of law; and judicial, legislative, and administrative efficiency; accountability, parity, openness, privacy and respect for human rights.

To ascertain how technology can contribute towards upholding the rule of law, students will gain a deep understanding of the role of ethics in engineering practices, students will be able to critically address topics, such as defining what AI and robots are, and what they can do or be expected to do in the foreseeable future; whether AI agents and robots have rights and if so, what those rights might be; relationships between AI agents or robots and their human counterparts; who is liable when "good AI goes bad"; issues of algorithmic bias and transparency, particularly in the criminal law context. Through this, students will develop a set of protocols that set out ethical statements for design and engineering of technologies. Students will adopt an interdisciplinary set of themes from philosophy, science, humanities, anthropology and law, to examine the current legal framework for the protection of human rights with regard to social and automated technologies. Theories of epistemology and ontology of human beings will be examined in conjunction with the philosophy of technology, and the capability of technology to mediate our experience and identity. Students will review existing ethical guidance in light of human rights recommendations, and enhance these with further research drawn from the various threads in this module to develop ethical guidelines and standards for the design, development and implementation of technological systems, with a recognition towards the capability of behaviour-influencing technologies and their

(Continued)

Table 15.2 (Continued)

ethical aspects and how technology influences and constitutes human nature and human existence.
Selected module example: Lawyering in a Digital Age Experiential programme
This module addresses grand challenge 2. It consists of interdisciplinary threads from: S, T, E, P, D, L Chapters 3, 4, 5, 9, 10, 11, 12 also provide examples of innovation in this area.
With the aim of using technology to innovate and prepare students to become future-ready for a wide range of professions that will benefit from the affordances of a law degree, students work in teams with clients, under the supervision of a team of interdisciplinary academic staff, to build a technological solution to solve a real-world "access to justice" problem identified by their client. Working together with computing and graphic and games design students, law students will co-create, design and develop, for example, an app, online portals with user friendly resources, or digital storytelling of complex legal areas, to gain practical experience and understanding of the concepts of proportionality, equitability and accessibility in a real-world situation; and making them meaningful, within and beyond the tech-solution for use by clients offers an in-depth understanding of how the rule of law and technology complement each other. Drawing on the interdisciplinary theoretical underpinnings of basic ethics, engineering science and philosophy of technology from the other modules studied in the law degree to scrutinise the access to justice crisis and balance the crisis with the challenges and liability issues which can arise from legal tech solutions, including issues of professional regulation. The model of this experiential learning module is built around principles of sharing responsibility and making substantive decisions in a joint cross-disciplinary team, using interdisciplinarity to find and solve authentic real-world problems, constructing and developing interdisciplinary knowledge in an authentic context of the real-world where problem-finding and problem-solving become messy, complex and contrary, creating solutions which have actual and relevant value for use and implementation in the real world and communicating solutions using data visualisation, design thinking, and other forms of multi-modal communication for a range of audiences.

been proposed in this model which may be useful for your students in a digitally transformational law degree? What are the practical and pedagogical challenges of an interdisciplinary law degree?

- With Model 1, a fully fledged redesign of the content and structure of a law degree is required. What are the benefits of studying law through thematic lines of enquiries framed as grand challenges of digital transformation? How will you prepare academics and administrators in your law school to embrace this new model of learning and teaching? What are the challenges and risks with this extensive change to academic practice? Could Model 1 adequately support students to become future-ready? How do you design a module that balances key principles of the module with new developments and new ways of thinking about existing principles? Creative and authentic assessments are key instruments to help bring the process of learning and the outcome of learning to life – consider innovations in assessments that help students become future ready within the context of the new way of learning.

- With Model 2, whilst also involving interdisciplinary study of law, it sets apart the legal knowledge modules from law-tech and law-tech experiential modules, particularly where a wholescale redesign is not possible. What are the benefits of studying law through neatly packaged modules – some law specific and some interdisciplinary law-tech modules alongside each other to address various grand challenges of digital transformation? How will you prepare academics and administrators in your law school to embrace new interdisciplinary modules? Would these modules become electives or core and how will this be determined? What are the challenges and risks with this extensive change to academic practice? How will students be supported to balance law only and interdisciplinary law-tech modules where methodologies of study could differ and could be seen as separate from the study of law? Could Model 2 adequately support students to become future-ready?

A full set of proposed modules and module descriptors for both models are available at request from the author.

References

Barnett, R (2004). Learning for an Unknown Future. *Higher Education Research and Development, 23*(3).

Bernstein, B (1971). "On the classification and framing of educational knowledge." In *Knowledge and control: New directions for the sociology of education*, edited by M. F. D. Young. London: Collier-MacMillan Publishers.

Bernstein, B (1999). Vertical and horizontal discourse: An essay. *British Journal of Sociology of Education, 20.*

Bernstein, B (2000). *Pedagogy, symbolic control and identity: theory, research and critique* (revised edition). Lanham: Rowman and Littlefield.

Bhaskar, R (1989). *Reclaiming Reality: A Critical Introduction to Contemporary Philosophy.* London: Verso.

Bradney, A (Winter 2000). Society of Public Law Teachers, Reporter 21.

Bradney, A (2011). *How to Live: Aristocratic Values, the Liberal University Law School and the Modern Lawyer,* 2 Web JCLI http://webjcli.ncl.ac.uk/2011/issue2/bradney2.html

Bradney, A (2003). *Conversations, Choices and Chances: The Liberal Law School in the Twenty-First Century* (Hart Publication).

Boud, D (2010). "Relocating reflection in the context of practice." In *Beyond reflective practice: New approaches to professional lifelong learning*, edited by H Bradbury, N Frost, S Kilminster & M Zukas. Oxford: Routledge.

Coonan, E & Pratt-Adams, S (2019). *Building Higher Education Curricula Fit for The Future: How Higher Education institutions are responding to the Industrial Strategy.* York: Advance HE. https://arro.anglia.ac.uk/703769/6/Coonan_Pratt-Adams_2018.pdf

Dearing, R, (1997). *Report of the National Committee of Inquiry into Higher Education*: http://www.leeds.ac.uk/educol/ncihe/

Department for Business, Energy & Industrial Strategy, (December 2018). *Policy paper on The Grand Challenges* https://www.gov.uk/government/publications/industrial-strategy-the-grand-challenges/industrial-strategy-the-grand-challenges

Department for Education (April 2019). *Realising the potential of technology in education: A strategy for education providers and the technology industry* https://www.gov.uk/government/publications/realising-the-potential-of-technology-in-education

Deloitte Legal (2017). *A Changing world requires a new approach to law* https://www2.deloitte.com/content/dam/Deloitte/global/Documents/Legal/dttl-legal-deloitte-approach-legal-management-consulting.pdf

Deloitte (Feb 2016). *Developing legal talent: Stepping into the future law firm* https://www2.deloitte.com/content/dam/Deloitte/uk/Documents/audit/deloitte-uk-developing-legal-talent-2016.pdf

European Political Strategy Centre (EPSC 2016). *The future of work: Skills and resilience for a world of change*: https://ec.europa.eu/epsc/publications/strategic-notes/future-work_en

Freire, P (1970). *Pedagogy of the oppressed.* New York: Continuum.

Gettier, E (1963). Is Justified True Belief Knowledge? *Analysis*, *23*(6).

Guth, J & Ashford, C (2014). *The Legal Education and Training Review: Regulating socio-legal and liberal education?*" Vol. 48(1) The Law Teacher http://nrl.northumbria.ac.uk/20961/1/Guth_and_Ashford_LETR_article_final_submitted.pdf

House of Lords Select Committee on Communications (April 2018). 'Regulating the Digital World'. https://publications.parliament.uk/pa/ld201719/ldselect/ldcomuni/299/29902.htm

Her Majesty's Government (2017). *'Industrial Strategy: Building a Britain fit for the future'* https://assets.publishing.service.gov.uk/government/uploads/system/uploads/attachment_data/file/664563/industrial-strategywhite-paper-web-ready-version.pdf

Her Majesty's Land Registry, (October 2018). To explore the benefits of blockchain https://www.gov.uk/government/news/hm-land-registry-to-explore-the-benefits-of-blockchain; https://hmlandregistry.blog.gov.uk/2019/05/24/could-blockchain-be-the-future-of-the-property-market/

International Bar Association, *Presidential Task Force on the Future of Legal Services, drivers for change in the legal profession* https://www.ibanet.org/Task-Force-on-the-Future-of-Legal-Services.aspx

Jisc UK. (2019). Education 4.0 – transforming the future of education (through advanced technology) https://www.youtube.com/watch?v=aVWHp8FsV1w

Jones, E, Ryan, F, Thanaraj, A, & Wong, T (2021). *Digital Lawyering: Technology and legal practice in the 21st century*. Routledge.

Klein, P (1971). A proposed definition of propositional knowledge. *The Journal of Philosophy*, *68*(16), 471–482.

Klein, P (2015). *'Skepticism', The Stanford Encyclopedia of Philosophy* (Summer 2015 Edition), Edward N. Zalta (ed.), https://plato.stanford.edu/archives/sum2015/entries/skepticism/

Lehrer, K, and Paxson Jr, T (1969). Knowledge: Undefeated Justified True Belief. *Journal of Philosophy*, *66* (8).

Manyika, J, Chui, M, Miremadi, M, Bughin, J, George, K, Willmott, P, & Dewhurst, M (2017). *Harnessing Automation for a Future that Works, Mckinsey Global Institute* https://www.mckinsey.com/featured-insights/digital-disruption/harnessing-automation-for-a-future-that-works

Nedelkoska, L & Quintini, G (2018). *Automation, skills use and training*, OECD Social, Employment and Migration Working Papers, No. 202, OECD Publishing, Paris (https://www.oecd-ilibrary.org/docserver/2e2f4eea-en.pdf?expires=1554040951&id=id&accname=guest&checksum=06BC7F3A1E72160839AC2189A34B9B8F

Neuberger (2012). *Judges and professors – ships passing in the night?* Speech at the Max Planck Institute, Hamburg on 9 July 2012, https://www.judiciary.uk/wp-content/uploads/JCO/Documents/Speeches/mr-speech-hamburg-lecture-09072012.pdf

Olssen, M (2003). *Foucault and critique: Kant, humanism and the human sciences*, Paper presented at the British Educational Research Association Annual Conference, Heriot-Watt University, Edinburgh, 11-13 September 2003 http://www.leeds.ac.uk/educol/documents/00003388.htm

Prensky, M. (2001). Digital natives, digital immigrants, part 1. On the Horizon, *9*(5), 1–6.

Pritchard, D (2014). *What is this thing called knowledge?* Routledge.

Pinker, S (2018). *Enlightenment now: The case for reason, science, humanism, and progress.* Penguin Books.

Rawson, G *Plato: Meno*, Internet Encyclopaedia of Philosophy (a peer-reviewed academic resource, https://www.iep.utm.edu/meno-2/

Ruhloff, J (2004). Problematising Critique in Pedagogy. *Journal of Philosophy of Education*, *38*(3), 379–393. doi: 10.1111/j.0309-8249.2004.00392.x

Standish, P (2012). 2012, 163Teaching in the University the Day after Tomorrow (Chapter 12) in The Future University: Ideas and Possibilities, NY Routledge. Barnett, R., Ed.; Routledge: New York, NY, USA; London, UK, 2012. 24, p.163.

Stuart, M, & Shutt, L (2019). *A manifesto for the 21st Century University*. WonkHE blog, https://wonkhe.com/blogs/a-manifesto-for-the-21st-century-university

Susskind, R (2017). *Tomorrow's Lawyers*. Oxford University Press.

Susskind, R (2010). *The End of Lawyers?* Oxford University Press.

Sosa, E (1980). *The Raft and the Pyramid: Coherence versus Foundations in the Theory of Knowledge. Midwest Studies in Philosophy*. https://www.andrew.cmu.edu/user/kk3n/epistclass/Sosa%20-%20Raft%20and%20Pyramid.pdf.

Thanaraj, Ann (2017). Making the case for a digital lawyering framework in legal education. *International Review of Law, 3*. https://insight.cumbria.ac.uk/id/eprint/3324/1/Thanaraj_MakingTheCase.pdf

Turri, J, Alfano, M, & Greco, J (2011). Virtue epistemology. *The Stanford Encyclopaedia of Philosophy*. https://plato.stanford.edu/archives/win2011/entries/epistemology-virtue/

Universities UK (August 2018). *Solving Future Skills Challenges*, https://www.universitiesuk.ac.uk/policy-and-analysis/reports/Pages/solving-future-skills-challenges.aspx

Wegner, J (2015). The values of legal education. *Nottingham Law Journal, 24*. https://www4.ntu.ac.uk/nls/document_uploads/nlj_24.pdf

World Economic Forum (2016). *Grand challenge insight report: The future of jobs*. http://www3.weforum.org/docs/WEF_Future_of_Jobs.pdf

World Economic Forum (2017). *Accelerating Workforce Reskilling for the Fourth Industrial Revolution'*, Geneva http://www3.weforum.org/docs/WEF_EGW_White_Paper_Reskilling.pdf

World Economic Forum (2018). *The Future of Jobs Report*. https://www.talenttalks.net/world-economic-forum-2018/

World Economic Forum (January 2019). *Modern society has reached its limits. Society 5.0 will liberate us'*, https://www.weforum.org/agenda/2019/01/modern-society-has-reached-its-limits-society-5-0-will-liberate-us/

Chapter 16

Legal Academics and the Fourth Industrial Revolution

Kim Silver

The chapters in this collection demonstrate how innovative legal academics are preparing students to thrive in the Fourth Industrial Revolution and, at the same time, taking advantage of digital transformation within their own practice. In this chapter, I seek to summarise some of the themes relevant to being a legal academic in the digital age and outline the research agenda that will support the transition.

Susskind and Susskind (2015) argue that the effects of digital disruption follow a common pattern for a range of professional activities. Disruption theory as defined by Clayton Christensen is one of "competitive response", where new entrants to the market take advantage of an innovation which existing players either have not identified or cannot accommodate within their existing business model (Denning, 2016). Susskind and Susskind suggest that digital disruption is most likely to happen where there is cost pressure, external competition is permitted, and technology provides alternative ways of delivering the result that the client or funder is looking for. They predict significant change for seven exemplar professions – today's legal academics may be exhilarated or horrified to learn that law and education are two of them.

As Williams and Janeček argue in chapter 13, digital change will have implications both for the legal system as a whole and for individual practices; and in chapter 11, Otoyo et al explain the opportunities for law graduates who are able to bridge the gap between lawyers and technologists. For education, Susskind and Susskind argue that the advent of educational technology radically alters the position of both educational institutions and educators themselves, transforming not only what is taught but how it is taught. Innovative teaching ideas abound, both for understanding substantive law (see the virtual town for teaching land law set out by Marunchak and Dunk in chapter 2) and for developing skills (for example, Jones et al describe using virtual reality when teaching presentation skills in chapter 3).

Whilst this book was being put together, Covid-19 has made the need for change apparent and speeded up the process. Universities around the world have pivoted to online learning, lawyers have had to work remotely and even courts have gone online. Rive (chapter 7) contrasts the "incremental adoption

DOI: 10.4324/9780429351082-16

of aspects of online teaching and learning" pre-Covid with "unplanned but largely wholesale moves to online platforms" in 2020.

This chapter will consider the impact of the ongoing digital disruption on legal academics. We have to prepare students for the changing world, whether in legal practice or elsewhere, but how we do this might be subject to pervading change, affecting professional identity and development, the content and methods of teaching, research opportunities and methods, and the way in which higher education institutions organise themselves and serve their student body.

This chapter starts by considering who legal academics are and what they do and briefly looking at the debates about the proper purpose of legal education. It asks who will be involved in ensuring that our students are future-ready – whether self-selected technophiles or entire law school teams. It identifies the barriers to accepting change and the threats to wellbeing that change can present. Finally, it offers some suggestions as to how legal academics can be digitally empowered.

Whilst the focus is on the UK model of undergraduate law degrees, which are not solely, or indeed primarily, aimed at preparing students for careers as lawyers but have a wider educative role in common with the humanities and social sciences (Quality Assurance Agency for Higher Education (QAA)), much of this will also affect those in law schools which are postgraduate and more closely linked with entry to the profession.

Legal Academics

There appears to be no consensus on the term "legal academic" and at what point such a status might be achieved: as has been noted " … there is no typical legal academic and no typical role … " (Ashford and Guth (eds), 2016, p1). The literature on legal academics is relatively limited.

Career Paths

For *Legal Academics, Culture and Identities,* Cownie (2004) interviewed 54 legal academics from a variety of universities in order to analyse their 'lived experience' (p1). More than half of the interviewees had:

> (e)ither seriously considered practice, or had qualified as practitioners (and in a minority of cases had worked as lawyers). However, they were clear that they regarded academia as a preferable occupation. (p79)

Becher and Trowler (2001) note that in "applied disciplines" such as law, pharmacy and engineering, it was normal to enter academia later in life, after professional qualification and experience, with that background as, at least initially, a substitute for a doctorate (p134), contrasted with "pure" subject areas. Whilst this picture may well have changed at research-intensive universities, it does mean that legal academic careers are not homogeneous. The PhD route is established, but so is entry from the professions, whether as junior or seasoned lawyers. In *The Legal Academic's Handbook*, Ashford and Guth (2016) identified four fictional legal academics, using them to tie together contributions from authors with experience across the academy. Two were former practitioners, one had a pure teaching background and one had a pure research background. This reflects the wide range of entry points for legal academics, which will in turn affect the age profile of the legal education community overall. Whether age affects responses to digital disruption is discussed further below.

Legal Education

The debate on the purpose of legal education is long-standing (the two camps can be seen in the review by Bradney (2008) of the book *Transforming Legal Education* by Maharg (2007)) and is discussed further by Thanaraj et al in chapter 8. Is studying law an opportunity to "learn about legal phenomena" or should it be an experiential introduction to what it is to be a lawyer? The answer, in any given institution, affects what it is to be a legal academic.

The vignettes provided by Ashford and Guth (2016) indicate that their imaginary academics' characters go beyond the trinity of research, teaching, and administration, retaining a practitioner identity. However, Cownie (2004) drew a strict line between academic and vocational legal education and found:

> None of the respondents mentioned preparing students for entry to the legal profession as one of their educational aims (indeed, several specifically mentioned that they were *not* preparing students for legal practice); nor did anyone mention teaching vocational skills ... . (p77)

These interviewees had very limited involvement in the professional vocational courses in England and Wales: Cownie noted that "only a small minority of university law schools" offered these courses at that time (p18).

Significant changes in UK higher education and legal education over the last two decades have led to explicit policies to emphasise graduate employability (see, for example, Office for Students (2021)) and more varied university provision. The distance learning LLB introduced by The Open University in 1998 is now the most popular law degree in the UK (Open University, 2019). Between 30 and 40 universities offer the Legal Practice Course, about a third of the law schools in England and Wales (see https://www.sra.org.uk/students/courses/lpc-course-providers.page). The Solicitors Regulation Authority is replacing the Legal Practice Course and the prerequisite qualifying law degree with a Solicitors Qualifying Examination, which will no doubt affect what is taught on undergraduate law degrees and how it is taught. Nevertheless, the subject benchmark provided by the Quality Assurance Agency for Higher Education (2019) will continue to require "students to apply their understanding of legal principles, rules, doctrine, skills and values" in the context of "ethical, social, political, environmental, and economic norms" and that they should be given "opportunities to discuss ethical questions and dilemmas that arise in law and to consider the features of ethical decision-making". The benchmark also stresses the employability of law students in a wide range of careers. This provides a broad canvas for law schools and legal academics to develop and teach appropriate courses.

The continued growth of the clinical legal education (CLE) movement has also blurred the academic/vocational divide. CLE brings together experiential learning and a social justice agenda, with substantial literature (such as through the International Journal of Clinical Legal Education). Law schools offering CLE are growing in number. LawWorks (2019) reported 287 clinics in operation in England and Wales, 49% of which were part of law schools. CLE also extends to the provision of activities such as StreetLaw (a form of public legal education) and simulated delivery of legal services (Thomas and Johnson, 2020). In this book, Weinberg and Giddings describe the development of a virtual legal clinic at Monash University in Australia (chapter 5; see Thanaraj and Sales (2020) for the UK experience).

As a result of these developments, many legal academics are now straddling the academic and vocational fields, adding greater complexity to their roles.

Employment Patterns

Most discussion of legal academics assumes that they are full time and working in one institution. However, many institutions use part-time staff, particularly practitioners and PhD students, to supplement their permanent staff. In particular, The Open University student's main point of contact will be one of an army of part-time tutors, with widely varying careers and backgrounds. (The Open University environment is described by Jones et al in chapter 3). This significantly widens the pool of teachers who will be affected by digital disruption, including some of those closest to legal practice.

Roles

The mix and importance of the traditional academic roles of research, teaching, and administration differ according to the type of university or law school; and individual academics may at some point in their career be involved in only one. The advent of CLE and the involvement of practitioners in legal education or legal academics in practice through CLE adds another dimension.

Academics employed to staff law clinics are likely to have different interests and motivations than those doing purely black letter law and may well be employed on different terms, to reflect the needs of clinic (Thomas and Johnson, 2020). It appears that these "lawyer-academics" are not always valued within the academy. Literature in the USA openly discusses a perceived difference in status of clinical educators (see Adamson et al, 2012 and Gilman, 2019) but this is less frequently dealt with in the UK literature (but see Gregersen, 2019). However, these dual professionals are crucial in the response to digital change in law and legal practice.

The Need to be Inclusive

The variety of the roles and the people filling those roles, research or teacher, practitioner or theorist, full- or part-time, should not be a reason to create artificial hierarchies. All will be affected by digital change, some more than others but the best hope for the academy is to enlist everyone into managing change.

Future ready?

Challenges for All

Legal academics as individuals face change on all fronts.

- The traditional model of legal advice and practice is being challenged. For many academics with an identity based on the experience of practice, that will be based in the analogue world. The stories of practice they share with students, aspects of their claims to expertise and their approach to the law, were shaped in earlier professional experience. If the professional world they know alters radically, how does this affect them? Are relationships with students changed? How do they maintain currency and credibility?
- There is a parallel revolution in education, with traditional teaching methods supplemented and sometimes replaced by digital tools. Law schools are asking how they can digitally empower their students to work in a rapidly changing world. Legal academics are under pressure to embrace both changes in teaching methods and also what is taught. Marunchak and Dunk in chapter 2 suggest that: "Academics in legal education have a duty to embrace new practices". As well as the use of technologies such as virtual reality (Jones et al chapter 3) and 3D graphics technology (Marunchak and Dunk, chapter 2), contributors throughout this book have been reshaping their courses to include both practical and theoretical approaches to law and technology.
- Research is being affected as well. In addition to fresh areas of research about cutting edge issues (for example on smart technologies and criminal justice, Brownsword & Harel, 2019; see the proposed research agenda developed below), Lupton, Mewburn and Thomson (2018) highlight the many ways in which research and scholarship are now created and accessed digitally. This has led to changed models of discussion and dissemination, as shown in the contemporaneous debate by public law scholars on Brexit

through the UK Constitutional Law Association (2020) blog. Social media continues to offer both opportunities and threats to the academic, as discussed extensively in Rowell (2019), contributions to which were sourced on Twitter, where many higher education communities have made online homes (see @alt_law, #lthechat). In this collection, see Homewood (chapter 4) for further discussion of how Twitter can be used to develop communities of practice in the context of teaching. Whilst there are issues for researchers, such as how to manage their academic persona (Marshall, Barbour and Moore in Lupton, Mewburn, and Thomson, 2018)), arguably researchers are the group most empowered by the use of digital technologies.
- Universities are increasingly using technology comprehensively, from communications to student welfare to human resources, with implications for many aspects of academic life. Alongside operational and pastoral changes, many institutions are seeking to extend their geographical reach by using online education at home and abroad, whether commercially (there are 44 distance LLMs offered by 21 UK universities, Postgraduate Search, 2019) or as a free online course or MOOCs (Massive Open Online Courses) (relatively rare in law). Freund et al in Lupton, Mewburn and Thomson (2018) note the "complexity of the labour involved in making MOOCs, in particular labour that becomes invisible" (p121).

> " … no one and no institution in higher education gets a pass on these disruptive changes".
>
> (Smith, 2017).

At the most basic level, as higher education increasingly relies on technology, all academics are affected, whether they like it or not. It is no longer possible, in most universities, to refuse to engage with technology.

The Few or the Many?

Most of the authors in this book take a broadly positive view of the affordances of digital technologies, but any law school is likely to contain technophobes as well as technophiles, and a range of digital literacies. Whilst one strategy might be to allow technophiles to push ahead to introduce digital change, theories of change stress the importance of looking at different levels of action and interaction (Trowler, 2008) – here, the academic, the department, the wider institution and the external context of the legal system and profession. The innovators will be working within existing systems and facing several significant issues. If they cannot persuade colleagues to back them, their ability to introduce new initiatives, let alone digitally empower their students, is likely to be impeded by the following political and practical issues.

What are Law Schools for?

This old conundrum, noted above, is given new life by digital disruption and may be answered in different ways in different institutions. The Quality Assurance Agency for Higher Education (2019) benchmarks are very broad and can easily encompass digital development. Some academics will accept that the profession may well change out of all recognition, but, apart from an academic nod to the driverless car or the iniquities of facial recognition technologies, will still argue that it is not the business of the law school to react to that change. Others, such as Williams and Janeček (chapter 13), Otoyo et al (chapter 11), Kennedy (chapter 12), Cakir (chapter 14), and Offer and Cook (chapter 6) will see it as essential to prepare students for significant changes in the employment market.

Curriculum Design

The law degree of the future may well have new options in "legal engineering" or "law and AI", together with an emphasis on interdisciplinarity, transferable learning and developing skills and competencies as proposed by contributors such as Williams and Janeček (chapter 13), Otoyo et al (chapter 11), Kennedy (chapter 12), Cakir (chapter 14), and Offer and Cook (chapter 6). However, given the limited space in the degree, there are bound to be some losers. The leader of a cherished and threatened module is unlikely to welcome the new kid on the block. Decisions as to the balance of the curriculum may be taken at the law school level, whether by departmental heads or by the school as a whole, or it may be a response to institutional or outside imperatives. Either way, the decision will be essentially political and will have profound implications for individual academic careers and the success or otherwise of law schools to re-cruit.

Resourcing

Introducing law and technology modules is another call on the departmental and institutional budget. Who funds these initiatives, and how, is likely to be another highly political issue, dependent on the experience and beliefs of individual budget-holders. This is likely to be less of an issue with digital innovation in pedagogy as the development of digitally enhanced learning tends to be an institutional priority, particularly post-Covid-19.

Teaching and Learning

Many authors in this collection would suggest that, ideally, a course would embed lawtech at all levels of the curriculum, whatever the aptitude or interest of the individual or team delivering that level. Although it may be of value to present different perspectives, the digital lawyering message is likely to be diluted if it is only delivered in pockets of the curriculum. This has been the model of the first Law and Technology LLMs such as those described by Williams and Janeček (chapter 13) and Cakir (chapter 14) (also see Swansea University, 2020).

Those who have experimented with lawtech in their teaching also know that it offers the opportunity to encourage logical application through the use of decision trees and creative thought through exposure to legal design (see, for example, Cakir (chapter 14), Otoyo et al (chapter 11), and Williams and Janeček (chapter 13)). These are applicable across the curriculum and should not be restricted just to modules with interested members of staff. Many voices in higher education stress the need to encourage critical evaluation of the use of technology throughout the curriculum, in foundation subjects and optional modules alike (for example, Aoun, 2017). That means looking for opportunities throughout the curriculum and is an opportunity to harness the interest of the techno-sceptics!

Skills and Aptitudes

Linked to these issues are the wider skills that students need to be future ready. As discussed in Williams and Janeček (chapter 13), Otoyo et al (chapter 11), Kennedy (chapter 12), Cakir (chapter 14). and Offer and Cook (chapter 6), digital lawyers will need to work across disciplines and in teams, using the principles of legal design and communicating clearly with colleagues and clients using a variety of media. When developing any skill, a collective insistence on the importance of that skill can have a transformative effect, which means involving all colleagues.

Assessment

Assessment must reflect all these aspects. It seems unlikely that the unseen exam will test many of the attributes required of the digital lawyer – but it remains a favoured form of assessment. Historically privileged by the demands of the professional associations, will it simply be replaced by the multiple-choice test to give students experience prior to the new Solicitors' Qualifying Examination? The chapters from contributors who have introduced law and technology modules show how group work and reflection can be harnessed. Bramley (2020) discusses the advantages and challenges of group work, particularly from a student perspective.

Any alternative assessment forms will need to pass institutional and departmental hurdles, convincing colleagues that they are as rigorous as those employed in parallel modules at the same level. Students are, of course, also alive to any perceived discrepancy. For this reason, a collective approach is desirable.

Barriers to Digital Empowerment

If law schools are to work consistently towards future-ready and digitally-empowered students, an approach which permeates the whole teaching team is best. Why might legal academics not embrace digital lawyering initiatives? Some suggestions follow (but see Thanaraj and Williams (2016) for more detail).

Digital Literacy

Digital literacy seems to be something of an accident of age, temperament and opportunity. It is not necessary to be digitally literate to encourage students to embrace a digital future – but it certainly helps. Data is not readily available on age distribution within legal academia but most are not "digital natives" (a concept explained and challenged by Helsper and Eynon (2010)) and in most walks of life, there will be people of all ages who view the scale and speed of technological change with varying degrees of scepticism, apprehension or incomprehension. Covid-19 exposed the range of digital literacies in academia. JISC (2020) noted, "it is unclear how prepared many staff are to step outside their comfort zone, which involves not only changes to workload but also hard-won identity" (p22). Whilst Krenelka Chase (2018), a US academic, makes a strong argument for employing millennials (those born between roughly 1981 and 1996), this seems a simplistic (and potentially discriminatory) response. It would be better by far to identify the training needs of individual staff, perhaps by systematic self-audit, accompanied by training to increase individual skills and confidence. JISC (2020) suggested: "Building staff confidence and comfort in mastering both the tools and the pedagogy is essential. The ability to adapt and shift approach cannot be separated from digital skills" (p8).

Time

However, Wilson and Strevens (2018) in their review of the psychological well-being of law academics cite a range of literature on the pressures encountered by academics in general and note that increased workload will have an impact on the individual's sense of competency and their ability to control their environment. Thanaraj and Williams (2016) identified the impact on time and workload as one of the barriers to adopting digitally enhanced learning.

Identity

The revolution in legal practice will affect those legal academics with dual professional identities as lawyers and academics. If their academic identity is partially dependent on their lawyer identity, where do these potential changes leave them? Will their relationships with their students alter significantly? Will the confidence they derive from significant previous experience be dented? This is an area which warrants further research.

Fear and Loathing

For some, however, the introduction of AI particularly strikes a deeper chord. There are significant issues of principle about the introduction of AI into the legal system and legal services. Zuckerman (2020) suggests that despite savings in cost and time and potential gains in reliability:

> "Machine-administration of justice may open a gulf between human conceptions of the law and machine law, leading to alienation, loss of institutional legitimacy and damage to the rule of law". (p428)

Fears about the misuse of AI, widespread unemployment and the rise of powerful tech firms are common themes in media reports. In the field of lawtech, particularly in relation to access to justice, the depersonalisation of legal advice or dispute resolution and the risks of digital exclusion are known issues (for a survey, see Law Society, 2019). For some academics, the pressures of technology on multiple fronts may represent an issue of simple survival. If the world is changing so radically, it may no longer be recognisable. We have yet to see whether Covid-19 and the online pivot have changed hearts and minds or entrenched opinions on both sides. We cannot afford to ignore the understandable reluctance to participate.

Digital Empowerment for Legal Academics

Law schools and academics who want to bring colleagues along with them on the digital journey might want to consider some or all of the following strategies. For a more detailed road map to digital transformation, particularly from an institutional perspective, see Thanaraj et al in chapter 8 (and also Thanaraj and Williams (2016)).

Knowledge is Power

Much of the above is necessarily assumption and surmise. There has to be a much clearer picture of academics' perceptions and expectations of digital disruption before solutions can be proposed. Within individual law schools, have open discussion and debate about the ideas presented within this book. What do people really think? Where do their boundaries lie? There may be fewer doubters than expected – but more concerns about competency and workload.

Digital Literacy Levels

Law schools may need to invest in increasing both staff digital literacies, awareness of developments in lawtech, understanding of digital pedagogies, and of the principles of legal design (Hagan, undated website). This will increase confidence and will certainly enhance the use of online technologies for learning and teaching in general. This need not be difficult: for example, a training session in a computer lab with a single, reasonably simple goal (to use one new feature of a virtual learning environment for example), allows people to swop ideas, help each other – and at the end of the day, take away something ready to use in their teaching.

Time

Again, try to find out what colleagues actually need and what can reasonably be expected within current workload models. Institutionally, it may be necessary to argue for part of the allocation to be devoted to training and then to creating digital materials. Do the team need technical support or peer support? Can students be an additional resource, given that so many of them are digital natives? Try to include law tech within the curriculum rather than as a standalone extra.

Remember the Law in Lawtech

If a consumer protection app is based on a simple contract law decision tree, this needs no tech knowledge or experience. Anybody can be an expert by virtue of their legal expertise – in the law and technology courses described in this book, it is the job of the law student on the project team to act as the bridge to the technology experts, rather than that of their client. The client provides legal knowledge and experience. Becoming a co-producer of knowledge with the students may build confidence and provide practical reassurance to legal academics that there is still an important role for them to play.

Feel the Fear but Do it Anyway

An important part of making students future-ready is to ensure that they can critique technological developments. Who better to get involved in this than the sceptics? Encourage robust debates about the opportunities and threats with representatives from both sides of the argument.

Researching Digital Transformation

Research into the law relating to the Fourth Industrial Revolution is already underway and has been noted above. However, there must also be a research agenda on digital transformation in relation to the matters discussed in this chapter. These are some of the many possible areas, some of which are solidly rooted in current issues and conditions, whereas others require imaginative thinking about our readiness for the future:

- Researching the effects of digital disruption on legal practice and the legal profession, on education more widely and on legal education specifically. An important example is the Oxford University research project "Unlocking the Potential of Artificial Intelligence for English Law", described by Williams and Janeček in chapter 13. Rive's account of the effects of the pivot to online in the early days of the Covid pandemic brings out the opportunities and threats posed by this sudden and acute disruption (chapter 7) and compares it with the more measured and gradual adoption of technologies in the years before 2020. He stresses the need for reflection on those opportunities and threats.
- Empirical research to understand more clearly the digital literacies and capabilities of staff, students, and the profession, in order to identify strengths and gaps. For example, Marunchak and Dunk in chapter 2 point to the reluctance of the profession to embrace e-conveyancing, whilst the Oxford University study also investigates the skills graduates will need in the future. Weinberg and Giddings in chapter 5 remind us that both practitioners and students will need to understand the relationships that will exist between technology and legal practice. Thanaraj et al in chapter 8 make a powerful case for a creative approach to course design, underpinned by sound pedagogical theory. This in turn provides a wealth of research opportunities into changing practices in legal education.
- Extending existing research to consider the ideas in this collection in new depth. For example, Homewood suggests that the Twitter project described in chapter 4 could be researched in more depth to establish "the views and thoughts of the members of the community and the impact on their learning". Similarly, Jones et al suggest a variety of uses for virtual reality technology in legal education beyond clinical legal education, whilst also pointing out that the use of technology encourages students to critique that use (chapter 3). Otoyo et al (chapter 11) suggest that the local initiatives they have developed in South London could be replicated on a wider geographical scale and point to existing networks already considering how this can be implemented.
- Investigating and evaluating the possibilities of new and existing technologies, ideas, and applications. Marunchak and Dunk reference a wide range of techniques which enabled them to build the digital town described in chapter 2. There is scope for academics to consider how these methods could be extended to subjects outside land law. However, Murray and Edwards sound a warning note in chapter 9 that technologies have to be considered in terms of sustainability, in its broadest sense.

Chapters discussing lawtech modules (Otoyo et al and Kennedy, chapters 11 and 12) also stress the importance of considering legal design, which puts the user at the heart of the process.

- Considering existing problems in the legal system or in education in order to (re)imagine digital solutions. Piaskowska and Piesiewicz in chapter 10 stress the need for more research into online tools for legal advice clinics. Kennedy points out in chapter 12 that teaching lawtech courses requires constant attention to the developing and changing needs of the profession and of end-users.
- Continuing research into how change can be managed at different levels and the effects of change on individuals' identities and wellbeing. Cakir notes in chapter 14 that acquiring the skills needed for innovation requires a cultural shift and a change in thinking for lawyers. This is also true of students and academics – and changes can be uneasy. As noted above, legal academics with dual professional identities may be particularly vulnerable to a sense of shifting identity.

Conclusion

Legal academics are a disparate group, whose roles can be difficult to define. They work in a multiplicity of environments and have different ideas about what legal education should be doing. This can affect their perception of whether it is in fact their role to prepare students for a changing future. In addition, the legal academy is under challenge from digital disruption from several directions and not all academics have the skills or the disposition to meet these challenges. However, law schools need to try and involve as many colleagues as possible in their quest for future readiness and promote a research agenda which supports it. In doing so, digitally empowering as many legal academics as possible will help them to achieve their goal.

References

Adamson, BL, Colbert, B, Hessler, K, Kruse, K, Kuehn, R, McNeal, MH, Pang, C, & Santacroce, D (2012). The status of clinical faculty in the legal academy: Report of the task force on the status of clinicians and the legal academy. *Journal of the Legal Profession, 36*, 353–414.

Aoun, J (2017). *Robot-proof higher education in the age of artificial intelligence*. Cambridge, Mass: MIT Press Kindle edition.

Ashford, C & Guth, J eds (2016). *The legal academic's handbook*. London: Palgrave

Becher T & Trowler, P (2001). *Academic tribes and territories* (2nd ed). Basingstoke: Palgrave Macmillan.

Bradney, A (2008). Transforming legal education: Learning and teaching law in the early twenty-first century by Paul Maharg. *Journal of Law & Society, 35*, 565–570.

Bramley, G (2020). There is no "I" in "a team of lawyers": An evaluation of student perceptions of group assessment within legal higher education. *The Law Teacher, 54*, 55–68.

Brownsword, R & Harel, A (2019). Law, liberty and technology: Criminal justice in the context of smart machines. *International Journal of Law in Context, 15*, 107–125

Cownie, F (2004). *Legal academics: Culture and identities*. Oxford: Hart Publishing.

Denning, S (2016). Christensen updates disruption theory. *Strategy & Leadership, 44* (2), 10–16.

Gilman, M (2019). The future of clinical legal scholarship. *Clinical Law Review, 26*(1), 189–202.

Gregersen, E (2019) *The lived experience of a university law clinic supervisor: An autoethnographic inquiry*. Doctoral thesis, Northumbria University. Retrieved from http://nrl.northumbria.ac.uk/41722/

Hagan, M (undated website). Law by Design, Retrieved from http://www.lawbydesign.co/en/home/

Helsper, E & Eynon, R (2010). Digital natives: Where is the evidence? *British Educational Research Journal, 36*, 503–520.

JISC Learning and Teaching Reimagined. Change and challenge for students, staff and leaders. Retrieved from https://www.jisc.ac.uk/sites/default/files/ltr-report-change-and-challenge-for-students-staff-and-leaders-aug-2020.pdf

Krenelka Chase, A (2018). Upending the double life of law schools: Millennials in the legal academy *University of Dayton Law Review 44*. Stetson University College of Law Legal Studies Research Paper Series Research Paper No. 2018-4. Retrieved from https://papers.ssrn.com/sol3/papers.cfm?abstract_id=3167442

Law Society (2019). Technology, access to justice and the rule of law: Is technology the key to unlocking access to justice innovation? Retrieved from https://events.lawsociety.org.uk/uploads/files/2f5acdb0-4227-455d-9d55-ec3e6254a5da.pdf

LawWorks (2019). LawWorks clinics network report Retrieved from https://www.lawworks.org.uk/solicitors-and-volunteers/resources/lawworks-clinics-network-report-2019

Lupton, D, Mewburn, I & Thomson, P (2018). *The digital academic*. Abingdon: Routledge.

Maharg, P (2007). *Transforming legal education: Learning and teaching law in the early twenty-first century*. Aldershot: Ashgate.

Office for Students (2021). *Supply of higher level skills*. Retrieved from https://www.officeforstudents.org.uk/advice-and-guidance/skills-and-employment/supply-of-higher-level-skills/

Open University (2019). About the Open University law school. Retrieved from http://law-school.open.ac.uk/about

Postgraduate Search (2019). Distance learning LLM law and legal studies. Retrieved from https://www.postgraduatesearch.com/pgs/search?course=law-and-legal-studies&qualification=llm&study_mode=distance-learning

Quality Assurance Agency for Higher Education (2019). *Subject benchmark statement: Law*. Retrieved from https://www.qaa.ac.uk/docs/qaa/subject-benchmark-statements/subject-benchmark-statement-law.pdf?sfvrsn=b939c881_16

Rowell, C (Ed.) (2019). *Social media in higher education: Case studies, reflection and analysis*. Open Book Publishers. Retrieved from https://www.openbookpublishers.com/product/945

Smith, P (2017). Digital disruption: Transformational change is pushing higher education leaders to rethink the traditional organizational model in ways that align with the digital age. *Business Officer, 51*(1), 74–79.

Solicitors Regulation Authority (2019). Legal Practice Course (LPC) providers. Retrieved from https://www.sra.org.uk/students/courses/lpc-course-providers.page

Susskind, R & Susskind, D (2015). *The future of the professions*. Oxford: Oxford University Press.

Swansea University (2020). *LLM Legaltech*. Retrieved from https://www.swansea.ac.uk/postgraduate/taught/law/llmlegaltech/

Thanaraj A & Sales, M (2020). Lawyering in a digital age: Reflections on starting up a virtual law clinic in L Thomas, and N Johnson, (Eds), *The Clinical Legal Education Handbook* Retrieved from https://humanities-digital-library.org/index.php/hdl/catalog/book/clinicallegal-education

Thanaraj, A & Williams, S (2016). Supporting the adoption of technology enhanced learning by academics at universities. *Journal of Teaching and Learning With Technology, 5*, 59–86.

Thomas, L & Johnson, N (Eds.) (2020). The clinical legal education handbook. Retrieved from https://humanities-digital-library.org/index.php/hdl/catalog/book/clinicallegal-education

Trowler PR (2008). *Cultures and change in higher education: Theories and practice*. Basingstoke: Palgrave Macmillan.

UK Constitutional Law Association blog (2020). Retrieved from https://ukconstitutionallaw.org/blog/

Wilson, J & Strevens, C (2018). Perceptions of psychological well-being in UK law academics. *The Law Teacher, 52*, 335–349.

Zuckerman, A (2020). Artificial intelligence - implications for the legal profession, adversarial process and rule of law. *Law Quarterly Review, 136*, 427–453.

Chapter 17

Law Schools and the Fourth Industrial Revolution

Ann Thanaraj

Complementing Kim Silver's review of the legal academic and the Fourth Industrial Revolution (4IR), this chapter looks at the Law School's place in the Higher Education of the future and the role of technology as an enabler for the academic experience. Higher Education plays a pivotal role in preparing students to thrive in a society which is being reshaped by technology, and various institutions are re-imagining their learning experiences, pedagogy, and strategy in order to deliver education that equips students with the key skills, academic knowledge, and mindsets that are needed in a digital-first world. Although the future of the 4IR remains uncertain, we know enough to take sensible actions: chapters in this book invite relevant critical reflection and innovative action.

The legal world is changing dramatically, as Richard Susskind had predicted: new careers are evolving such as legal data architecture, legal software engineers, legal designers, and legal data handlers; there is automation and twenty-four-seven services from around the world for clients. Further automation will allow lawyers to avoid repetitive tasks and offer more accessible and creative ways of accessing legal services. The Internet of Things, Artificial Intelligence, and complex datasets combine to offer powerful opportunities to "probabilistically emulate [human] behavior under analogous conditions" (Katz, 2013), which would typically require flexibility, creativity, problem-solving, and complex communications. These changes have significant implications for all parts of society, including law and the legal system, creating new areas of legal practice with the need for expert knowledge and skills in these areas.

With technology bringing new careers and automating existing ones, graduates need the resilience and creativity to operate in evolving settings, the skills and attributes to become lifelong learners and creators of knowledge, and the knowledge to produce innovative ways of identifying and solving problems. Naturally, this assumes that Higher Education generally and Law Schools as a particular example should address the 4IR and adapt learning models to prepare students for the fast-changing world.

The digital transformation of a law degree is not simply using technology to teach or assess. Rather, it embraces and embodies key seismic drivers for

DOI: 10.4324/9780429351082-17

change: vision, people, and culture, which collectively require holistic support and transformation through leadership with credibility and trust (Thanaraj & Williams, 2016; Grajek & Reinitz, 2019). Digital transformation is a journey, not a destination, and so involves the continual understanding of why we are seeking change, who this change will benefit, and how to unlock the value proposition of a law degree as an anchor discipline in stewarding the challenges of the 4IR.

Whilst legal education in various countries has been through several reviews, relatively little change has occurred to the mode of delivery, structure, core modules, curriculum and themes of study, or assessments since the creation of law degrees in the 1800s (Sako et al, 2020). The changes brought about by the 4IR provide law schools with an opportunity to debate, collaborate, and redesign legal education to better equip prospective legal professionals for its impact. Various authors in this collection have addressed the construct of "future readiness" and identified their own definitions of this, and as a reader, you are encouraged to come up with your own as you read the case studies and interventions showcased. Further, several authors call for the transformation of law degrees, fundamentally revising the value proposition of law in the changing landscape, while also being respectful of the distinctive nature of legal education and the role of professional regulators as gatekeepers of the profession.

Various chapters in this book prompt reflection on how digital literacies are beginning to define creativity, and the need for continuous learning and mastery of new skills, given the rapid pace of technological development and its uses in practice. Three strategies to better equip students for the future and steer legal education forward emerge: (i) embedding digital literacies, (ii) developing interdisciplinarity, and (iii) nurturing creativity, collaboration, and communication opportunities. These should create future-ready students who are familiar with interdisciplinary real-world problems and can identify problems and solve them using and adapting knowledge in creative ways. This will require law schools to review and redesign their student learning experiences, refocus their research on areas of the law and legal system that can tackle the grand challenges of the changing world, and develop new areas of expertise in their teaching and research. Whilst existing areas of discourse, research, and motivations will continue to be valuable – for example, clinical and pro bono work, thinking like a lawyer, legal skills, and entrepreneurship and law – the changing needs of professions, industries, and sectors that require legal knowledge and skills require some level of priority.

Digital Literacies

In higher education, digital literacy is commonly found as a facet of an employability or transferable skills outcome within a programme of study. This is appropriate, given that digital literacy is now essential for successfully living, learning, and working in today's increasingly digitalised society and knowledge economy. However, digital literacy affords a much broader and holistic opportunity to reimagine the curriculum and prepare students to thrive in a digital society: this requires us to shift our thinking from digital literacies as tools to digital literacies as a body of theory, brought to life by practical and experiential learning that seeks to replicate the tasks and performance standards typically found in contemporary workplaces and equip students with real skills needed to solve in-demand industry and societal problems.

Such digital literacies require grounding in authentic disciplinary and professional values and identities to be operationally meaningful. Understanding some of the changes in legal or hybrid careers can empower students to shape the future of their professions. In addition, questioning what is required to thrive in a modern practice will rejuvenate the conversation around what knowledge and skills are needed by graduates, including interdisciplinary knowledge and adaptive abilities so that people can find creative solutions to new problems. Creative problem-solving skills are those perhaps less likely to be impacted by automation.

Whilst there is no broad consensus on the meaning of digital literacy, which hinders its uptake, a growing body of research is helping teachers and practitioners to navigate the continuous adjustments required by emerging technologies. The chapters in this book, in their own ways, share a vision about fostering digitally empowered skills. Accordingly, a bold and pedagogically meaningful innovation, a virtual reality (VR) app (Jones et al, chapter 3), allows students to experience a variety of professional environments and collaborate with various professionals in the justice system. Using social media tools, such as the use of Twitter as a community of practice for learning and teaching (Homewood, chapter 4), is another example of using technology to challenge students to use their academic knowledge to solve problems around them. Emerging technologies such as VR and social media as pedagogic tools are rich and authentic environments reflecting industry needs, and help academics support learner interactivity, collaboration, communication, reflection, and skills. The use of online platforms to teach Public law and International Environmental Law (Rive, chapter 7) offers insights into how to use them effectively as part of preparing students for the technologically advancing world of work.

Illustrations from Australia also show how to address current issues around access to justice and use technologies to build trust and interact with clients through a virtual law clinic (Weinberg and Giddings, chapter 5) and create knowledge-based apps for communities to understand their rights and help them with making decisions (Offer and Cook, chapter 6) by introducing the approach of putting real-world clients at the heart of designing technology for their benefit (and joining law and computer science).

The growth of the digital landscape and the technological disruptions in professional work and practice present invigorating opportunities to design curriculum content and delivery to equip students with the relevant knowledge, skills, and attributes for working and participating in the digital society. Otoyo and others (chapter 11) provided students with literacies in data, technology and humanities, communication and design, alongside broader skills in project management, teamworking, and legal design skills to be future-ready.

Kennedy (chapter 12) outlines another innovation where students worked on real-world app designs: whilst design thinking for the end-user features heavily as an underpinning of the success of the app design, this chapter shows us how students were able to critically assess the suitability of digital solutions to address practical legal and social issues and to work across disciplines to develop and design a systems solution through design thinking approaches and assessing its legal implications. It will become increasingly important for students to be aware of the potential of design thinking to make accessible legal services for everyone.

Piaskowska and Piesiewicz (chapter 10) take further the intersection between design thinking and access to justice to support how students build upon their digital literacies with confidence. Questioning the reliability, accuracy and creditability of the sources of legal knowledge found online expands the construct of design thinking and digital literacies to be well prepared to exercise their professional judgement in the future.

Together, these chapters suggest that digital literacies involve using digital solutions to find problems, solve problems, communicate in a variety of ways, collaborate with others, create new ideas and develop deep thinking. The chapters also support developing authentic experiences which allow students to take ownership of initiatives and tasks, drawing on their curiosity to analyse, refine and evaluate existing knowledge to create unique and cogent ideas and artefacts.

Viewing digital literacy as providing confidence to navigate through uncertain futures and confront and engage with the (un)known opportunities and challenges of the future, using critical thinking and problem solving, the aim should be to create an understanding of what technology works best in a given situation and how to optimise and use it with fairness, transparency, and equality. In embedding digital literacies into the curriculum, different law schools will recognise and value different forms and combinations of digital literacies suited to the ethos and telos of their law degree. In each case, it should be noted that developing students' digital literacies from awareness to fluency requires incremental steps: this allows students to experiment and build opportunities to confidently articulate their creativity.

Key points for reflection about how to incorporate digital literacies into a law degree, contextualised to the needs of the various careers likely for our graduates include the knowledge, skills, and future readiness required to thrive in these settings, and how these settings are changing. Crafting and embedding digital literacies into course and module design requires more than the technical use of tools, and involves considering the other dimensions of learning that students should be able to articulate and showcase. Rive (chapter 7) reflects on using online environments and tools for learning and teaching. Thanaraj et al (chapter 8) explore how digital solutions can be used to create authentic and creative learning experiences and assessments, and inculcate future readiness and digital empowerment in learners; and how to meaningfully embed digital literacies contextualised to the needs of the discipline and the profession within the curriculum and learning design. This rests on the importance of creativity and resilience in realising authentic future-facing learning, through an ability to take ownership of knowledge and learning and approaching these in new ways, as a construct of digital literacies.

Interdisciplinarity

In the future of work, legal careers are likely to be pluralistic, diverse, global, and multidimensional, and people are likely to have a portfolio of careers within the legal sector and beyond. Several authors in this collection reference a reimagined law degree for this future resting on three pillars, sustainability, creativity, and using the law for good. There is also a need for interdisciplinarity, as the significant challenges of the 4IR and its evolving environments cannot be addressed by any one discipline in isolation. As such, cross-boundary and interdisciplinary learning grounded within the episteme of law is necessary. The recently coined term "Digital Lawyering" (Thanaraj, 2017, 2018) offers an insight into the theory that begins to formulate the sorts of learning that are required for law students and future professionals to thrive in a digital age. Various authors in this book take the position that technology has the potential to go beyond a technical tool and become a subject of teaching and research within the episteme of law and the law degree.

A crucial question here is whether it is worth teaching about technology that might soon be obsolete, and if so how should it be integrated? Murray and Edwards (chapter 9) explore why legal tech is used and so what skills need to be developed. Through the lens of sustainable teaching and learning practices that will develop sustainable graduates with the skills to adapt to an ever-changing professional environment, they invite students to reflect on the pillars of sustainability, using technology as their lens, in order to develop skills of adaptability, critical thinking, and the ability to navigate change. The pillars of sustainability also afford an understanding of the commercial realities of legal tech and consequently build an additional dimension of their digital lawyering skills.

Otoyo and others (chapter 11) take a different approach by advocating for collaboration between law lecturers, computer scientists, and local lawyers to introduce students to lawtech to address diverse client needs by breaking down legal solutions into a set of simple rules brought to life by technological solutions. The module develops new ways of thinking in both law students and computer science students, particularly around the impact of technology on legal services and careers in law and computing.

When introducing an interdisciplinary dimension into the parent degree, it is sensible to consider the extent to which it prepares students to thrive in a technologically mediated legal practice. This requires an analysis of the sorts of knowledge and skillsets that law students require to enter the professions that make use of legal skills, but also the practical and pedagogical challenges. These include how to prepare academics and administrators to embrace new models of learning and teaching and identifying the challenges and risks arising from extensive change to academic practice. It is also necessary to determine whether the modules are core or elective and to consider innovations in assessments that help students become future-ready.

In setting the direction of change towards future-ready disciplines and curricula, authors have considered the exponential growth of knowledge and the rapid and radical development of technology. Williams and Janeček (chapter 13), Cakir (chapter 14), and Thanaraj et al (chapter 8) explore how we ensure that curricula remain relevant and responsive to contextual challenges and to student needs. These authors argue that law schools have a responsibility to understand and assist this digital transformation by preparing students: this involves interdisciplinary knowledge and working for students to exercise leadership on critically important debates at the intersection of law and digital technology by achieving fluency in the key legal frameworks and an understanding of the technical, philosophical, ethical and humanities aspect of technologies and the ways society can work to ensure those technologies serve the public good.

Williams and Janeček (chapter 13) describe and reflect on their practice-oriented Oxford LawTech Education Programme and the academically-oriented Law and Computer Science Programme, strongly advocating for developing an interdisciplinary mindset focused on the use of data and design-thinking with robust ethical grounding to the use of technology for lawyering. Cakir (chapter 14) demonstrates the impact of in-depth study of how technologies are changing the legal sector, incorporating STEM subjects into the study of law and developing design-thinking in lawyers and law graduates. The chapter presents a case for the value of interdisciplinary knowledge to shape law degrees as stewards as the world navigates through the 4IR and to train and prepare students for the digital transformation of society by giving students the means to understand and face the challenges of the digital world, using law as a lens to identify challenges and develop potential interdisciplinary solutions.

Through the design of two models for a law-tech curriculum, I argue in chapter 15 that a reimagined law degree can contribute to these challenges by giving students the means to understand and face them and also bringing together different perspectives and processes to generate and integrate something new in problem-finding and solving. The models allow law academics to consider the need for different knowledge and skills from those currently being developed through the academic and vocational stages of legal study.

Creativity, Communication, and Collaboration

As higher education plays a pivotal role in creating the next generation of highly skilled, adaptable, innovative, digitally literate, and creative graduates entering the workforce, the curriculum should empower our students to develop the self-awareness and wide-ranging qualities, abilities, and behaviours needed for rewarding professional lives. The ability to think and work creatively – which may involve different elements in different disciplines – is widely recognised as a catalyst for innovation, adaption, and resilience in modern professional contexts. In a technologically rich and constantly evolving knowledge economy, a sense emerges that knowledge cannot, by itself, provide the core of an authentically future-facing higher education. Creativity will be the super skill which can help students thrive in change. While automation is replacing some of the work skills we have been training students to do, what cannot be digitised is most valuable and should be cultivated and developed.

What kinds of pedagogic practices and environments are best suited to nurturing creative learners? What works depends on the types of thinking and learning we want to encourage at any particular moment in the student's learning journey. It is also heavily dependent on the learner and their progress. Students need sufficient time and space in the curriculum to allow them to develop their creativity: incremental opportunities for students to develop confidence in their ability to explore and experiment are needed. The learning opportunities and environments should support the development of each individual learner's creative capabilities to seek out and face everyday problems, as well as enhance their capacities for future success. We must provide a clear reference point for creativity in our learning designs, allowing sufficient space for innovation, appropriate risk-taking, and experimentation. We must also find ways of valuing the role of 'relative failure' as an integral part of the creative learning process since initial mistakes will eventually allow for improved outcomes. The acceptance of failure and experimentation, as much as the reward for success, plays a key part in developing individual resilience and offers an incentive for innovation.

Creativity is a theme that runs throughout this book. Authors provide thought-provoking reflections on approaches to engage meaningfully with such questions, providing insight into the ways academic colleagues might embed and nurture creativity through curriculum and learning design. In various chapters, we see how students are given the autonomy to choose to work in new and interesting ways, enabling students to be creative in ways appropriate to their own experiences and learning situations. Innovative examples around the creation of digital tools and applications, and preparing students for the changing legal profession through virtual law clinics and interdisciplinary models of learning law, challenge students through authentic, demanding, and meaningful work. Students are encouraged to embrace unfamiliar tasks and working practices, be open to new ideas and perspectives, and recognise opportunities to create new and build on existing knowledge and insight in real-world learning situations. Learning through design and creative outputs allows learning to be intentionally designed to allow for outcomes which are not narrowly predetermined or fixed, which emphasises assessment of "process" to draw together and apply their learning throughout a module or course and provides important opportunities for students to demonstrate their creativity.

Creativity is the ability and confidence to take ownership of a task and approach it in a new way, often in a collaborative fashion. Problems are not neatly compartmentalised in linear disciplinary areas and neither are solutions: problems have to be redefined, innovative solutions found and action taken. As such, creativity is at the heart of learning experiences in higher education. But there is no "creative strategy" or "creative environment" that we as educators should generally use, because "what works" depends on the types of thinking and learning we want to encourage at any particular moment in the student learning journey. This is also heavily dependent on the learner and their progress. Creativity can be supported and nurtured, as well as weakened and suffocated, by the climate for learning we create through our curricula and learning designs.

Students' own creativity, in the way they relate to convoluted terminologies and principles, visualise arguments and identify complex inter-relationships, can be seen in the digital 3D 'Virtual Town' (Marunchak and Dunk, chapter 2) as well as in the gamification and Virtual Reality app (Jones et al, chapter 3). The latter made a shift towards connecting academic knowledge with real-world applications, and developing students' soft skills, such as interpersonal skills and working as a team; this fosters the development of in-depth technical knowledge, industry readiness and transferable skills in graduates who "know that" and also "know how". Both these examples also highlight how students are being equipped with future-ready thinking to identify legal and ethical challenges that arise from technological innovations and critically examine how developments in technology may protect or undermine the rule of law. Students are often confronted with unique and unstructured problems, forcing them to think outside the box and look for answers beyond their textbooks.

The chapters in this book encourage the reader to consider the ways in which a course or module currently helps students to develop flexible and creative ways of thinking and working that empower and prepare them for their future. This includes questions about the extent to which students are encouraged to critique, shape, and position authentic narratives about their own creativity and learning development, and do so through interaction and collaboration with other people and networks that enable students to make meaningful contributions to a wider community of practice. Or the extent to which students are allowed to resolve complex problems and situations, or confidently navigate changing professional industry contexts.

The features of future readiness threaded throughout the chapters of this book suggest several hallmarks of the future-ready law graduate, equipped to thrive and creatively use their learning and skills in ways that they anticipate - and some that they have not yet imagined:

- Able to transfer learning to new and dissimilar contexts through a lifelong-learning frame of mind
- Commercially aware to thrive in uncertain futures and ready to change
- Adaptable to human-led and automatised ecosystems working together, including criticality and skills that cannot be digitised
- Digitally fluent, and able to use technology to optimise performance and client needs, including the impact on digital lawyering
- Comfortable with interdisciplinary collaborations and methodologies to contribute towards solutions for wicked problems
- Having an aptitude and mindset of an active creator with purpose
- User of sustainable and ethical thinking and action

The Need for an Institutional Culture that Supports Transformation

Institutions can encourage transformative, research-informed academic practices (Education 4.0 (Thanaraj et al, 2021)). Digital transformation in law schools needs change at the level of the enterprise so as to empower staff. Continual investment in professional development requires more than teaching people how to use a new device which may become obsolete. The upskilling experience involves staff learning how to think, act, and thrive in a sustainable way through confidence and fluency in the digital environment. Embedding creativity, resilience, and adaptability into subject disciplines, along with sustainable practices, will help to prepare staff also to tackle grand challenges in the world through a broad law curriculum, supported by an opportunity to reimagine the purpose of assessments within the curriculum and how we design them.

The table below identifies components that law school leaders can take into consideration when leading authentic transformation of a law degree by exploring a variety of contexts, inputs, and drivers, shifting practices and exploring enablers for change. As digital transformation is a journey, not a destination, it involves the continual understanding of why we are seeking change, whom this change will benefit, and how to unlock creative learning methodologies. This is a pedagogic and cultural challenge, the latter requiring a collaborative effort that is values-driven and authentic, led by engaging and empowering others towards inclusive decision-making. Any successful transformation requires a collaborative process, taking people on the journey. A collaboration driven by thoughtful considerations around student experience and the academic goal of learning, rather than the systems and tools which are simply the canvas upon which transformative experiences are created, allows a design for the maximum tailored learning and support (Table 17.1).

Table 17.1 Leading authentic transformation of a law degree

Leading authentic transformation of a law degree

Innovation and reimagination of the law degree must be done with a purpose. It is a journey not a destination

Context, inputs and drivers	*Shifting practices*	*Enablers*	*The journey*
Affordances and impact of the 4IR across industries, professions and disciplines, ways of work, life, and culture	Building on the episteme of a law degree	A compelling and meaningful vision rooted in the episteme of law as an instrument for good	Changing the value proposition of a law degree
Market needs for future-ready graduates	Needs of industry 4.0 through education 4.0	Taking people on a journey with direct impact on preparing students for change and creating a supportive environment allowing barriers to be raised and addressed. Management buy-in is essential to progress any strategic and transformational projects – so there is a need to bring different parts of the university together, with people who have the ability to make change and decisions, to make things happen with a shared vision.	Drawing on a digitally transformed law curriculum and learning experience
Data-driven decision making	The relevance of law in a changing world	A clear vision and purpose that is authentic and aligned to the institutional values, aims, mission, - and needs of its learners Outstanding leadership and credibility to drive digital transformation	Mapped onto the dimensions of future readiness

(*Continued*)

Table 17.1 (Continued)

Leading authentic transformation of a law degree *Innovation and reimagination of the law degree must be done with a purpose. It is a journey not a destination*			
Context, inputs and drivers	*Shifting practices*	*Enablers*	*The journey*
Impact of development and use of technologies for societal good, ethical functionalities and value enabled practices	Need to tackle challenges through interdisciplinary means	Building on the culture of the organisation, including fearlessly changing approaches to curriculum, structure, design, and delivery, thereby causing a culture change ready for the 4IR	Knowledge, skills, and the habits of mind to address the grand challenges of a digitally mediated world.
Safeguarding of rights and responsibilities including privacy and freedoms	Digital literacies are beyond functionalities and address the synergies between technology, law, regulations, values and ethics.	Strategy and how it translates to students' experience is enabled by the academic who is supported in a variety of ways to turn the strategy into meaningful actions within their learning designs. Opportunities including professional development of staff and students to master the technology and tools at their disposal.	The expansion of the learning ecosystem that is both physical and virtual allows students to collaborate in several ways, with creativity embedded into assessments and learning opportunities

The table above offers an illustration for law school leaders to enable change. Nurturing a culture of shared purpose and a collective direction for staff and students is essential. The vision for the law school, what it wants to be known for and how it wishes to get there, needs to be built on values that facilitate the future readiness of both its staff and students. Students need authentic opportunities to develop skills that are relevant to both their course and the workplace of the future. Several examples, from interdisciplinary learning to digital literacies, are key factors in thriving in a complex and changing professional setting. Technology can improve access to learning and enhance the academic experience, drawing on the opportunities and affordances of digital technology for providing high-quality teaching and innovating in teaching and assessments. In doing so, it can transcend the boundaries of our learning ecosystem through seamless integration of physical and digital tools and spaces for active high-impact collaborative learning and assessments.

In Chapter 16, Kim Silver discusses the multifaceted and changing role of being a legal academic in the digital age. If law schools wish to develop cultures of innovative digital fluencies, they need to develop academics as leaders in the digital learning experience through a culture of innovation in which academic staff are empowered and enabled to advance their teaching practices in a rapidly changing digital environment. Institutions will need to focus on collaborative staff development and training, with particular emphasis on rapidly building capabilities and empowerment, within the context of the 4IR. Teachers can be supported better to design excellent learning experiences by leveraging, differentiating, and pioneering a wide range of digital solutions with confidence and fluency to educate effectively and prepare themselves and their students for the digital future. This requires a robust programme of professional development, coaching, and mentoring with a focus on pedagogically sound learning design. Such a programme will ensure course innovation is sustainable, inspiring and innovative by (i) sharing examples of educational innovation and good practice and (ii) profiling excellence in design, practice and impact on student learning experiences via case studies. The aim is to equip teaching staff with the capabilities to deliver cutting-edge Education 4.0 learning experiences in a rapidly changing education and employment context and to move the teaching practices of staff from digital literacies to digital fluencies.

A policy-led large scale incremental adoption of digitally transformative learning and teaching practices (Thanaraj & Williams, 2016) can help to re-imagine academic practice and teaching and envision new models of learning. The right institutional culture will enable the use of digital technologies to encourage institution-wide evolutionary and transformative change to learning and teaching design and delivery: it will do so by building on new digital practices and opportunities for integrating culture and operations for a new learning ecosystem.

An understanding of technology, its affordances, and limitations and how it can best be utilised is a key component in building a future-ready portfolio and in delivering learning experiences that reflect the needs of the changing world. It also includes embedding digital lawyering knowledge and skills holistically into the curriculum, creating a space for interdisciplinary collaborations and learning. Creativity is fundamental here in fueling critical thinking, problem-finding and solving, and finding new ways of tackling complexities. As such, future readiness can be interpreted as confidence and fluency embedded into curriculum reform and this requires institutional support for academics to design a curriculum which supports students to develop their digital capabilities to ensure that they are able to thrive in new working and learning environments. Inclusivity by default is also necessary so that everyone is able to benefit from all aspects of learning.

Research Agenda: Looking into the Future of Legal Education

This book is a step towards embedding creativity in legal education. The ever-changing, dynamic landscape encourages flexibility and resilience in order to drive progress and extend the areas of excellence in digital learning design and bring transformational change in educational design and delivery.

We hope the modernisation agenda for legal education is an ongoing conversation across the globe, in which we begin to identify a future-ready law graduate and what we can do as educators and education leaders to support excellence in learning. We also hope that this is a start to the conversation and research around what digital literacies and creativity mean within the context of legal education; and also to making a case to establish the role of legal education in influencing and shaping the progress of the 4IR and to position legal education as an anchor discipline in Higher Education, as a provider of stewardship and intellectual force at a time of exponential change to a variety of professions, industries, and sectors.

The journey towards reimagining legal education requires consideration around the future role of lawyers. As we draw this book to a close, we ask you to consider what motivates you as a law academic or law leader and what theories influence your module creation and teaching. Throughout the book, we have set out some key reflective questions; here, I revisit some of them, with some thoughts and ideas for further research:

1 Are we always teaching to fit what's required now rather than thinking of ways to change the system to fit the new realities?

   Cakir's work (chapter 14) offers us a blueprint for developing a new model of studying law. She makes a case for breaking boundaries within legal knowledge and introducing interdisciplinarity into the study of law to empower lawyers for the digital age through an in-depth study of how technologies are changing the legal sector and equipping them with the relevant knowledge to understand challenges and develop innovative solutions. Cakir's work focuses on Postgraduate studies, and therefore you may ask, how can traditional subjects in law become modernised?

In Chapter 15, I offer models of interdisciplinary law degrees which show how a law degree can provide stewardship towards the challenges imposed by the 4IR. They move away from focusing on work-readiness and legal practice alone to a wider contribution to the regulatory, legal and ethical debates and challenges arising from the blurring identities, disciplines, professions, and structures of what we know, and the operations and impact of exponential digital transformation. The first model is developed using the episteme of law through thematic lines of enquiry as an integrative interdisciplinary methodology for law, and the second model offers interdisciplinary modules alongside law modules. Both models offer different approaches to modernising a law degree, yet offer a vision towards interweaving law (L), science (S), technical understanding (T), ethics (E), philosophy (P), humanities (H), design (D), and entrepreneurship (Ex) into the law degree. This affords revolutionary insights and positions a law degree to contribute towards tomorrow's technological breakthroughs.

Whilst we have established the value of interdisciplinarity in law, there is much research required in the field of interdisciplinary learning within legal education. The difference between an interdisciplinary module and a multidisciplinary one is a useful starting point for investigating how we empower our students to become future-ready. Areas for further research include how the teaching approaches and learning experiences of interdisciplinarity are supported at module and programme level, across the institution and more widely across legal education. At the programme level, how are learning experiences engineered to create integration (ie, how does a multidisciplinary programme become an interdisciplinary one)? At the institutional level, what are the best practice examples that demonstrate how interdisciplinary teaching is supported by an institution, and what are the risk factors, barriers, enablers, and recommendations for success? At a broader subject discipline level, how do larger interdisciplinary projects aim to integrate knowledge from various sources, disciplines, or subjects to break down the silos of knowledge? What learning processes are used to support and advance integration at module and programme level? How is it possible to assess the integration of disciplines, practices, or knowledge and what are student perceptions of interdisciplinary assessments? Following on from this is the question of what does it mean to be a law academic engaged in interdisciplinary teaching that is going to help our students become future-ready and digitally empowered?

2 What does creativity mean in your law school?

Creating learning opportunities where students can bridge the gap between theoretical research and industry applications in the form of solving an industry problem equips students with real skills needed to solve industry and societal problems. Offer and Cook (chapter 6) share the example of how apps created by students for real-world purposes use emerging methodologies of design thinking in solving legal problems. Similarly, Marunchak and Dunk (chapter 2) exhibit creativity brilliantly by bringing land law to life through the design of a digital 3D virtual town: this allowed new ways to present information to a variety of audiences, making legal concepts more accessible and user-friendly to clients and organisations. It helps students to visualise arguments and strategise their cases differently, allowing for a relationship between numerous elements of facts, propositions, and challenges to surface in more emergent fashions.

Within the context of creativity, how do new digital experiences and pedagogy deliver learning and teaching in legal education that meets the changing needs of the profession and society? To address this, exploratory research is required into how we structure and construct law degrees. In the chapter on Designing Creativity into Digital Learning (chapter 8), colleagues from Teesside University and I discuss that the development of creativity and resilience in our students is not only necessary but essential if they are to thrive in an increasingly unpredictable and complex world. It is for us as educators to decide the role creativity plays within our courses and modules in preparing our students for increasingly uncertain future professional lives. Ongoing work is required to answer how might a law degree be designed to develop attributes needed for the familiar and unfamiliar circumstances of the future – building student confidence, allowing collaboration, and allowing students to demonstrate creativity and be assessed for that, are some of the questions to be explored.

3 How will law schools re-design curricula to support lifelong learning to tackle the world's biggest challenges?

Chapters 13 to 15 question how we ensure that curricula remain relevant and responsive to contextual challenges and student needs. What competences do future graduates need and how do we anticipate these? How do we prepare graduates to be future-ready in a constantly changing digital world, and for the challenges of artificial intelligence? Williams and Janeček (chapter 13) discuss law and technology education, demonstrating that through collaborative interdisciplinary approaches to learning, learners are being prepared to become future-ready. Their reflections and findings identify gaps within legal education and they advocate for the curriculum that lends itself to developing an interdisciplinary mindset, one that is focused on the use of data and design thinking with robust ethical grounding in the use of technology for lawyering. Piaskowska and Piesiewicz (chapter 10) take a different but notable approach to supporting lifelong learning. Through their access to justice initiatives, their study tackles digital literacies in students by advocating that the law curriculum should go beyond teaching how to use the digital tools: instead, they argue that with the internet being a source of information and misinformation, the ability to recognise the truthfulness of news, and in particular of legal information, will allow students to be well prepared to exercise their profession in the future. This will help the implementation of the guarantee of Access to Justice and better prepare the students to be future-ready.

The introduction to this book (chapter 1) sets the scene on how the legal profession is changing. The emergence of artificially intelligent lawyers, DIY law (offering cheaper solutions to clients) and legal platforms and applications offering legal solutions reflect some of the changes permeating the legal sector. As with all change, questions inevitably arise as to whether the future of the legal profession is viable, perhaps in an adapted form, and the ways technology aids or hinders the role of the future lawyer. The research focus from a learning and teaching perspective is around the sorts of graduate attributes a digitally proficient lawyer requires – knowledge, skills, and attributes which help future lawyers to interpret legal issues from a new perspective, keeping an open mind and considering the newer, untapped possibilities that convergence of the law with technology now bring. The modern lawyer must be receptive to new concepts, and eager to continually learn and upskill as newer digital tools and technologies permeate the legal sector. In your research, you may consider how legal education can afford developing skills for future employment such as flexible and innovative thinking, design thinking, and actively learning to assimilate and work with change, problem solving, judgement, and decision making?

4 What are the models of learning which prepare students to become future-ready?

Law students require proficiency in fact-finding and investigation, interviewing techniques, legal research, analysis, and writing skills in order to reach sound and valid conclusions; and they must acquire persuasive negotiation and oral and written advocacy skills. A law degree must provide excellence in maximising student learning and professional development, aligned to an evolving profession, guided by maturity and ethics as well as intellectual and analytical prowess. Authentic student work and assessments implant real-world impact and help students transition from their role as novices and learners to developing professional and emerging practitioners.

In addition, creativity, collaboration, and communication are key elements of a future-ready curriculum and graduation. Graduates also need to be resilient in order to survive and thrive in the future workplace. In determining some of the core curriculum components to build resilience, the authors advocate for three pillars of future readiness in law students: sustainability, creativity, and using the law for the greater good. Murray and Edwards (chapter 9) explore how to develop sustainable graduates with the skills to adapt to an ever-changing professional environment and understand the commercial realities of legal tech and consequently build an additional dimension of their digital lawyering skills. Otoyo and others (chapter 11) collaborate with computer science to aid students' development of new literacies in data, technology, humanities, communication, and design to address diverse client needs by breaking down legal solutions into a set of simple rules brought to life by technological solutions.

To help focus our thinking, research could examine the sorts of problems that the next generation of lawyers need to solve, given that many tasks will be automated but there will still be a need for humanity in legal processes. The need for lawyers to enjoy their roles is also important: and the same goes for legal academics!

References

Arntz, M, Gregoryi, T, & Zierahni, U (2016) 'The risk of automation for jobs in OECD countries: A comparative analysis' (OECD Social, Employment and Migration Working Papers No. 189) https://www.oecd-ilibrary.org/docserver/5jlz9h56dvq7-en.pdf?expires=1578172632&id=id&accname=guest&checksum=A098B5E211CAC63D4D88A0DB93857F8F

Grajek, S & Reinitz, B (2019). Getting ready for digital transformation: Change your culture, workforce, and technology, EDUCAUSE.

Katz, DM (2013). Quantitative legal prediction – or – how I learned to stop worrying and start preparing for the data-driven future of the legal services industry, *Emory Law Journal, 62.*

Menkel-Meadow, C (2001). Aha? Is creativity possible in legal problem solving and teachable in legal education? *Harvard Negotiation Law Review, 6.*

Sako, M, Armour, J, & Parnham, R, (March 2020) 'LawTech adoption and training – Findings from a Survey of Solicitors in England and Wales'. https://www.law.ox.ac.uk/sites/files/oxlaw/oxford_lawtech_adoption_and_training_survey_report_18_march_2.pdf

Susskind, R (2010). *The end of lawyers?* Oxford University Press.

Thanaraj, A (2017). Identifying students' perspectives on skills and attributes gained from working in a Virtual LawClinic to create an impact on 'the digitally proficient lawyer': A grounded theory study, US-China Law Review, *14*(3), 137–167. http://www.david-publisher.org/index.php/Home/Article/index?id=31289.html, http://insight.cumbria.ac.uk/id/eprint/2978/7/Grad%20Skills.pdf

Thanaraj, A. (2018). Studying Law in a DigitalAge: Preparing Law Students for Participation in a Technologically-Advanced, Multidisciplinary and Complex Professional Environment. *Nottingham Law Journal, 27*(2). http://www.nlscle.org.uk/publication-of-nottingham-law-journal-2018-special-legal-education-edition/, https://www4.ntu.ac.uk/nls/document_uploads/nlj-vol-27-2-2018.pdf

Thanaraj, A & Williams, S, (2016) Supporting the adoption of technology enhanced learning by academics at universities. *Journal of Teaching and Learning with Technology*, 5(1).

Thanaraj, A, Durston, P, & Elkington, S, Building blocks for Education 4.0, BETT (8th July 2021), https://www.bettshow.com/bett-articles/building-blocks-for-education-40

The Economist Intelligence Unit Ltd. (2018). The automation readiness index: Who is ready for the coming wave of automation? http://www.automationreadiness.eiu.com/static/download/PDF.pdf

Index

For Product Safety Concerns and Information please contact our EU representative GPSR@taylorandfrancis.com Taylor & Francis Verlag GmbH, Kaufingerstraße 24, 80331 München, Germany